Double Passage

Double Passage

The Lives of Caribbean Migrants Abroad and Back Home

George Gmelch

Ann Arbor

THE UNIVERSITY OF MICHIGAN PRESS

Copyright © by the University of Michigan 1992
All rights reserved
Published in the United States of America by
The University of Michigan Press
Manufactured in the United States of America

1995   4   3

A CIP catalogue record for this book is available from the British Library.

Library of Congress Cataloging-in-Publication Data

Double passage : the lives of Caribbean migrants abroad and back home
    George Gmelch [interviewer].
        p.   cm.
    Includes bibliographical references and index.
        ISBN 0-472-09478-5 (alk. paper). —ISBN 0-472-06478-9 (pbk. :
    alk. paper)
        1. Barbados—Emigration and immigration. 2. Return migration—
    Barbados.   I. Gmelch, George.
    JV7331.D67   1992
    325.72981—dc20   92-29733
                                                                    CIP

Acknowledgments

I began work on this book in 1985, and along the way many people have contributed to its creation. For their critical reading of various chapters I wish to thank Maggie Boitano, Karen Clark, Peter DiCerbo, Margaret Deutsch, Steve Hackenberger, Joyce Harrison, Sharon Felson, Ron Farrell, Ellen Frankenstein, Arleigh Griffith, Victor Johnson, Miriam Lee Kaprow, Susan Keefe, Sheila Otto, Andrew Marchant-Shapiro, Ann Roberts, Bill Schneider, Andor Skotnes, Carol Wallace, Dwight Wallace, Tom Weakley, and Bob Wells. Their suggestions have made this a better book. I am particularly grateful to Loran Cutsinger, Bill Schneider, and several anonymous reviewers who read the manuscript in its entirety and who challenged me to think about my material in new ways.

Many people in Barbados have also helped. Dawn Marshall, Trevor Marshall, Tory Pilgrim, and Theo Williams all gave substance to my understanding of Caribbean migration. The Bellairs Research Institute and its director, Wayne Hunte, provided me with a stimulating environment in which to work. Others at Bellairs who assisted in various ways are Norma Alleyne, Julie Horrocks, Robin and Susan Mahon, Hazel Oxenford, and Esther Blackette.

I owe an intellectual debt to Andor Skotnes and Bill Schneider for showing me the ways of oral history; to Hugh Foley for explaining the psychology of memory; to Rich Felson for being a sounding board for my ideas; to Warren Roberts and Tom Weakley for their unflagging enthusiasm and wise counsel about book manuscripts and publishing; to Joyce Harrison, my editor, for gently pushing me to add a final chapter of reflections about doing oral history; to Mary Cahill, Bruce Connolly, Dave Gerhan, and Maribeth Krupczak, of the Union College library, for a great deal of help finding references and verifying details; to Richard Nelson for the example he has always set for me through his devotion to good writing; and to Sharon Gmelch, my wife and colleague, for listening to me, for critiquing the many drafts, and for the inspiration and high standards that she provided with her own life history, *Nan: The Life of an Irish Travelling Woman.* Her friendship has enriched my life and this book in numerous ways. Credit is also due to Morgan Gmelch, age eight, for providing refreshing distraction from the work.

I have also benefited from the Union College students that Sharon Gmelch and I have taken to Barbados over the past ten years. As apprentice anthropologists in our field program, they lived in villages with local families and did full-time fieldwork. Their insights and experiences contributed to my understanding of the Caribbean in more ways than they will ever know. I thank Union College both for a faculty research grant and for its Dana Fund for Summer Research Fellows.

The most productive period of writing was a summer spent in New Mexico, and I am grateful to Ron Farrell and Carole Case, then of New Mexico State University, for bringing me there and providing an office and secretarial support. Martin Benjamin, Johanna Campbell, Ellen Frankenstein, and the British Broadcasting Corporation's (BBC) Hulton Picture Library kindly provided photographs, which add an invaluable visual dimension to the oral histories.

My deepest gratitude, of course, goes to the Barbadian narrators—Siebert and Aileen Allman, Norman and Ann Bovell, Roy Campbell, Tony Carter, Richard Goddard, Valenza Griffith, Errol Inniss, Cleve and Rose Thornhill, Janice Whittle, and John Wickham—whose experiences are what this book is all about. My heartfelt thanks to them for the trust they showed me by sharing their life stories and for their patience with a process that must have seemed interminable to them. *Double Passage* is dedicated to them.

Contents

Part 1
Setting the Stage

Chapter 1
Introduction

In the 1830s slavery was legally abolished in the British Empire, and with it untold thousands of black West Indians were given the freedom to move. Since then probably no other region of the world has experienced as much human movement as the Caribbean.[1] In the eastern Caribbean, particularly, where small, resource-poor islands predominate, migration is a way of life, a common household strategy for dealing with economic scarcity. Young people learn early that often the quickest means to getting ahead in life is through emigration, although few ever intend to leave permanently. On many islands migration is so pervasive that nearly every household has a relative living in Britain or North America. An estimated half-million West Indians live in Britain today and three times that number in the United States and Canada.

This book is about the lives and experiences of migrants from the island of Barbados. Through oral histories thirteen men and women describe their decisions to leave the familiarity and security of home for an uncertain future in Britain or North America. They tell what it is like to be black and immigrant in the predominantly white societies they settle in and of their struggle to find good-paying jobs and decent housing, to develop new relationships, and to save enough money to be able to return home and attain the life-style—a "wall" house and car—that emigrants aspire to and that is expected of them by people at home. Their narratives also show us the difficulty of returning home, of reconciling tradition and island ways with the new ideas and attitudes they acquired while abroad. Their ways of adapting are as diverse

3

1. Map of the Caribbean

as the migrants themselves—men and women, working class and middle class, peasant and urbanite, worker and student.

Many books have been written on Caribbean migration, particularly on the movement to Britain following World War II. In the 1950s and 1960s most research concentrated on the assimilation of new immigrants: how black West Indians fit into all-white Britain and the impact they had on society.[2] Indeed, the subject of "race relations" received a great deal of attention in British academic circles in the 1960s.[3] Marxist writings focused on immigrant labor and the immigrants' relegation to the bottom stratum of Britain's class structure. A few studies were concerned with the impact the migrants' absence had on the homelands they left behind, since most migrants were able-bodied and industrious men and women in the prime of life.[4] Other studies focused on the larger structural forces at work, such as international capitalism, for example, which had caused the population movement. Generally speaking, these analyses were not concerned with the experiences of the migrants themselves. Rather, they were inclined to view emigration as a dependent variable in the larger equation involving economic imbalances between European and North American metropoles and the developing, dependent societies of the Caribbean.

Such perspectives are indispensable for understanding the national and international forces that influence migration and determine the position of immigrants in the host societies. Where these analyses fall short, however, is in the uniform way they treat emigrants, who often become no more than a faceless mass of new proletarians or, in the words of one critic of these writings, "automatons mindlessly reacting to forces over which they have no control."[5] At the very least they homogenize migrant lifeways that are very different and thus overlook the individual emigrant's perspective. As the following oral histories show, the experiences of migrants, even those from the same class and cultural backgrounds, are enormously diverse. People's motivations, experiences, and ways of internalizing the experience of migration vary widely. In most respects there is no typical West Indian or Barbadian migrant story.

The aim of this book is to delve beneath the abstractions of migration theory to uncover and look at this movement from the migrants' own perspective. I have chosen to do this through oral history,[6] that is, through first-person accounts of West Indians who emigrated to Britain, North America, or both and later returned home to Barbados to stay. In the words of one observer, "To understand why someone behaves as he does you must understand how it looked to him, what he thought he had to contend with, what alternatives he saw open to him."[7] By showing context, illuminating motivation, conveying personality, and revealing inner thoughts and perceptions, it is hoped that the narratives in this book can help fill in gaps and flesh out our understanding of Caribbean migration.[8]

They offer the reader an insider's understanding of what it means to be black and West Indian in such places as London, New York, and Toronto and later to return home to a small island society. And in listening to their voices we come to see the migrants as active players who make decisions and not merely passive pawns manipulated by the world economy, labor recruiters, or governmental decrees.

Oral histories are subjective documents that lack some of the detachment and objectivity of historiography, ethnography, or social survey, though even here the *a priori* notions and biases of the researcher often leave their imprint. The aim of oral history, however, is not *explanation*, as is generally the case with the etic approaches already mentioned, but rather, *understanding*, which is gained through firsthand knowledge. Indeed, the idea for this book grew out of disappointment with survey research I had done earlier in Barbados. In 1982–83 I conducted a survey of Barbadian returnees, focusing on their demographic characteristics, their reasons for returning home, and their readjustment after having lived abroad for many years.[9] The results of the survey, in which the data were reduced to statistical patterns, seemed far removed from the reality of the migrants' lives that I knew. I had gotten to know dozens of returnees and spent countless hours in their homes interviewing them, but I saw little of their experiences reflected in the material I was then writing. Most important, the generalizations I made glossed over the enormous variation I knew to exist in their adaptations abroad and at home.

The narratives in this book are similar to anthropological life history.[10] There is, however, a small difference. Most life histories deal with the whole of a single person's life, such as Marjorie Shostak's account of an Ikung woman in *Nisa,* John Niehardt's Ogala Sioux medicine man in *Black Elk Speaks,* or Hans and Judith-Marie Bucheler's story of a Galician Spanish woman.[11] The stories in this book come from thirteen individuals rather than one. And they do not deal with the whole of the subjects' lives; rather, they focus on that part of the life cycle that relates to migration or that provides useful background to the reader in understanding the individuals and the adaptations they have made.[12] But, otherwise, the method for compiling the narratives, as well as the objective—to provide an "inside view" told by "insiders"—is the same.

A unique feature of the oral life histories in this book is that they deal with both ends of the migration chain. My original intention was to focus on the experiences of Barbadians returning to the Caribbean, or what it meant to come home. It became clear very quickly, however, that return migration could not be divorced from what had happened to the migrants abroad, and in order to understand that it was important to know about their reasons for leaving Barbados in the first place. Hence, the object of the study soon became the entire migration cycle. The individuals whose stories are recounted here have been both "immigrants" abroad and "return migrants" at home. They have all had to adjust twice, first to the radically different metropolitan environments of England, Canada, or the United States, then to the deceptively familiar environment of their island home. Because these men and women were interviewed after the completion of their migration cycle, with both time and space between them and the lives they had lived abroad, they have the detachment necessary to discern some of the patterns and meanings of their overseas experiences. In short, they are able to see migration in a way that West Indians who are still abroad cannot yet perceive.

Their narratives, which both begin and end in Barbados, also say much about the life and culture—folk beliefs, diet, living conditions, pastimes, sport, schooling, and race relations—in one Caribbean society. Through the migrants' comparisons of the island they left as young adults with the society they returned to decades later, we learn something of the changes that Barbados has undergone as a result of gaining independence from Britain, the decline of the sugar industry, and the growth of tourism.

Barbadian values and customs are also brought into relief both in the migrants' stories of their efforts to find their way in the complex world of a foreign metropole and in their own reexamination of and readjustment to Barbados upon their return. Their accounts also tell us something about North American and British society, for the social situations they describe and must adapt to are our own. They see certain aspects of our lives, such as the congestion and fast pace of our cities, the impersonal way we treat one another, our general mistrust of strangers, that we seldom notice because they are so familiar.

The Interview Process

The oral histories involved selecting the subjects of the study, conducting the interviews, transcribing the audio tapes, and editing the transcripts of the interviews into coherent stories. The last step also involved reviewing the edited narratives with the subjects. In choosing people for the study a primary consideration was finding individuals who would openly and willingly talk about their lives and who were willing to give me the considerable time required by the interviews. Some of the migrants, especially "country people" from the villages furthest from the city of Bridgetown, found it difficult to understand why I would want to record their lives. Not being politicians, performers, athletes, rich, or famous, they had difficulty grasping why their lives would be of interest to strangers. I explained to them that the typical subjects of oral history are "ordinary" people, such as the former housewives whose lives and work experiences in the wartime industries are recorded in Shurna Gluck's *Rosy the Riveter;* the textile workers in a New England mill town whose lives are recounted in Tamara Harevan's *Amoskeag;* the rural Mexican family in Oscar Lewis's *Pedro Martinez;* and the black GIs whose experiences in Vietnam are chronicled in Wallace Terry's *Bloods.* I also explained that the work aimed to enter into the historical record the everyday lives of migrants, who have heretofore been uninvolved in the creation of documents about their pasts. That is, the interviews would preserve the voices of "the Little Tradition."

I tried to make my selection of the subjects roughly representational of all Barbadian returnees in terms of gender, class, and the countries to which they had emigrated, as best I understood it. Since, however, returnees are not identified in the Barbadian national census (nor are they in most national censuses), there was no reliable profile of the return migrant population to use as a guide. Instead, I relied on the demographic profile that emerged from the survey I had done three years earlier. Some readers may wonder if the high level of education and literacy of most of the narrators is representative. I believe it is not far off: Barbados has a literacy rate of 97 percent, one of the highest in the world, and an excellent school system. For many years Barbadians were recruited to other islands to teach school. And migrants generally have had more education than those who stay home. � oppertunity while in Europe or America

All of the interviews were done between 1985 and 1990, during which time I spent a total of twelve months in the field. The interviews were conducted with an "interview guide," a sort of shopping list of major topics and questions to be covered. Oral history research is, above all else, an extended process of asking questions yet permitting the narrators to take them wherever they want. The interview guide was divided into three parts, each reflecting a different stage in the migration: the first concerned childhood and early adulthood prior to emigrating from Barbados; the second concerned the journey, experiences, and adaptations to life abroad; and the last concerned the decision to return home and the individual's readjustment to Barbados. The interview guide, which functioned more as a "topical road map" than an explicit set of questions, was constructed from the ground up. That is, most of the topics were ones that the subjects considered important and that had come up in the many informal conversations I had had with migrants before the oral history work began. In short, I wanted their narratives to reflect as much as possible their own perspectives and concerns, rather than mine.

Most migrants talked far more about their lives abroad than their lives before emigrating or after their return. This was, of course, the part of their past that had involved the most discovery, challenge, and personal change. Living abroad was also something that made them stand out from the Barbadians around them who had never "traveled." It made them more interesting individuals. Also, their time abroad was by now a completed life event and one about which, upon reflection and after comparing their experiences with those of others, they had arrived at some conclusions. Their analyses, so to speak, could vary from the abstract notions about migrants collectively, which sound much like generalizations made by social scientists, to specific reminiscences and recollections of people and events.

As part of the interview process, I looked through the narrators' family photograph albums and scrapbooks. Old photographs and press clippings often helped jog their memories or brought back details that had been forgotten. Snapshots of family, events, home, and neighborhood were invaluable in increasing my own understanding of the narrators. They also enabled me to ask better questions. I have gathered together the best of their pictures, along with documentary photographs from the British Broadcasting Corporation (BBC) Hulton Picture Library, to illustrate their stories and to offer the reader something of the insight the photographs provided me.

Most of the migrants were interviewed three times with the use of a tape recorder. In general, each set of topics (i.e., before emigration, the overseas experience, and the return) was covered in a different interview, although the narrators were free to skip around or circle back to follow whatever associations came up. In fact, usually I began each interview, after the initial one, by going over the transcripts from the previous session in order to let the subjects elaborate on or clarify points that were fuzzy.[13] In my introductions to each oral history I describe the narrators and the contexts in which the interviews took place. The subjective nature of oral history makes it important for the reader to know something about the conditions under which the story was related.

In the narratives related by married couples—the Bovells, the Thornhills, and the Allmans—the husband's story is always the dominant one; this occurs despite the fact that the woman in each family was the better storyteller. The reason for this may be that in each family it was the man who had emigrated first and who had been abroad the longest; indeed, in all three cases the men had lived in both Britain and North America, while their wives had been immigrants in only one. Also, I would not rule out the possibility that my being a male researcher may have influenced whose story the narrators focused on.

My task in editing the transcripts was to ensure that the stories were faithful to the oral testimony while also making the language intelligible to readers outside of the Caribbean. The editing involved pulling together broken pieces of the narrative and organizing the stories so that they followed the general chronology of the migration and return. A chronological organization, as I explain in chapter 16, was natural to the narrators. It is also useful to the reader because, when events are presented in the sequence in which they occurred, cause and effect becomes clearer. The transcripts were also condensed, usually by half or more, to enhance clarity and to eliminate material that was unimportant to our understanding of either the migrants' backgrounds or their migration experiences.[14] As a general rule, I tried to preserve the dialect and style of Barbadian speech. Unfamiliar terms and idioms are defined in brackets, such as *carb* [to hit] or *gap* [a road] or, when longer explanations are required, in footnotes.[15] The reader will notice that Barbadians often describe themselves using the second person rather than the first. In a typical example Errol Inniss (chap. 13) talks about his first day outside Barbados:

> Okay, it's your first time off the island, and here you are in Calgary, a city with 300,000 people, more people than all of Barbados, and they are all white, and it's snowing. All those white people looked the same to you—you didn't even know if you is seeing the same person twice.

As the quotation above also indicates, many Barbadians use the present tense rather than the past when recounting their experiences.

The migrants were asked to check the final edited narratives for accuracy and were given the opportunity to delete embarrassing detail. Only a few minor changes were requested.

My role, apart from getting the migrants to tell me their stories and editing them into a coherent form, has been to provide a framework—to describe for the reader the historical and social contexts of their migrations, to introduce the individual migrants, and at the end to offer my own observations. Otherwise, I interrupt the migrants' narratives as little as possible. I ask the reader to keep in mind that these are cultural narratives as much as they are individual stories of migration. (I will have more to say about the methods of oral history, its strengths and limitations, in chap. 16.)

The Returnees

The first people I approached—Norman and Ann Bovell (chap. 4), Cleveland and Rose Thornhill (chap. 8), and Errol Inniss (chap. 13)—are returnees whom I had interviewed in my earlier survey research. I chose them because they had been particularly good interviewees: they had interesting experiences and were able and willing to talk about them. They could tell a good story.

I had also known Siebert and Aileen Allman (chap. 11) before this study began. I met them in 1983 when I was looking for families in rural villages to accommodate American university students in an anthropology field training program that Sharon Gmelch and I directed in Barbados. I stopped in the Allmans' general store in Sutherland and asked if they knew of anyone in the village who might want to house a student for ten weeks. That was the beginning of a long relationship. I chose to interview the Allmans, in part, because I knew they would be very open about their experiences, including their disappointments in returning to Barbados. But also important was the fact that Siebert had worked as a conductor on London buses, one of the primary occupations of Barbadian immigrants in England in the 1950s and 1960s.

Thirteen migrants, aside from those just mentioned, were recommended by others. I did not continue working with five of these individuals after the initial interview. One did not have the time the study would require, and three were reluctant to talk freely about their lives.[16] The fifth was an excellent respondent but had to be dropped when I learned that she spent nearly all of her childhood on another island, where her Barbadian parents had been schoolteachers. More frustrating was having to abandon another subject after three interviews and sixty pages of transcripts. A highly respected, middle-aged businessman, he became concerned about the reaction that people in his field might have to his critical comments about Barbados and the white-dominated business sector that he worked for. We discussed changing his name and any revealing details in his biography, but, on a small island and with so few blacks in his particular position, even that would have been problematic. Moreover, the large number of changes that would have been necessary to conceal his identity would undoubtedly have weakened the narrative.

The remaining returnees who were recommended proved to be good choices. John Wickham (chap. 7), one of Barbados' most respected writers and senators, was recommended to me by then governor-general of Barbados, Sir Hugh Springer. A well-educated, middle-class professional, John Wickham has written several short stories and a novel that treat, in part, his experiences as an immigrant. Unlike the other migrants in this study, he has lived for many years elsewhere in the Caribbean.

The Mighty Gabby (chap. 10), Barbados' famous calypso artist, was recommended by friends at the Barbados museum who knew that many of his songs were influenced by his experiences working in the garment district of New York City. I thought Gabby would also be a good choice in that he would probably talk about calypso, an important Barbadian institution whose popularity he has helped to revive. He also proved to be an excellent storyteller.

Roy Campbell (chap. 5), a working-class returnee from London, was suggested by one of my students on the basis of his outgoing personality and because he had played a great deal of cricket while abroad, a sport that many West Indian immigrants participated in.

I learned about Janice Whittle (chap. 9), who had gone to England for her university education and is now an art teacher, from a friend involved in international cultural exchanges. Apart from being articulate and reflective, Janice seemed perfect because I wanted another student migrant, preferably a single woman, to round out the sample. My only reservation was that she had studied in Newcastle, in the north of England, while most West Indian students went to London or Birmingham.

Late in the study I added Richard Goddard (chap. 12). He is the only white subject. I had planned to only interview black returnees because 95 percent of Barbadians are of African descent, and the story of Barbadian migration is predominantly a black one. White Barbadians also emigrate, however, and, as the project progressed, I realized that the narratives were about more than migration. They were also about Barbados—its culture and society—and what it means to live on a small island. But to maintain a balance, given the small minority white Barbadians comprise, there was place for only one white returnee in the study. I believe Richard Goddard was a good choice because his family background spanned the social spectrum. A few generations earlier his ancestors had been poor whites, members of a stigmatized group known as "Redlegs." Richard's grandfather had moved away from the east coast where the Redlegs live to Bridgetown where through entrepreneurial talent he built a business empire and entered the ranks of the white elite.

Finally, when I had completed a first draft of all the oral histories, I added Valenza Griffith (chap. 6). I was attracted to Valenza both because she is a superb storyteller and is representative of the many young women who went to England in the 1950s and early 1960s to learn nursing.

Of the thirteen Barbadians we hear from in the following narratives, five emigrated to England, four to North America, and five were immigrants on both continents. The time they spent abroad ranges from two to thirty years, with an average of fourteen.

The Plan of the Book

The book is divided into four parts. The first part, which includes this introduction and the following two chapters, provides the background for the oral histories. Chapter 2 describes Barbados, the setting and society in which the people in this book grew up and to which they later returned. Chapter 3 examines the patterns and structural causes of West Indian migration to Britain following World War II and to the United States and Canada in the 1960s and 1970s.

Part 2 comprises the oral histories of the Barbadians who emigrated to Britain, and part 3 of those who went to North America. Since some of the emigrants lived on both sides of the Atlantic, I have categorized them according to the society where they lived the longest. Finally, part 4 contains three chapters of analysis and reflection. Chapter 14 deals with the immigrants' experiences and adaptation in the host societies; chapter 15 concerns the migrants' readjustment to their homelands and the impact they have had on Barbados, as agents of cultural change, by bringing home new skills, attitudes, and ideas. The final chapter offers my reflections on doing oral history and its relevance to the study of migration.

NOTES

1. It has been estimated that Caribbean net emigration since 1950 has constituted about 20 percent of all voluntary international migration, legal and illegal. The number of citizens who have left their Caribbean homelands to settle elsewhere is the equivalent of 5 to 10 percent of the total population of nearly every Caribbean society, a higher proportion than any other world area (Segal, quoted in E. Chaney, "The Context of Caribbean Migration," 8).
2. D. Marshall, "Toward an Understanding of Caribbean Migration."
3. J. L. Watson, *Between Two Cultures*, 11–13.
4. See, for example, S. B. Philpott, *West Indian Migration: The Montserrat Case;* and D. R. Hill, *The Impact of Migration on the Metropolitan and Folk Society of Carriacou, Grenada.*
5. Watson, *Between Two Cultures*, 12.
6. Ken Plummer notes in *Documents of Life: An Introduction to the Problems and Literature of a Humanistic Method* (26), that, while oral history is as old as history itself, it has only been since the 1940s that an "oral history movement has emerged around tape recordings." The movement got its impetus from Alan Nevis's work at Columbia University. Despite its increasing popularity, oral history is still viewed by many historians as a marginal enterprise because it is limited to the memories of living people. It has also been criticized for its users' tendency to amass quantities of narrative without providing much analysis of it.
7. Sidney Mintz, in "The Anthropological Interview" (310), argues that whether or not a subject of a life history is "representative" may not be terribly important. Rather, what is important is that the life history reveal patterns that are typical of that culture. Also, James Freeman in *Untouchable: An Indian Life History* (399) has argued that using representativeness and generalizability to evaluate life histories is, if not wrong, then at least misleading.
8. The narratives may also contribute to the descriptive base for constructing the social history of these mass movements, particularly the 1950s migration to the United Kingdom. The recollections of every life provide information about how the migrants conceptualized their experiences, and these perceptions have not been described in many other sources. As John Whitehead and Bill Schneider observe in "The Singular Event and the Everyday Routine," individual oral histories can lead to more general cultural insights because "there is a direct relationship between individu-

als sharing their personal experiences and the generalized attitudes of a cultural group" (78).

9. This study was a controlled comparison with earlier research I had done on return migration in Ireland and Newfoundland. The Barbados survey is described in more detail in chapter 14.

10. L. Watson and M. Watson-Franke define *life history* as "any retrospective account by the individual of his life, in whole or part, in written or oral form, that has been elicited or prompted by another person" (*Interpreting Life Histories,* 2). Life histories are ordinarily recorded in a sequence of sessions within a limited time span so that the individual reviews his life from a more or less consistent perspective.

11. A few other excellent anthropological life histories are Paul Radin's *Crashing Thunder,* of a Winnebago Indian; Bill Schneider's *Kusiq,* of an Eskimo man; Margaret Blackman's *Never in Our Time,* of a Haida woman; Sharon Gmelch's *Nan: The Life of an Irish Travelling Woman;* and Leo Simmons's *Sun Chief: Autobiography of a Hopi Indian.*

12. Some excellent life histories that involve more than one narrator include Caroline Brettell's *We Have Already Cried Many Tears,* of three Portuguese women in Paris, and Oscar Lewis's *Children of Sanchez, La Vida,* and *Pedro Martinez,* all of which combine individual accounts of different family members.

13. In the beginning my transcriptions of the interviews were verbatim. But, as I got a better sense of each narrator and the story, I often did not transcribe repetitious descriptions, fragments, or anecdotes about events or minor people that were unrelated to the account.

14. While nearly all anthropological life histories are edited, a few critics have argued that editing often distorts the narrator's meaning and makes any serious analysis of the initial production difficult. There is some truth to this, but I believe failure to edit in this case would have meant that these narratives would be repetitive, tedious, and dull.

    For examples of unmediated life histories, see Vincent Crapanzano's *Tuhami* and Kevin Dwyer's *Moroccan Dialogues.* These works, which are mostly long conversations between the anthropologist and the narrator, may solve the problem of the researcher mediating or influencing the material in ways unknown to the reader, but they do so at considerable cost. The reader of these "dialogues," as Jonathan Spencer notes in "Anthropology as a Kind of Writing," becomes so mired in particularistic data that he or she is left more helpless and dependent upon the anthropologist to explain what has happened than is the case with the edited life histories.

15. I have used two different systems for notes. In the oral histories I use footnotes because most of the information contained in them is substantive, explaining or clarifying terms or places mentioned in the narratives. Because they are often important to the reader's understanding of the narrative, I wanted them at the bottom of the page, where they will be

most accessible to the reader. Endnotes, consisting mostly of citations to literature, are used in the other chapters.

16. They willingly recounted the facts of their migration—when they went, why, where they lived, and so on—but they did so without revealing their subjective feelings about the experiences. Put differently, they were unable or unwilling to reveal much of their inner selves, and perhaps they had not reflected much on their past.

Chapter 2

Barbados—
The Island Homeland

Barbados is the most easterly of the Caribbean islands. It lies outside the great arc of volcanic islands that sweep a thousand miles from the Virgin Islands in the north to Trinidad and Tobago in the south. Unlike its volcanic neighbors, which are steep and mountainous, Barbados is a coral island and is relatively flat, rising to only a thousand feet in a series of limestone terraces. The terraces are a major structural feature of the island. Each terrace was once a fringing reef, like the one that surrounds Barbados at present. Legend has it that it was the flatness of Barbados that caused Columbus to miss the island, though it was later visited by Spanish explorers. The low relief means that trade winds blow unimpeded across Barbados, tempering the heat of the sun. The island's topography is especially favorable to agriculture, enabling nearly two-thirds of the land surface to be cultivated. Indeed, all that remains of the island's original vegetation is one small, forty-acre patch of semievergreen tropical forest at Turner Hall Woods at the center of the island.

Barbados has a nearly perfect climate. The temperature varies little, from an average low of 77° F in January to a high of 81° F in August and September.[1] The proximity of all parts of the island to the sea ensures comfortable, year-round sea breezes. This, combined with the purity of the groundwater, said to be second only to Malta's, and the absence of pestilence, led one nineteenth-century English travel account to rate Barbados the healthiest place in all the British empire, which then included half the nations on earth.[2]

Barbados, the Colony

The history of Barbados is tied to England and to sugar. The first
European contact with Barbados occurred in the early 1500s,
when Spanish sailors captured some of the island's Carib Indians
to use as slaves in the fields and mines of larger Spanish islands.
The first English party arrived in 1620 and reported the island to
be uninhabited. The aboriginal population had totally disappeared. The reasons are still unknown, but the likely possibilities
are famine, disease, and/or Spanish enslavement.[3] Barbados
avoided actual colonization until a century later, when in 1627 the
British returned with eighty settlers and ten black slaves captured
en route from trading vessels.[4] During the next two decades,
twenty-five thousand English settlers arrived in a mass migration
similar in scale to that of Britain's other colony in New England.[5]

The early settlers were primarily smallholders who grew tobacco, cotton, and other crops for export. This peasant economy,
however, was short-lived. Sugarcane, introduced from Brazil in
1641, produced a major social revolution as the settlers' small
holdings were swallowed up by ever-expanding sugar estates. Plantations became the center of the island's existence, and, as their
need for field hands grew, their owners quickly discovered that
African slaves could work harder in the tropical climate and at less
cost than British indentured servants.[6] Between 1645 and 1680 the
population of slaves increased from 5,680 to over 60,000.

With the expansion of the plantations many white smallholders emigrated to other British territories, particularly the
Carolinas.[7] In a mere four decades after the introduction of sugar
thirty thousand white settlers had gone, and Barbados' population
had become predominantly black, with blacks outnumbering
whites by three to one. With the spread of sugarcane across the
island Barbados became a classic colonial monocrop society, with
thousands of enslaved Africans producing sugar, molasses, and
rum for sale in the metropolitan markets of Europe, while political
power was concentrated in the hands of a hundred or so large
landowners, the "plantocracy."[8]

In 1838, after forty years of agitating by British humanitarians
and nearly two centuries after the beginning of the slave trade,
Barbados' seventy thousand laborers of African descent were

emancipated. The white plantocracy opposed emancipation, be-lieving that, once given their freedom, the ex-slaves would refuse to work on the estates and that, with the loss of cheap labor, the sugar industry would collapse.[9] The sugar estates survived eman-cipation, however, and the white planters retained their positions of wealth and power.

Barbados' flat, fertile landscape had allowed planters to put most of the island under cultivation, leaving very little land avail-able for black freedmen. Unlike on many other Caribbean islands, there was no area of idle, unclaimed land in Barbados. In Jamaica and the Windward islands ex-slaves could go into the highlands and pursue subsistence agriculture and establish their own free settlements.[10] But not in Barbados. Most Barbadian blacks were forced to continue working for the planters, becoming one of the world's first agricultural proletariats. Others, however, left the island "to resist, to escape, and generally to assert their individual freedom."[11] In search of a new livelihood these first black migrants stretched their kin networks to other islands, establishing migra-tion avenues for future generations of Barbadians to follow.

Sugar Is No Longer King

Although sugar is still important to Barbados' economy, it is no longer the major earner of foreign exchange.[12] Faced with a decline in world demand for sugar, fluctuating export prices, and the high cost of production, Barbados has had to diversify its economy. Since the 1960s it has begun to do so by developing tourism, light industry, and new agricultural products. Some for-eign manufacturers have opened shop in Barbados, attracted by its political stability, well-developed infrastructure, educated labor force, and tax incentives. Today the manufacturing sector is split between local firms and the subsidiaries of multinational firms who export to destinations outside the Caribbean.[13] In the most recent census, taken in 1980, 13 percent of the labor force was employed in manufacturing.

Government and planters have tried to find crop substitutes for sugarcane. Sea island cotton, maize, coconut, and a variety of vegetables have all been tried with varying degrees of success. Because rainfall is irregular and seeps below the surface so quickly

Cutting cane. (Photo by Ellen Frankenstein.)

and because the trade winds dry the soil, no crop seems as well suited to Barbados as sugarcane. But with income declining year after year, many cane farmers, particularly smallholders, have stopped farming, and large tracts of cane land have been sold to developers for new housing.[14]

The biggest boon to the economy, making up for the loss of sugar dollars, has been tourism. The number of overseas visitors to Barbados has grown rapidly since the early 1960s, as Caribbean vacations have become more popular with North Americans and Europeans. With fine sandy beaches, ideal climate, and a population considered the "friendliest" in the Caribbean, Barbados has become one of the favored destinations. More Britons now vacation in Barbados than anywhere else in the Caribbean. The number of foreigners who visit Barbados each year now exceeds the island's population, and tourist revenues have grown from BDS

$13m in 1960 to an estimated BDS $568m in 1984.[15] Largely because of tourism, the service sector is now the leading source of employment in Barbados.

Tourism has greatly increased the average Barbadian's exposure to the outside world. Contact with tourists, while perhaps broadening one's "horizons," can also make the young dissatisfied with their homeland and want to go elsewhere. Gabby, Barbados' famous calypsonian (chap. 10), recalls how mixing with North Americans on the boats he worked on as a singer led him to emigrate:

> They'd talk about things I had no experience of—fascinating things, like their countries, the size of them, the fastness of them, and the kind of things that you could do. . . . I was a young man having all this information fed to me. . . . I was fascinated, and I wanted to go see for myself.

Tourism has some other negative consequences at home. It is linked to a rise in materialistic values among young Barbadians, crime, drug use, and prostitution, overdevelopment of the coastline, pollution of the sea, and the killing of the coral reefs by the runoff from the hotels. If unchecked, destruction of the island's coral reefs will eventually erode away the beaches and send the tourists packing to other destinations. Economists caution that tourism is a shaky foundation for an economy, because it is tied to external circumstances and fluctuations in the disposable incomes of, in this case, North Americans and Britons.[16] And, because many of the hotels are foreign owned, a sizable percentage of tourist dollars do not stay on the island.

A steady growth in the economy over most of the past two decades has given Barbadians one of the highest standards of living in the Caribbean. Annual per capita income of $5,250 in 1988 is surpassed only by that of Trinidad. Today more than 85 percent of all Barbadians own the houses they live in, a figure even higher than the 62 percent of Americans and 47 percent of Britons who own their homes. Furthermore, 90 percent of all Barbadian households have running water, 79 percent have televisions, 79 percent have refrigerators, 55 percent have telephones, and 24 percent have cars.[17] Such living standards have been significant in encouraging many Barbadians who had emigrated

Tourist and local at the Southwinds Resort, Christ Church. (Photo by Martin Benjamin.)

overseas in the postwar years to return home. Talking about his first trip home to Barbados, Roy Campbell (chap. 5) said:

> I could see great improvements—there were many more cars, the roads were much better, and the people were doing better. They had things, like fridges, that they didn't have when I'd left.

Population

Two hundred and fifty-four thousand Barbadians live in one of the most densely populated societies on earth. On a pear-shaped land surface just twenty-one miles by fourteen miles at its widest, there are 1530 people per square mile. That is five times denser than India, and nearly three times denser than Britain or Japan. Among islands, only Malta has more people per square mile.

In recent times, however, Barbados has been able to hold its population in check. While most developing countries are burdened by rapid population growth, averaging 2.0 percent to 3.0 percent increases per year, Barbados population increases have fortunately been low, currently only 0.5 percent per year.[18] Only 29 percent of Barbadians are under fifteen years of age, which compares favorably with the developed world; 23 percent of Britons, for example, are under fifteen. Barbadians have fewer children than their Caribbean neighbors due to a very effective family planning program begun in the 1950s, which has made birth control methods available to all Barbadians and has encouraged their use.

Several West Indian writers have suggested that the small size of Barbados and the density of its population have shaped the character of its people. "The inability of people to remove themselves from one another," writes John Wickham, "has led to a concern for public order, a compassion for others, and a compelling sense of a neighbor's rights and integrity."[19] The small size of the island means that in most settings, even on the downtown streets of Bridgetown, Barbadians are known or recognized by others. Without anonymity the pressures to conform, to always act in socially acceptable ways, are great.

The absence of a hinterland that on other islands offers a refuge for criminals, social misfits, and the strongly independent has meant Barbadians must find ways to get along with one another. It is not surprising that Barbadians are said to be less than straightforward in their dealings with one another, are reluctant to openly criticize, and take pains to avoid confrontation. About small West Indian societies, in general, David Lowenthal notes that familiarity makes it hard to sustain uncompromising hostility and that "from an early age West Indians learn how to get along with those from whom they differ."[20]

Also shaping the character of its people has been Barbados' long and exclusive association with England. Barbados is the only Caribbean nation to have had a single colonial master. The description of Barbados as "Little England," a hackneyed phrase of the tourist trade, has some legitimacy. It has been coined in part from comparisons between the two landscapes, both green and rolling and everywhere showing the hand of humans. And Bridgetown's most prominent landmark, a statue of Horatio Lord Nelson, resembles its counterpart in London's Trafalgar Square. Barbadians, more than any other Caribbean people, are similar to the English in their reserve, civility, and in having an unshakable belief in their own superiority. In the words of John Wickham they have a "distinct penchant for priding themselves on their moral excellence."[21] Overseas, where West Indians from different islands live side by side, Barbadians are commonly thought of as being "smug," "prideful," and "know-it-alls." In trying to assess national character, however, we need to be reminded that personalities range greatly in every society, many individuals deviate from these patterns, and the range of character traits produces wide overlaps with other cultures.[22]

Race and Class

Barbadians are racially less heterogeneous than are the people of most other Caribbean islands. About 70 percent of the population is black, direct descendants of the Africans who were transported to the island to work as slaves. About 20 percent are "colored," of mixed black and white blood. Approximately 7 percent are white, and the remaining 3 percent are mostly recent immigrants, many being Hindus and Muslims from south Asia and the Middle East.

Barbados' whites are primarily descendants of the early English settlers and their indentured servants, many of whom came from not only England but also Scotland, Wales, and Ireland. Many of them were on the losing side of the English civil war or were convicted of crimes and exiled, or "Barbadosed," to the Caribbean. As bonded servants, they were required to work a specified number of years for their masters before being granted their freedom.

Whites have always controlled Barbados' economy and, until the island's independence in 1966, its politics as well. Before this century a small clique of twenty powerful families of the plantocracy controlled the lion's share of the island's commerce. An almost exclusive group, the white planter class controlled the legislature, dominated the Anglican vestry councils, served as justices of the peace, and bestowed knighthoods on one another.[23] The white elite finally lost political control. When Barbados became independent from Britain nonwhites moved into all the important positions of government. While the economic power of the whites has been diluted in recent times, they still control the majority of Bridgetown's large businesses.

Not all Barbadian whites are or were on the top of the social pyramid. Many descendants of the indentured servants never fared well. Thinking themselves to be above manual labor, especially jobs that blacks worked, and without much land of their own, most scratched out subsistence livings. One early twentieth-century account describes their condition:

> We passed through the hilly districts . . . and observed working in the fields or sitting in the doorways of miserable shacks, not the Negro figures to which the eye is accustomed . . . but ragged white men with blue eyes and tow coloured hair, bleached by the sun. This little population of Redlegs, as they are called . . . [have remained here] in the same humble plight as when they were first herded ashore.[24]

Today most "Redlegs," also contemptuously called "Ecky-Becky," "white niggras," and "poor backra-Johnnies," still live in isolated poverty in villages on the east coast. Higher-status whites find them unacceptable because of their backwardness and alleged indifference to work, and, therefore, the Redlegs have become highly inbred. Very few poor whites have been upwardly mobile. A well-known exception is the Goddard family, described in chapter 10. In the late 1800s a young member of the family moved to Bridgetown and managed to open a small shop and pub. The family expanded into other businesses, and within two generations the Goddards owned one of the island's largest corporations and joined the ranks of the white elite.

The ancestors of Barbados' majority black population came from territories in West Africa that are now the countries of Ghana, Nigeria, Sierra Leone, Guinea, Ivory Coast, and Cameroon. Because they came from different tribes and spoke different languages, they were unable to retain much of their traditional culture in the New World. These cultural differences also made it difficult for them to collectively resist the oppression of their slave masters. Slaves revolted on four occasions—1649,

1675, 1692, and 1816—but never succeeded fully. Since gaining independence in 1966 some educated Barbadians have campaigned for a popular appreciation of African traditions, to give all black Barbadians an understanding and a sense of pride in their African heritage. Two cultural foundations, Black Night and Yoruba Yard, were organized in the late 1960s and early 1970s to herald Barbados' African heritage. In schools children are now exposed to African folklore and music and read the African-inspired poetry of Edward Braithwaite.

In between whites and the blacks are colored Barbadians. Although some regard themselves, and are often regarded by whites, as a separate socioracial category, they are internally differentiated in terms of physical appearance. They are variously labeled "brown-skin," "light-skin," "fair-skin," "high brown," "red," and "mulatto" on the basis of skin shade. Brown or light colored Barbadians who emigrate to Britain or North America are often dismayed to find they are labeled as black, color diversity is not recognized abroad. In North America and Britain a crude dichotomy of white and black replaces the range of racial categories found in the Caribbean.[25] In Britain, for example, Indians, Pakistanis, Africans, and West Indians who are nonwhite are lumped under the single label of "black."

Education and overseas experience have since World War II done much to level out the influence of race in Barbados, putting nonwhites on a more equal footing with whites. Educational opportunities expanded rapidly as central government first took control of schools and then made primary and secondary education free to all Barbadians.[26] In 1963 Barbados acquired a branch of the University of the West Indies, its first full-fledged comprehensive university.[27] While most white families have always been able to afford to send their children through school, most blacks could not. Being neither large landholders nor owners of businesses, black families for several generations have viewed education as the primary means to their children's social mobility. Most Barbadians have successfully instilled in their children a desire to do well in school. This holds true for girls as well as boys. Today all but 15 percent of the island's children aged eleven to seventeen are enrolled in school, and the percentage of students who graduate from secondary school exceeds that of many indus-

Prayer session after recess at St. Augustine Boys School, 1986. (Photo by Martin Benjamin.)

trial nations, including North America and Britain. The adult literacy rate of 95 percent reported by the Ministry of Education is one of the highest in the world.

But even before the postwar expansion of education Barbadians were regarded within the Caribbean as being well educated. Since the 1930s some islands have recruited schoolteachers and police officers from Barbados. Similarly, some British companies and government agencies in the 1950s chose Barbados as a place to set up offices to recruit workers.

Overseas experience has been the other leveler of race. During World War II many black Barbadians served in the American, Canadian, and British armed forces, and after the war many more migrated to metropolitan centers in those countries to work or to attend university. Working overseas, black Barbadians acquired new knowledge and work skills, but, more important, their experiences in these predominantly white societies gave them a better understanding of racism and colonialism, which led to an awakening of racial and political consciousness. Upon returning home, some of these people became the prime movers in Barbados' movement to gain independence from Britain and in efforts to improve the status of blacks.[28]

Today there is a comfortable tolerance between blacks and whites. The racial exclusivism—seen, for example, in the country's racially separate cricket, soccer, tennis, and bridge clubs, which were once common—are largely gone.[29] And the last all-white school, St. Winifred's, was desegregated in 1970. Still there remain institutions that are controlled by one racial group or another, but this dominance is largely by tradition and rarely are there attempts, at least overtly, to exclude members of the other race. Yet, while blacks and whites may mix freely in public and may even be invited to the same dinner parties, blacks are still not fully accepted as social equals by most whites. This inequality is reflected in the relative absence of interracial marriages. There are mixed race couples in Barbados, but the white partner is typically non-Barbadian. Indeed, whites have maintained their separateness chiefly through endogamy. For the Caribbean as a whole, David Lowenthal notes, nowhere is miscegenation legally banned or publicly censured, but, nonetheless, white intermarriage remains customary, if not mandatory.

City and Country

Like most small developing countries, Barbados has one principal city, which overwhelms the island's few other urban places in size and importance. Bridgetown, located on the sheltered Caribbean side of the island, is built around a small harbor called the careenage, the place where sloops and trading schooners were once hauled ashore and "careened" on their sides to be cleaned and painted. Two bridges span the careenage. In fact, the city takes its name from a primitive bridge first built by Indians.[30] Large ships no longer use the harbor, yet there is still a great deal of activity as small interisland traders discharge yams, bananas, mangos, papaw, and other produce from the neighboring islands of St. Vincent and St. Lucia. Local fishers unload their daily catch of flying fish and dolphin from bright blue and yellow boats. Before the age of air travel, when the sea was the only means of

Board, or chattel, house. (Photo by Bill Case.)

communication with the outside world, the center of trading was the harbor area. All goods, as well as ideas and news from the outside world, entered here before spreading across the island.

A deep-water harbor was built on the northwestern flank of the city in 1961 so that large oceangoing ships could take on sugar in bulk, directly from the shore. Previously, the sugar had to be put in bags, loaded onto lighters, and ferried out into the bay to ships anchored offshore. The new harbor, which has a half-mile of protective backwater, also made it possible for cruise liners to dock. Passengers no longer had to transfer to launches to get ashore. Within a few years of the harbor's completion Barbados became a primary port of call for Caribbean cruise liners. Today the arrival of cruise ships is marked by the flood of white tourists on the streets and in the duty-free stores in Bridgetown. Most passengers, with only hours in each port, do not venture far beyond Bridgetown; many leave the island with as slanted an impression of Barbados as that of the visitor to the United States who only sees Manhattan.

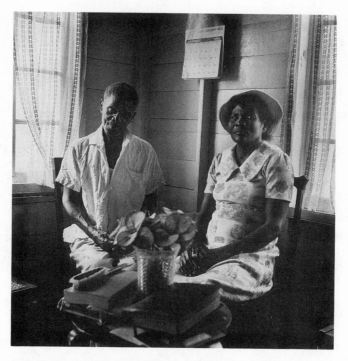

At home, near Mile and a Quarter, a village in St. Peter.
(Photo by Ellen Frankenstein.)

Nearly half the population of Barbados resides in Bridgetown, which has all the hustle and bustle of a major Caribbean city. The sidewalks are narrow and in places abruptly disappear into the road. On these walks fish and vegetable hawkers and Rastafarian coconut sellers jostle with well-dressed businessmen, tourists, and the many country folk who come to town to shop. Twice each day thousands of children from all over the island pass through the city's open-air bus terminals on their way to and from school.[31] Most congested are the roads. Founded in 1628, the year after the initial English settlement, Bridgetown's unplanned narrow and winding road system can scarcely handle the explosion of automobiles that has come with the island's recent prosperity. The prevailing sentiment is that riding the bus is beneath the dignity of the middle class.

Because Barbados' population is concentrated in Bridgetown and the adjacent coastal strips, the rest of the island is fairly rural.

Teenagers at the Holetown Festival. (Photo by Ellen Frankenstein.)

Here the settlement pattern consists predominantly of small villages separated by large tracts of sugarcane and, in places, by gullies.

Barbadian villages are typically an agglomeration of houses on small parcels of land. Houses are strung out single file along the main road with others scattered randomly beyond, connected by footpath more often than road. Villages rarely have a definable center. This is unlike the villages on the islands and Central American rimlands colonized by the Spanish. There new settlements were laid out in a grid with a plaza and Catholic church at the center. In place of a single monolithic church Barbadian villages typically have several small houses of worship. The number and small size reflect a wide diversity of religions. More than 140 different denominations and sects are represented on the island. Villages in Barbados tend to have a low and fairly uniform roofline. In Catholic lands, in contrast, the village church, with its belfry rising well above the surrounding houses, can be seen from miles away and is the focal point of the community.

Besides churches, most villages have several rum shops. Islandwide, there is an average of one rum shop for every 150 adults.

Getting a haircut in Mile and a Quarter, St. Peter. (Photo by Ellen Frankenstein.)

The rum shop serves as a pub and small grocery as well as being a gathering place and domino parlor for village men. For women the churches, with their frequent services, serve a similar function. From a good distance one can hear men slamming dominoes into place and conversing loudly at the outdoor makeshift tables. In many respects the Caribbean rum shop is the counterpart of the neighborhood English pub, except that its patrons drink rum rather than ale, often sit outdoors rather than in, and play dominoes instead of darts.

There are basically two types of village housing, "wood" and "wall." The former, also known as the "board" house, is constructed of a single layer of planks. Its roof was traditionally

Cricket and soccer are the major outdoor sports, though in recent years basketball has also become popular. Here boys play on a makeshift court in the village of Chalky Mount. (Photo by Martin Benjamin.)

covered in wood shingles but is now more commonly covered with sheets of galvanized iron that, unless the house is shaded by trees, creates ovenlike conditions inside. An unusual feature of the wood house is that it can be dismantled and moved to a new location. Some villagers do not own the land their houses sit on. If the landowner raises the rent, there is a disagreement, or if the home-owner saves enough money to buy a plot of land elsewhere, he or she may dismantle the house and reassemble it in another location.

Most Barbadians prefer the wall house. More common in the suburbs and new housing estates than in the villages, it is built of cement blocks and stucco and often encircled by a small cement wall. Both durable and costly, the wall house confers status, and, not surprisingly, it is the type that all emigrants expect to build upon their return home. All of the migrants in this book who

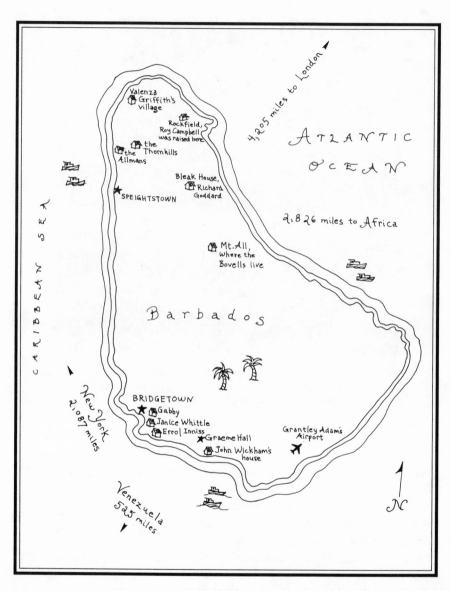

2. Barbados.

Girls returning from school and an agricultural laborer on the road near the village of Chalky Mount. (Photo by Martin Benjamin.)

came from rural or working-class backgrounds were raised in board houses. They hoped that by working abroad they would be able to save enough money to build a wall house when they returned to Barbados. And they all did. Because of the cost, most families other than migrants do not build a wall house all at once but, instead, add cement block additions onto their wood houses, one room at a time. The conversion may take many years; hence, a great many houses are in a constant state of transition, combinations of wood and wall.

There is a certain uniformity to village life, irrespective of location. Lifeways in St. Lucy, in the remote northern part of the island, are not really very different from those in villages of comparable size in the south. In contrast, on most other Caribbean islands, particularly the mountainous ones, there are sharp differences between lowland and highland environments, each requiring a different human adaptation.

Similarly, rural-urban differences are much less pronounced

in Barbados than elsewhere in the Caribbean. The small size of the island and gentle terrain, which makes travel easy, have allowed many Barbadians who work in the city or on the hotel belt to live in the country. No commuter is more than an hour-long bus ride from work. Because of the easy access to Bridgetown coupled with a lowered rate of population growth, Barbados has escaped the massive rural-to-urban migration that today is characteristic of most developing nations. The rural areas are not in danger of losing their population nor starved by neglect.[32] And, although Bridgetown is congested, it has no squatter settlements or shanty-towns and few homeless people. The easy movement of people between country and city has also helped to homogenize Barbadians. Villagers may be more traditional and less sophisticated than their urban compatriots, but the gap between them is strikingly small compared to the other nations of the Caribbean.

The following chapter examines the reasons why Barbadians, like many people from other small Caribbean islands, so often leave their homeland. It widens the focus beyond Barbados to consider the causes and patterns of migration for the British West Indies as a whole, as stories of migration from these islands are all variations on a common theme.

NOTES

1. H. Hoefer and R. Wilder, *Barbados*, 292.
2. J. H. Moxly, *An Account of a West Indian Sanatorium and a Guide to Barbados*, 25.
3. V. T. Harlow, *A History of Barbados, 1625–1685*, 3.
4. Hoefer and Wilder, *Barbados*, 23.
5. A. Chandler, "The Expansion of Barbados."
6. S. Mintz and S. Price, *Caribbean Contours*, 9.
7. According to Trevor Marshall, Carolinian descendants of these early settlers have been returning to Barbados regularly over the last twenty years to dig into birth and baptism records to reconstruct their genealogies and Barbadian ancestry (Marshall, quoted in Hoefer and Wilder, *Barbados*, 56).
8. A similar transformation was repeated throughout the Caribbean. Just as the economy of the Canadian prairies once centered on wheat, the American Midwest on corn, and the Middle East on oil, the economy of Barbados was centered on sugar (B. C. Richardson, *Panama Money in Barbados, 1900–1920*).

9. S. Greenfield, *English Rustics in Black Skin,* 50.
10. B. C. Richardson, *Caribbean Migrants: Environment and Human Survival in St. Kitts and Nevis,* 17.
11. Ibid., 18.
12. The period from 1963 to 1970 marked the transition to when the economy shook free of its three hundred year dependence on sugar as the source of economic growth (D. Worrell, *Small Island Economies,* 52–53).
13. Ibid., 61.
14. The loss of agricultural land to development was slowed after 1974 when a public outcry led to the reintroduction of legislation to protect it (Worrell, *Small Island Economies,* 60).
15. The Barbados dollar is tied to the United States dollar at an exchange rate of approximately two to one.
16. Worrell, *Small Island Economies,* 61.
17. G. Dann, *The Quality of Life in Barbados,* 54, 133.
18. Statistics provided by the Barbados Statistical Service.
19. J. Wickham, "The Thing about Barbados," 226.
20. D. Lowenthal, *West Indian Societies,* 141.
21. Wickham, "The Thing about Barbados," 227.
22. In complex and stratified societies anthropologists have largely given up the idea of trying to get at national character traits because there is so much variation within each population.
23. Hoefer and Wilder, *Barbados,* 61.
24. J. Sheppard, *The Redlegs of Barbados,* 4–5.
25. Mintz and Price, *Caribbean Contours,* 8.
26. See Greenfield, *English Rustics in Black Skin,* 74; and Dann, *The Quality of Life in Barbados,* 88–90.
27. Barbados' Cave Hill branch is one of three campuses in the University of the West Indies system. The other campuses are in Jamaica and Trinidad.
28. Among those returnees who worked for independence were Errol Barrow, the island's first prime minister, who had served in the Royal Air Force (RAF) and later attended university in London; Sir Grantley Adams, trained in London as a lawyer; and Sir Winston Scott, the first native governor-general of Barbados (1967–76), who went to medical school in the United States (Marshall, quoted in Hoefer and Wilder, *Barbados,* 63).
29. Ibid., 62.
30. In the early years of the colony the town was referred to as Indian Bridge, Indian Bridgetown, or simply The Bridge (ibid., 104).
31. The school a child attends is assigned or chosen not on the basis of proximity but, rather, according to qualification based on the child's performance on standardized tests. Hence, many children travel considerable distances to school.
32. Wickham, "The Thing about Barbados," 8.

Chapter 3
Patterns of
West Indian Migration

In the first fifty years after emancipation, from the late 1830s to
the 1880s, the major movement of West Indians was away from the
plantations on which they had been enslaved.[1] They moved to
small landholdings to work themselves, to towns in search of wage
labor, and to other islands. The interisland migration was mainly
to other British colonies within the Caribbean. Much of this movement was in response to the expansion of sugarcane cultivation
and the consequent demand for labor in the newer British colonies of British Guiana and Trinidad.

In the second phase of Caribbean migration, from 1885 to
1920, West Indians still migrated within the Caribbean region but,
in contrast to the earlier people, they went to Spanish and other
non-British territories. They went to Cuba and the Dominican
Republic to work on large sugar estates, to Central America to
work on banana plantations, to Bermuda to construct a dry dock,
and to various other islands to build industrial and military in-
stallations. Their mobility largely followed the pattern of foreign
investments in the region.[2] Most notable in this period, both in
terms of the size of the migration and the number of countries
that participated, was the movement to Panama to excavate and
build the Panama Canal. Able to earn ten cents an hour as "pick
and shovel" men, twice what they could earn on the seasonal
sugarcane estates in their home island, 130,000 British West Indians traveled to Panama between the 1880s and the canal's completion in 1914. Among them were 45,000 Barbadians, or about one-
quarter of the island's total population.[3] Except for Jamaica and

Trinidad, all of the islands saw their populations decline, particularly among men, during this period of out-migration. By the 1920s the out-migration had slowed to a trickle due to the loss of work opportunities with the completion of the Panama Canal, a crash in the world price of sugar in 1921, the introduction of legislation restricting immigration in the United States and in some Central American republics, and, finally, the Great Depression.[4]

Over the next two decades, until World War II, there was little migration. Moreover, this was a time when many earlier migrants returned to their home islands from the United States, Cuba, and the Dominican Republic. During the depression years, with few jobs to be found anywhere, it was generally better to scratch out a living on a small parcel of land at home than be unemployed abroad.

The outbreak of World War II caused a new wave of migration as Britain, the United States, and Canada required workers to help in the war effort and to fill in for the jobs of citizens who were temporarily serving in the armed forces. Some West Indians joined the military as well—eight thousand served in the Royal Air Force alone. In many ways the war was the prelude to the mass migration to Britain and North America that followed. The wartime migration "opened a window on the world, at least the north Atlantic world, which black West Indians now saw in a more familiar, inviting, and accessible light."[5]

The Postwar Migration to Britain

The major migration of West Indians since the end of World War II has been first to Britain and then to North America. While the migration of West Indians to Britain began in the early 1950s, the conditions for it were set during the war: the enormous loss of human life, the devastation of many British cities, and a backlog of neglected work all required additional laborers. A booming economy in the postwar years added to the need for outside labor.[6] The British government, recognizing the need for additional manpower to assist in the reconstruction of the economy, began to recruit workers from its former imperial territories, particularly from the Caribbean and the Indian subcontinent. At the same time, many of the West Indians who returned home after the war were discouraged by the lack of opportunity and deteriorating economies of their islands.[7] Their favorable experiences in Britain, and word that their compatriots who had chosen to be demobilized in Britain were doing well, encouraged them to re-emigrate, and they in turn encouraged their friends.

It was in the 1950s that West Indians emigrated in large numbers. In fact, the movement was of such scale that it is commonly referred to as a "mass migration"; its numbers exceeded all previous movements in the Caribbean. In 1951 the number of West Indians arriving in Britain was estimated at just 1,750, but the figure increased rapidly until in 1955 over 27,000 new migrants disembarked at British ports.[8] The number of new arrivals then declined for several years as the British economy felt the effects of a credit squeeze and the Suez crisis in 1956.

Beginning in 1960, however, the stream of migrants surged again, this time in response to legislation, the Commonwealth Immigrants Bill, which promised to restrict future immigration to the United Kingdom. Over 100,000 West Indians rushed to Britain in 1961 and the first half of 1962 to beat the ban. All told there were approximately 450,000 West Indians in Britain by 1966, with 260,000 having arrived between 1955 and 1962.[9] The total population of Britain at this time in round terms was about 50 million.

The enormity of this migration can best be appreciated in relation to the small size of the sending societies. In less than a decade many islands lost upwards of 5 percent of their populations to migration; in just six years, from 1955 to 1961, Barbados saw nearly nineteen thousand, or 8 percent, of its citizens leave.

Other territories in the British Commonwealth also participated in the mass migration. While Caribbean migrants comprised over half (56 percent) of the total net inward movement (1955–62), they were followed by India (16 percent) and Pakistan (14 percent), with Cyprus, Hong Kong, and the African territories together making up the remaining 12 percent. From within the West Indies the largest migration came from Jamaica. Jamaica, whose population of 1,640,000 (1960) was about 25 percent of the total estimated population of all the West Indian territories, contributed about 60 percent of the migrants.[10]

Most West Indian governments permitted their citizens to leave, some of them seeing migration as a way to relieve their island's overpopulation and keep unemployment down. Barbados actually gave assistance to the migrants; the Barbados Ministry of Labour collaborated with British companies and government agencies wanting to recruit workers. London Transport Executive and the British Hotel and Restaurant Association, for example, set up an office in Bridgetown where Barbadians from all walks of life could come in and interview for a job. As Siebert Allman describes (in chap. 10), any villager could come into Bridgetown and apply for a job three thousand miles away as a conductor on a London bus, a ticket taker on the platform at Euston Station, or a dishwasher in a Lyons restaurant. If they measured up, which most did, the recruiting office would place them in a job, train them, provide them with information about living in England, and help arrange their transatlantic transportation.[11] For its part the Barbadian government helped finance their travel with loans. Upon arrival in England a company's agents would meet the new migrants, provide them with accommodations, and help them to get settled.

The Passage to Britain

In the early years of the emigration to England the West Indians traveled by sea; later they flew. In 1953 there were only three ships making five sailings per year.[12] Two years later there were thirteen ships making more than forty sailings.[13] In addition to more ships and sailings, the number of passengers carried on each voyage had increased as well: in 1953 no ship carried more than three hundred passengers, while five years later each carried up to a thousand migrants.

Over half the ships were Italian; in a curious reversal of migration streams some of the ships carried Mediterranean emigrants to Venezuela on the outward voyage then picked up Britain-bound West Indians for the return crossing. The fare was expensive, and many emigrants had to sell some of their possessions and turn to relatives to raise enough money. Most had never been on a ship before, but once they got their sea legs they enjoyed the voyage—the new experience of being at sea, nightly entertainment, and meeting passengers from other parts of the Caribbean,

West Indian immigrants arriving at the Southampton docks in June 1956. The newspaper (*Picture Post*) that ran this photograph captioned it "Thirty Thousand Colour Problems," referring to the number of West Indians who were expected to arrive that year. The caption is ironic in that the English government was then going to great lengths to recruit West Indian and other immigrant labor. (Photo courtesy of The Hulton Picture Library.)

all on top of the anticipation about what their new lives in England would bring.

The Italian ships did not call at British ports but sailed directly to the Continent. After a week at sea the West Indians disembarked at Genoa or some other Italian port, then boarded a train for the overland journey through Italy and France to the English Channel, then traveled by steamer to Folkestone on the English coast. After being screened by British officials they continued by train to London.

The arrival of a party of West Indian immigrants on the English Channel in November of 1958 was described by sociologist Ruth Glass:

This young woman was one of seven hundred West Indians to
disembark on 9 June 1956, at the port of Southampton, on the
south coast of England. (Photo courtesy of The Hulton Picture
Library.)

The West Indian passengers came ashore last, many of them
still in summer clothes, with some improvised extra covering
to meet the harsh November day. They went quickly through
passport control while two London officials stood by, in case
there were any special questions. Two coaches on the boat-

West Indian immigrants arrive at Victoria Station in London, 1956. (Photo courtesy of The Hulton Picture Library.)

train had been reserved for the West Indian party so that the officials could go around and ask everyone whether they had a place to go to. Everybody had an address to give.

At Victoria [Station] the platform was crowded. There was a mass of dark people; about a hundred friends and relatives were waiting to greet the newcomers. Soon they were all dispersed. No official body has a record of where they have gone to; and no official body knows for certain where they are now.[14]

By the early 1960s charter flights had become the most common means of transport for the transatlantic migrants.[15] Where the sea voyage often became the stuff of family folklore, the plane trip was comparatively free of adventure. Being transported, however, in a single day from the tropical colonies to the European

A West Indian family in a two-room dwelling in Colville Gardens, London, 1967. (Photo courtesy of The Hulton Picture Library.)

mother country was a shock to many. Air travel, by making it quicker and easier for West Indians to go overseas, may have contributed to the out-migration. It certainly has made it easier for the migrants to return home, whether on holiday or for good.

Where They Settled

The arriving West Indians went mainly to cities that were losing population and where the prospects for work were good. Over half settled right in London; the others gravitated toward the cities of the English Midlands—Birmingham, Nottingham, Derby, and Leicester—or they went over the Pennines to Manchester and Liverpool. They avoided Scotland, Wales, and those parts of England where unemployment was high.[16] In contrast to both the white and the Asian immigrant populations, West Indians became concentrated in the inner areas of British cities.[17] With time and

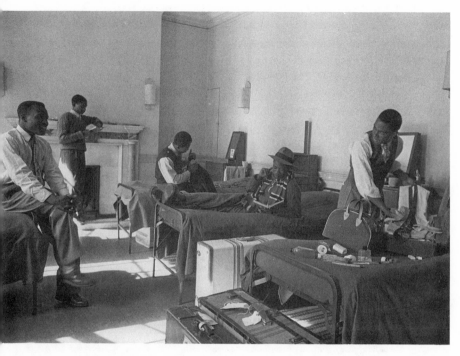

Newly arrived West Indian workers unpacking, 1949. (Photo courtesy of
The Hulton Picture Library.)

improving fortunes some immigrants, such as the Thornhills (see
chap. 8), were able to move out of the city into suburban housing.

Who Went

During the 1950s the doors to Britain were wide open to all
immigrants from the commonwealth, though the British government did try to ensure that passports were not given to people with
serious criminal records, old people, or unaccompanied children.[18] Although just about any commonwealth citizen could
enter, the migrants were, generally speaking, better educated and
more skilled than those who stayed behind.[19] A survey of emigrants leaving Barbados in 1955, for instance, found that 70 percent of them were skilled workers; although *skilled* was broadly

Street scene in Notting Hill, England, 1958. (Photo courtesy of The Hulton Picture Library.)

defined, this was nevertheless double the proportion of skilled people in the population of Barbados as a whole.[20] A 1958 survey of West Indians living in London found that one in four of the men and one in two of the women had been nonmanual workers at home (e.g., professionals, shopkeepers, salespeople, clerks, typists), and that, among the male manual workers in the sample, half were at least skilled or semiskilled.[21] Only one in ten had been farmers or fishers.

As the migration to Britain wore on, however, the number of skilled migrants declined.[22] G. W. Roberts and D. O. Mills, to cite just one study, noticed that the proportion of unskilled workers in the out-migration from Jamaica steadily increased over the three years of their study in the mid-1950s.[23] This finding seems logical in that early on the skilled workers were more likely to have had the financial resources to afford the passage to England. Later, lower fares and the growth of travel agencies made it possible for the less well-off and less skilled to emigrate.

In the early stage of the emigration to Britain men far outnumbered women. Seven of every ten immigrants from 1952 to 1954 were men. After 1957, however, the proportion of women, and also children, in the migration stream increased steadily. And after 1962, when the new immigration act went into effect, the movement became primarily dependents of those who were already settled in Britain, and thus women and children predominated.[24]

Most West Indians migrated as individuals, not as couples or families. And, as the above data on the sex ratio of the emigrants suggests, in most households it was the man in the family who emigrated first, later followed by his wife or girlfriend and some, but seldom all, of the children. Why did the men go first? Were they more ambitious, adventurous, and independent than West Indian women? Definitely not, according to Nancy Foner in a study of Jamaican migrants in New York and London.[25] Rather, she points out, in most households there simply was not enough money for the whole family to emigrate together, and, since men were the principal breadwinners, it was natural that they would go first, while the women would remain behind to maintain the home and look after the children. Then if employment and housing conditions abroad were favorable and enough money could be saved for the additional fares, the women and as many children as could be afforded would be sent for. Another factor was that information about job opportunities was more readily available for men in the Caribbean than for women.

One of the most striking features of West Indian migration was the number of men and women on some islands who were forced to leave many or all of their children behind. The adults who arrived from Jamaica from 1955 to 1960, for example, brought only sixty-five thousand children with them while leaving more than ninety thousand behind.[26] Only one West Indian emigrant in twenty to arrive in Britain during the 1950s was a child. Children were generally left in the care of grandmothers or other relatives, with the parents regularly sending money home for their care.

Slamming the Door

The pattern of emigration from the West Indies, as well as from other tropical commonwealth territories (India, Pakistan, and Africa), was radically changed by the passage of the 1962 Commonwealth Immigrants Act, which restricted immigration. The act was the outcome of a widely publicized campaign begun in the mid-1950s by extreme right-wing groups and some Conservative members of Parliament and widely publicized by the press to control immigration, in particular the immigration of "colored" people. Support for the act came largely from those who believed, first, that immigrants were flooding the labor market, taking jobs away from the native British, and, second, that too many colored immigrants were creating a "race problem" in Britain.[27] In the summer of 1958 white youths armed with a variety of weapons attacked colored immigrants and their homes. Their actions led to counterattacks and much racial tension in London and Nottingham. The following year a young West Indian carpenter was murdered by white youths as he walked home. Although instigated by whites, these incidents fueled fears of racial violence and indirectly increased popular support for restrictions on immigration. By 1961 a Gallup poll found that 73 percent of the Britons interviewed favored some control on immigration.[28]

The introduction of immigration control led to some unexpected results. Namely, it encouraged many people who previously had no commitment to emigrating, but who thought they might someday want to go to England to work, to make immediate plans to depart, before the ban went into effect. The number of arrivals in the year and a half prior to the June 1962 starting date of the emigration ban shot up dramatically: in those eighteen months the influx of new immigrants was almost as great as that of the previous six years combined.[29] Moreover, the migrants arrived at an economically difficult time because the job market was contracting. Had the migration stream been left to respond to labor conditions, the immigration rate actually should have dropped during this period. Another effect was that many migrants already in England who were considering returning home feared that further controls would make their reentry to England difficult and decided to stay on. Paradoxically, the proponents of the immigration control bill had created the very situation they had tried to prevent.

Migration to North America

As Britain closed its doors to new commonwealth migrants, with the exception of dependents of the immigrants already settled in Britain and those who had special job skills, the direction of the outflow from the West Indies shifted to North America.[30] In the 1960s both Canada and the United States eased their immigration restrictions. In 1962 Canada adopted a more "universalist policy" for immigrant admissions, resulting in a large increase in the arrival of Caribbean migrants. From a trickle in the 1950s the number of West Indians migrating to Canada grew to approximately 4,000 in 1966, 12,500 in 1970, and a peak of nearly 24,000 in 1974.[31]

The scale of the "new" migration was even greater in the United States. In 1965 the United States amended its Immigration and Nationality Act of 1952, which had imposed an annual quota of no more than one hundred immigrants from each West Indian territory. By abolishing the national origins system the amendment made it possible for many more West Indians, as well as Latin Americans and others, to enter the United States. The 1965 act has allowed 120,000 immigration visas to be issued annually to citizens from the West Indies and Latin America.[32] New York City, particularly Brooklyn, has had the heaviest settlement of West Indian immigrants, and there are now more West Indians living there than in all of Europe.[33] In Canada, Ontario—and, within that province, the city of Toronto—has been the most popular destination.[34]

While Canada and the United States were admitting more immigrants than before, they were being more selective than Britain had been. Canadian policies based entry on skill, education, and training, and, as a result, these policies had a built-in bias toward skilled workers and professionals. Hence, among the West Indians going to Canada there were many scientists, veterinarians, medical doctors, nurses, dentists, pharmacists, and other skilled and educated workers. An unintended effect of this immigration policy was a "brain drain" and the depletion of the most valuable sector of the labor force in the West Indies. The stricter requirements for admission also resulted in an unprecedented rate of illegal immigration into North America.

Some unskilled West Indians were, and still are, able to emigrate to the United States and Canada as seasonal contract laborers.[35] But, unlike the skilled migrants, these seasonal workers go to a specific job for a fixed period of time, after which they must return home. Most of them do agricultural work and live in camps, and they have minimal contact with the host society. Typically, they remain from two to eight months, depending upon the work they have been contracted for, but they may reenlist the following year, and some make a dozen or more trips to North America during their careers.

Another difference between the mass migration to Britain and the more selective migration to North America was that women outnumbered men. This was particularly true in the early years of the "new" (post-1965) immigration.[36] In 1967 and 1968, for example, among Jamaican migrants to the United States about three in every four were women.[37] Because of the high demand for nurses and domestic workers in U.S. cities, it was then easier for women to qualify for "labor certification." When the demand for domestic labor declined around the end of the decade the proportion of men and women in the migration stream evened out.

In contrast to the movement to Britain, the migration to North America also involved less sentiment. West Indians had long had strong links to Britain: they came from an English subculture, and their religion, laws, school curriculum and textbooks, and many of their customs are British. Although they journeyed to Britain mainly in search of jobs, they were just as eager to see and experience "the mother country." In contrast, movement by West Indians to North America had more to do with its proximity and economic opportunities. The United States offered jobs, good wages, and cheap passage, but absent were the cultural affinities and allegiance the emigrants felt toward Britain. Of course, sentiments are subject to change, and they often did, as the experiences recounted in the following chapters amply show.

How Permanent Was the Postwar Migration?

Very few of the West Indians who went to Britain or North America intended to stay for good. They went to make their "fortunes" as quickly as they could then return home. In the case of Britain, due to the long and costly passage and the relatively high cost of accommodation, most migrants expected to be away at least several years. But, most stayed away much longer than they had ever planned, and a majority have yet to return home. Why have not more gone home? Some have made better lives for themselves in the host societies and do not want to return; others have been so successful at work that returning to the West Indies would require too large a financial sacrifice. Still others have simply been stranded for whatever reason—difficulty finding a good job, low wages, profligacy, illness, a second family—and have not been able to save enough money to come home and fulfill their dreams. Nevertheless, many of them hang onto the hope that someday, perhaps when they retire, they will be able to return.[38]

On the Causes of the Postwar Migration

When discussing the causes of human migrations social scientists often use the terms *push* and *pull*. "Push factors" are simply those conditions or attributes of the homeland that induce individuals to leave, such as difficulty in finding a job, land shortage, poor crop yields, or political strife. "Pull factors" are the attractions of the destination that draw, or pull, individuals to it, such as the availability of jobs, better schools, and the promise of a better life. Although the push-pull framework has been criticized as being simplistic, it is nevertheless a useful device for thinking about the causes of West Indian migration.

Push & pull

On the push side of the equation—the conditions in the Caribbean that make islanders willing to go abroad, willing to give up the security and familiarity of home and old friends—are poverty, deprivation, and overpopulation. Population growth has outstripped economic development, and on many of the islands there are simply too many people for the available resources. On some islands, such as Jamaica, population growth rates of up to 4 percent per year, double that of the nineteenth century, have caused the rural population to become so concentrated on small-holdings that further increases are not possible without a substantial drop in the standard of living or movement off the land.[39]

But movement to where? Unemployment and underemployment have been chronically high in the urban as well as rural Caribbean, so, with jobs in nearby towns and cities already scarce, migration overseas became a common outlet. Urban dwellers were pushed toward emigrating by the same lack of economic opportunity, and, while jobs have been more plentiful in the towns, wages have typically been low, particularly when compared with wage levels in Britain and North America.[40]

Clearly economic deprivation in the Caribbean created the push condition necessary for a mass movement of population. Yet, as William Peterson has rightly argued, hardship can only be termed a *cause* of migration if one can demonstrate a correlation between hardship and the propensity to emigrate.[41] No social scientist has yet shown that such a correlation exists. There now appears to be wide agreement that the postwar migrants were reacting not to internal conditions in the West Indies but, rather, to an external stimulus—namely, the demand for labor in the United Kingdom.[42] In a landmark study of the postwar migration to Britain, Ceri Peach examined migration rates from the different islands then compared them to indices of population pressure, income, unemployment, economic growth, and so on. He found no correlations to show that these push factors were the predominant causes of the movements. Rather, he concluded, adverse conditions in the West Indies had allowed the migration to take place, but they had not caused it.[43]

In fact, rates of migration from different Caribbean islands have tended to follow the same pattern, irrespective of local conditions. The migration rates of Barbados, Grenada, and St. Kitts, for example, might mirror one another in a given year, despite their economies and employment levels failing to rise and fall together. The inescapable conclusion was that the migrants were responding to "factors external to the West Indies."[44] And, again, that external factor was the demand for labor in Britain. When labor demand rose in Britain immigrant arrivals increased, and when labor demand fell, as it did in 1957 and 1959, arrivals decreased.[45]

The sole exception to this pattern was the final year and a half before the imposition of the 1962 Commonwealth Immigrants Act when, in the rush to beat the ban, the number of arriving migrants swelled out of proportion to labor demands.

Looking back over the course of Caribbean migration since emancipation, several patterns are clear. Perhaps the most obvious is that over time the migrants moved further and further afield, first off the plantations but within the British colonies, followed by wider movements to the non-British Caribbean and Central America, and then in this century to Britain, the United States, and Canada.[46] Second, the movements have been in the direction of available jobs. And, not infrequently, the migration was actively encouraged by foreign governments and companies, such as the Isthmian Canal Commission, plantation owners, fruit growers, and the London Transport Executive, which directly solicited workers. Indeed, many migrants had work contracts in hand even before leaving home. The destinations of the migrants have also been determined by the immigration policies of the foreign governments. Whether the migrants could go at all and how many could leave depended as much on the willingness of the host governments to admit them as on the availability of jobs. In short, West Indian migration, like migration from most Third World societies, has generally been a consequence of the dependent and underdeveloped position of the Caribbean economies vis-à-vis the wealthy metropolitan societies. Finally, the West Indian migrations generally have been of a temporary nature.[47] Although many workers did remain behind in the host countries, nearly all left their homelands expecting to return, and many of those who remain abroad today hang onto the notion that someday they will go home. With an understanding of some of the macro level causes and patterns of West Indian migration, we can now turn our lens on the lives of individual migrants, told in their own words.

NOTES

1. B. C. Richardson, *Caribbean Migrants: Environment and Human Survival in St. Kitts and Nevis,* 6; D. Marshall, "Toward an Understanding of Caribbean Migration," 124.
2. D. Lowenthal, *West Indian Societies,* 216.

3. Ibid., 216.
4. This brief review of the history of Caribbean migration is based on the work of Marshall, "Toward an Understanding of Caribbean Migration"; Richardson, *Caribbean Migrants;* and C. Sutton and S. Makiesky, "Migration and West Indian Racial and Political Consciousness."
5. Richardson, *Caribbean Migrants,* 146.
6. While Britain was in need of additional workers many women and elderly, who had taken jobs to help in the war effort, were leaving employment, adding to the labor shortage (C. Holmes, *John Bull's Island: Immigration and British Society, 1871–1971,* 211).
7. S. Patterson, *Dark Strangers: A Study of West Indians in London,* 38.
8. Ibid., 38.
9. R. Harper, *Colour in Britain,* 7.
10. E. J. Rose et al., *Colour and Citizenship,* 44.
11. In the seven years from 1955 to 1961 nearly forty-five hundred assisted migrants left the shores of Barbados. Although they constituted a minority of the overall number of migrants, they did have an impact on the British population well out of proportion to their numbers. As Sheila Patterson explains, this is because so many of them were employed in public transport and the hotel industry, where they came into frequent contact with the British public. On the whole they made a very favorable impression (Patterson, *Dark Strangers,* 38).
12. Ibid., 40.
13. S. Allen, *New Minorities and Old Conflicts,* 38.
14. R. Glass, *Newcomers: The West Indians in London,* 9–10.
15. Patterson, *Dark Strangers,* 40.
16. C. Brown, *Black and White Britain,* 54; Holmes, *John Bull's Island,* 227.
17. D. K. Midgett, "West Indian Migration and Adaptation in St. Lucia and London," 173.
18. F. Field and P. Haikin, *Black Britons,* 8.
19. Richardson, *Caribbean Migrants,* 152.
20. Cited in Rose, *Colour and Citizenship,* 50.
21. Glass, *Newcomers,* 22.
22. Rose, *Colour and Citizenship,* 50–52.
23. G. W. Roberts and D. O. Mills, "A Study of External Migration Affecting Jamaica: 1953–55," 124.
24. N. Foner, "Sex Roles and Sensibilities," 138.
25. Ibid., 138.
26. Lowenthal, *West Indian Societies,* 220.
27. R. B. Davison, *Black British: Immigrants to England,* 7.
28. Allen, *New Minorities,* 39–42; N. Deakin, *Color, Citizenship and British Society,* 49.
29. Holmes, *John Bull's Island,* 261.
30. As an example of how dramatic the shift was in the destination of the migrants, E. Thomas-Hope cites figures from Trinidad. While a large majority of all Trinidadian migrants prior to 1962 went to Britain, only a

mere 7.6 percent went there in the first seven years after the ban went into effect. After the ban, between 1962 and 1968, 58.7 percent went to the United States and 29.0 percent to Canada (Thomas-Hope, "Caribbean Skilled International Migration and the Transnational Household," 424).

31. It is also argued that the immigration control changed the migration from one primarily composed of worker migrants to one of families coming for settlement. In general families have been less likely to consider returning home than single males or females (Deakin, *Colour, Citizenship and British Society*, 54).

32. A. Marks and H. Wesson, eds., *White Collar Migrants in the Americas and the Caribbean*, 89.

33. Richardson, *Caribbean Migrants*, 157.

34. From 1966 to 1970 nearly 350,000 West Indian immigrants arrived in the United States, and during the following decade (1971–80) nearly 760,000 arrived (U.S. Immigration and Naturalization Service, 1980 Annual Report).

35. Marks and Wesson, *White Collar Migrants*, 91.

36. The United States, for example, has been recruiting seasonal farm workers from the English-speaking Caribbean since 1943. The largest employer of West Indian farm labor are sugar growers in southern Florida, who hire up to ten thousand cane cutters annually from Barbados, Jamaica, St. Lucia, St. Vincent, and Dominica. The program is restricted to males, with preference given to those from the poor, small-farm population. See C. H. Wood and T. McCoy, "Migration, Remittances, and Development: A Study of Caribbean Cane Cutters in Florida."

37. Foner, "Sex and Sensibilities," 138.

38. Because most West Indians keep open the option of return migration in case things go bad for them abroad, there is no sharp line that separates permanent from temporary migrants among West Indians.

39. Lowenthal, *West Indian Societies*, 69.

40. Ibid.

41. W. Peterson, "A General Typology of Migration."

42. See, for example, Rose, *Colour and Citizenship*, 74; Watson, *Between Two Cultures;* and C. Peach, *West Indian Migration to Britain: A Social Geography.*

43. Peach, *West Indian Migration*, 92.

44. Ibid., 36.

45. Also affected was the sex ratio of the arriving migrants. As migration rose, the proportion of men in the migration flow also rose. Men were more responsive to the demand for labor than were women or children. Many women and children were migrating to join husbands or boyfriends already established in Britain and therefore were less sensitive to fluctuations of the labor market (ibid., 36).

46. Marshall, "Toward an Understanding of Caribbean Migration," 123–25.

47. Ibid., 116.

Part 2
Barbadians in Britain

Chapter 4
Norman and Ann Bovell

Norman Bovell is eighty-two, and his wife Ann is seventy-five. Norman is tall and thin, while Ann is very short, just four feet ten inches by her own yardstick. They both wear brown felt hats, and Norman is often barefoot. One would hardly suspect that he had spent nearly two decades in London.

Norman first left Barbados during World War II as a contract laborer to the United States, where he worked in a paper factory in Arkansas for six months. He left Barbados again in 1956 for England and did not return until eighteen years later. He held a succession of menial jobs and struggled to save enough money to bring over his family. Ann joined him five years later, but it was a few more years before they were able to save enough for the passage of their children.

When the Bovells returned to Barbados in 1974 they settled in Mount All, a village of several dozen houses strung out single file along the top of a hilly ridge near the highest point on the island. The ridge drops away so sharply that the houses abut the edge of the road, few having enough land for a front yard. Consequently, much of the village's activity—women washing clothes, children bathing, men slaughtering the odd pig or cow—takes place on the road itself. The Bovells' house, with its sturdy cement block construction, red iron railings, and bright blue and burnt orange colors, strongly hints that its occupants have lived abroad. In fact, it was the appearance of the house that made me pause on the road one day and ask if the owners were returnees. The view from the house is among the best in Barbados. To the east you look down into a rich green valley of cane fields and palm trees and beyond that to the villages of Baxter and Cane Garden. At the far side of the valley is Chalky Mount, the village of potters, and a few miles beyond that the vast Atlantic. To the west the view takes in Mt. Hillaby, the highest point on the island, and Turner Hall Woods, the sole surviving patch of primeval tropical forest. The Bovells used to sit on

Norman and Ann Bovell, 1988. (Photo by Ellen Frankenstein.)

the cliff to watch the sunset, but now they no longer notice the view. A few years ago an American wanted to buy their property. "He offered me more money than I'd ever see in me lifetime," said Norman, "but I didn't sell."

I first interviewed the Bovells as part of the survey of return migrants I did in 1983. Two years later I returned to their house to ask if they would be willing to do a series of in-depth interviews on tape. They were reluctant. Ann asked, rhetorically, if she hadn't already told me her story, and they both wondered why anyone would be interested in their experiences, as they were just "common people." Probably more as a favor to me than of their own desire, they finally agreed. I interviewed them three times for this book and later twice on camera for a documentary film. Each time I went back I had to reconvince them that they had more to say. But once they started in they both quickly warmed to the task, and, in describing experiences, they would often get up from their chairs and act, changing voice and manner to suit the characters they were portraying. Often Norman would start to answer one of my questions, and Ann would cut him off and finish the story. Often they talked over one another, and I wouldn't know who to listen to. The interviews were always long, never less than two hours, and they were interrupted by one or the other going off to feed the chickens, water the cow, or just finding something that they wanted to show me. Despite their initial reluctance, I felt they always enjoyed telling their experiences, and they were never in a hurry for me to go.

The story they tell is rich in ethnographic detail and reveals much about the adjustment that was required of peasants in cosmopolitan London. Ann Bovell, in particular, is overwhelmed by the strangeness of the new society and the customs of its white people. But she is able to see the humor in her own naive attempts to get along in London, such as answering back at the loudspeaker that had paged her at Heathrow Airport. The Bovells say much about the kind of work West Indian immigrants performed and of the difficulties of being separated from children left behind in the Caribbean.

Today the Bovells are retired, but Norman spends many hours each· day working in his garden and tending his cow, turkeys, and chickens. Ann cooks and sells soda pop from her front window, about twenty bottles a week for a profit of two dollars.

Norman Bovell

So you want to know how I got caught up going to England. Well, I went there to make money, or, as some people would say, to look for my fortune. In my boy days in Barbados you couldn't reach [earn] the money here you could reach in England. There was many folks here who never had money to buy things or to fix things up. Then the emigration scheme came along, and I saw all the young folks going up to England, and I said I would give it a try. Plus, in the olden days you heard a fair bit about England, and you wanted to see it with me own eyes. I was about forty years old then, but most of them that went was twenty and thirty.

I left here in November 1956 on the Italian ship called the *Napoli*. The fare was £66, that amounted to 300 Barbados dollars in those days. That was a heap of money.

When I arrived in England I was to meet my friends at Victoria Station, but they never come. I wait and I wait, but I don't see them. I don't know where to go, but then I see a fellow I know from Barbados, and he tells me he can give me lodging. This is Tuesday night. On Wednesday I go right out, and I pick up a job at the emigration [labor] office. The emigration chap asks me if I can start work the same day. I tell the chap to let me look around first, that I am a visitor to England, and that I need to know my way back to my digs. You wouldn't want to get lost your first day in London. I go back Thursday, and they have a job lined up for me, putting on paint. I was working from that day in 1956 until I left England eighteen years later. But not the same job—I skipped from job to job.

The first job I had was being a painter at the Farraday School in London. Painting was hard. When I get there the boss presents me with a brush and some paint and takes me to the spot. Then he say, "Start painting." We is working under contract, so you is always being rushed. The boss stays down below in the basement of the school, where they keep the paint. And every now and then he comes up from underneath to see how far you got. As soon as you got to your destination, before you could put the brush out of your hand, he presents you with another brush and another color of paint. There was no letting up. I stayed a few weeks, then I said to myself, "This job will kill me if I don't leave."

So I leave the painting and go to an engineering firm, to a firm that is making nuts and bolts for television. Then I leave that job and go to work at Lyons Hotel in Oxford Street. Then I leave there and work in the buildings carrying cement. When I leave that I go back to Lyons Hotel. Next I work for a large firm whose name I forget. At this place I do labor, and when the toilet cleaners don't turn up for work the foreman asks me if I will clean the toilet. I did everything; I never turn work down. So I say, "Yes, I will clean the toilet." But my countrymen, my own color, say funny things to me. They say they didn't come to England to clean toilets.

I leave London when work get a bit scarce. I write to my friends in the country to know what jobs are up there, and they write back and tell me to come up. So I go on the train at Kings Cross. I don't know where I am going except that thirty-two miles away is my destination, a place they call Letchworth. Some white people told me what I had to do. You can give me white people anytime. They can be great; they use their ability. When I got off the train I didn't know what bus would take me to Letchworth, but I had a mouth to speak. When I got off the bus the conductor tells me how to get to Green Lane, where my friends lived. Now, you know, a lot of people wouldn't take that chance of traveling in a strange place; they'd be afraid of never finding the way.

Well, my friends aren't home, but the landlady let me put down my suitcase. I went right out and start to hustle a job. The first factory I come to is where they make the mouths [barrels] for guns. No job here. But at the next place I ask the chap [guard] at the gate what the factory does.

He says, "They make bacon."

I say, "What is bacon made of?" 'Cause I'd never seen bacon made before. I did buy bacon in the city, but I never knew where it came from.

He say, "They kill pig."

I say, "That my line."

He say, "Could you kill pig?"

I say, "Yes, I used to slaughter them back in Barbados."

He say, "Well, you is the man they are looking for. Let me take you around to the manager." So the bloke took me around to the manager, and the manager say, "You can start work here Monday morning at seven o'clock." And he take me through the factory, and he introduce me.

I work with this other chap. Our job was to kill one thousand pig a day. We have a thing that give out strong electric shock. We'd go like that [he motions as if putting a large pair of scissors behind the ears of a pig]. When pig gets shock he falls down. The other chap give the shock, and I put a chain around back feet of pig and hang him up. Then the pig is pulled up near ceiling where he slide him along to the machine that have hot water. The machine scrub all hair off pig, and when he come out the pig as white as paper.

I enjoy that job until the end of time, but I leave it because one day they bring in a big boar. You know, a big great pig with two tusks [he uses his index fingers to make like tusks]. The boar fixes himself in the corner [he backs into the corner of the room making like a pig], and the boar looking at me. So me and this chap go in and herd him. The chap says to me, "You take a chance with the electric thing."

I say, "No, it your job. My job is to wrap chain around pig's feet after he go down." Now I am thinking about a chap at another bacon factory that was killed by a boar that put his mouth on him and tore him up with his two tusks. And this here boar in front of me have a neck like a pumpkin. Well, the chap pokes the boar with the electric thing, and he fall down. But only for a short time. He then jump up. He is ravenous, and he make terrible noises. He run wild around the place. He come after me, and I thinking he going to tear me down if he get his mouth on me. Well, that was my lot. I quit. I walk right out.

I leave Letchworth bacon factory then and go to a factory in Hitchen Herts. There I get work feeding the machines with oil. And I work there ten years, until I come home to Barbados in September 1974.

The only thing that really upset me in England was the climate. Leaving a hot country like Barbados to go into a cold country, you'd expect an upset. In London I used to ride a bicycle seven miles from where I live to where I work, and sometimes when I get off the bicycle I'd seize up with the cold. I so cold that I'd make for the big oven where they bake the bread and cakes, but I had to ask for a space to get near oven because there are so many men standing around it trying to get heat into their bodies. I used to see some push their hands up in the fire.

But, as for living with the English folks, I never have no trouble at all. I work shoulder to shoulder with them. They give me a hard joke, like they ask me why I don't go back where I come from. But I give them a hard joke back. They have prejudice toward the colored, but they try not to show it. I think there will come a time when there will be no more prejudice, you see the Bible tells that the lion and the lamb will lie together. Nowadays when I watch sport on television I see the colored man in it; nearly all the fellows you see in the picture, in the sports, do be colored. Well, in the year nineteen hundred forty you wouldn't see that. Oh no, you wouldn't see nothing like that. Today you even see a colored man on the moon.[1]

I got along alright with the English, and I go to their house, and I take tea with them. And I got on splendid with the Irish, but the Indians is terrible. They lived near me, and they didn't know a word I was saying. When I first go to Letchworth, where I got work in the bacon factory, I knocked on the door of my friends, and these Indians came to the door and start to speak to me. I don't have no idea what they is saying. I learn the Indians don't eat

---

1. He is referring to the United States space shuttle *Challenger*, which had a black crew member. It exploded around the time of the interview.

meat; they don't use no knife and fork; they don't use spoon either.

And if you living in one of their houses, they don't let you carry meat into the house. Now, how is a West Indian who likes beef and pork going to live in the Indian house when he cannot eat his own food? You see, where they come from, in the country of India, they worship sows, so they don't want you eating cow in their house.

Indians have a very cheap way of living; they don't spend no money. An Indian or a Pakistan come into England one year, and the next year they have about two houses. I am glad I got to know them or I wouldn't be able to sit here and tell you this.

Like most of the male West Indians who emigrated to Britain in the 1950s, Norman Bovell left his wife and children at home, intending to send for them if the work conditions and accommodations were satisfactory. After five years in London Norman had saved enough cash to send for his wife, though he could not yet afford to bring his four children. Here Ann Bovell tells her story.

Ann Bovell

I leave Barbados the last week in May in 1960, and I got to England the twelfth of June. I figure it'd be two weeks on the sea. I went by boat of the name *Serrienta*. To tell the truth, I had a very lovely voyage. But when I leave here I was scared. I feared that I would get sick and that, if I died on the sea, they would throw me body overboard. My mother told me that I no be sick. She did tell the truth because, when the boat came into the harbor in Bridgetown to carry us to England, a doctor came aboard and sprayed [germicide] all about, and so I no get sick on the sea.

The boat take us to Genoa, and then we take the train and boat and train again to England. When I get off train at Victoria Station I meet my husband and my sister and some friends. We take a taxi to Letchworth, where me husband is living. We go there at night and in the morning, when I open my eyes and look around, I say to my husband, "Hey, they got a lot of factories down here."

He say, "They isn't factories. They is the people's houses, and they live in them."

I say, "What? Them places all have chimneys, and we pass a very lot of them where smoke do be coming out the top."

He say, "Yes, but they is the people's houses, and the smoke coming up is the chimney where the people make fire inside the house to keep the house warm."

I say, "But I don't see no house."

He say, "That is because they are attached, one to the other, but that each man has his own door to go in."

The next day I see everything for myself. I see how Mrs. Cumberbatch, the landlady, light the fire and put coals on it. Then I go outside and look up and see the smoke going up the sky out of chimney. Then I see all the people come out of the houses that I think are factories.

Well, I land in England on the Sunday, and on the Monday me husband, Norman, tell his boss that he would like a day or two off to show me around. On Tuesday Norman carries me down the town. My eyes are big like so with seeing all the things that I never see before. After we come back home I go out by myself. I want to see if I can go around the block and find my own way back. So, while Norman is busy cooking in the kitchen, I slip up the road. Off I go. I watch the cars and the lorries go round the roundabout. Then I go down the hill, this way and that way. After a while I do a big circle and reach back to where my own gap [road] is, just where I first started out. I see Norman coming down the road looking all over for me. He look very worried; he think I get lost. He shout at me.

Norman went back to work then, and I stood home. The landlady took me out to look for work, and at the labor [employment office] they give me a card and tell me to go to a hostel, a place where plenty of people live. But my landlady tell me not take that job, that I would be a maid and that I would have to go into people's rooms and tidy them and pick up ladies whatnots. She say it not a nice job. And I say, "That not my line of work."

But I get fed up staying home because each morning the landlady leave her children with me to look after while she go to town. I tell Norman, "I don't come to England to sit down. I come to England to work, so help me find a job."

Norman ask his boss to give him a few days so that he could carry me around to get employment. The next day we start walking until we come to this big factory called Casibondar. I say I will try my luck here. But I am a bit scared, so Norman go forward and say to the policeman [guard] at the fence, "Good morning, we are looking for a job." I stand back in case there be trouble. But the white man, the policeman, talk to Norman very nice. When I hear the nice talk I step forward. The policeman take us up to the office. I sit down in a chair and a lady [secretary] take down my details. She ask me many questions. I can't understand the language so nice, so she ask Norman to fill out a form for me. The lady very nice and ask me about me children in Barbados and if I like England. Then she take us to another room, and another woman question me the same way. How long I be here? If I like it? If I have children? Who looking after them? If I want to bring them here when I settle? I tell her, "Yes, I'd love to get me children here."

She say, "We want people to come to work who want to stay and not to come today and leave tomorrow." Norman tell her that I won't be leaving tomorrow, that I am eager for work.

She say to him, "Could your wife start today?"

He say, "No, let me take her back home today and show her way around, how to get to bus, how to get home, and how to get to factory." He tell the lady that I come the next day.

She say, "We'll be looking for you but don't go yet." She press a button and a tall gentleman appear. She say to me, "Mrs. Bovell, this is your boss. Mr. Barker his name." When I look up at him, he say, "I am going to call you 'Shorty.' That is your name, Shorty."

The woman say to him, "Take her down to the department and show her around to the girls, so when tomorrow come she will know them." In the factory I was the only one of my color.

When we leave Norman show me all the gaps and little corners that cut through to the factory. When we got home, I say the Lord really work for me this morning. I thank the Lord. Well, I work there for fourteen years, until I leave to come back here. That be the only job I do in England, and I never did clean up the ladies' whatnots at the hostel.

The factory made clothing. They knit material there, and when they finish it it go into a big trough where they wash it. After the wash it go through a steam roller. I am at one side of the roller, and another lady is at the other side. As the material comes out of the roller, we fold it onto a cart, and when the cart full of material we take it away and pull up a new cart.

The first day I work there one of the ladies tell me that she going to take me to lunch. I say alright, but what kind of food it going to be? It is cabbage, beans, boiled potatoes, boiled fish, and a drink in a bottle with a straw. You know, we Barbadians cook our food with salt. Well, the English don't. They have the salt on the table, in a salt jug. I never knew that English food have no salt, and the first piece I put in my mouth don't have no taste at all. No taste at all. I look at her. She say to put a little salt and a little pepper on it and see how nice it is. I say, "I am sorry, but I can't eat it." She say that she is sorry that I can't use the food, and she tell me how in England they don't cook with salt because not all people take salt. Now I never heard of such. The next day I tell her I have my lunch with me, and from then onwards I carry me own lunch.

When I first went to the factory a white lady, she talk so nice, she ask me, "Annie, you want to save money?" I laugh.

She say, "I'm not joking. I ask if you want to save money."

I say, "Yes, I like save money."

She say, "I am going to show you what to do." And she show me how I could let the company take out so much from me pay and put it aside. I tell the company what to take out, and they save it for me, and when I get ready for the money I can ask for it.

The white people was lovely. Some talk with me, some bring me presents, some want to know if I have children back home. A lady bring me a lot of small clothes that her girls grow out of. They nice clothes, and they fresh—she washed them out. Yes, white people can be lovely.

I was two years folding the material when the firm bought a factory up north and took the knitting department away. Then I went upstairs to do socks. When they make socks they put in a seam, and you got to check to see if it got holes. If it got holes, you put them aside. They call that sorting out, and that was what I did. I was there a year, and then they carry me to the stockings department. They teach me how to stitch the toes of stockings on the big machines.

There was twenty-four machines and twenty-four ladies in one big place. The work didn't worry me because we all talk and make jokes with one another, and if your machine break down, you would come by me and help me shake down [compress] the stockings in my bag. The only thing I didn't like was when it got very hot. I did like that job. But while I was there I had a baby, and it born dead.

On Saturdays and Sundays, after I finish making the dinner and do the wash, then we would go out for a ride. Norman had a big bike, and I would ride on the back. One time he took me to a pub with some of his friends from work. His friends were with their wives, and they told him to go get his wife, so he bring me along. I don't mind telling you that there was a lot of people in the pub, some sitting down and some standing up and some of them throwing the darts. I was very scared that I might be stabbed by the dart. You see, me and me husband were the only two colored among the lot, and you know how the English don't like the colored, and they carrying them darts. I get so scared that I whisper to Norman to take me home. When we get home I tell him that I not accustomed to the pub. I tell him, "Don't carry me to no pub at all again."

I went to the theater two times, but I'd never go back after that. One time he took me to see Cliff Richard and the Chubby Checker doing the rock 'n' roll and another time to see Cliff Richard singing with the dancing shoes and the children. It was very nice, but to tell the truth I didn't feel right. In Barbados I never practiced going to the theater, and then to go over to England where there are ruffians, where the people might carb [hit] you, well, I did be afraid that I could be stabbed. So I tell Norman, "No more theater."

When I got settled in England I started going to church. It was St. Anne's Church, the Church of England. This fellow dressed in the clothes of a priest come to our door one day. Norman let him in, and we have a long chat. He reads some Scriptures and then he invites us to his church. Our home was number 3, and the church was number 7—same street, same side. When the service finished he come right down, and he stand by the door, and he shake everybody's hand. He miss nobody. He even shake the little ones.

But some white people in the church don't like it; they don't like him shaking hands of the colored. They think he is too friendly with us. Yes, I hear the people whisper that the reverend is very friendly with the colored. The white people didn't like that, and they had the priest sent away to another church.

We got a new priest then. But he was a very young man, and he was friendly mostly with the young people. He never mind the old ones much, not even the old white ones. There was no unity left in the church then, so we left the Church of England and joined the New Testament Church [Pentecostal]. It was all colored, all West Indian, but the pastor was a white man. Yes, Pastor Robinson was a white man. It was just like the church I'd left here in Barbados, so I was very happy. They baptized us, and we did fellowship with them until we came home.

During the early years in England we didn't have our own house. Living with a lot of other families in somebody else's house could be real rough. There was four families of us living in the one place, and we all used the same kitchen and dining room. Everybody would be in the kitchen at the same time trying to cook. Now that is a big vexation. You'd have on your saucepan, I'd have on my saucepan, she'd have on her saucepan, and every time you would turn around you'd butt into somebody. And then the children be running through, and they weren't even your own. I'd say to Norman, "Look, I didn't leave my clean, happy house in Barbados to come here to butt in the kitchen with these people."

He'd say, "You try and make out until we get money for your own home." I used to feel happier at work than at the house, and that shouldn't be.

Norman Bovell

I wanted a house of my own, because my wife wasn't happy living with so many other people. Plus, she and the landlord's wife could not get along. Plus, the landlord wanted our money, but he never wanted to give service. My wife kept jamming down me throat, "Get some place for us to live." Every day, "Get some place to live." I'd say, Lord I am in trouble if I don't get a house. So I go to the land agent's office—we had been in England nine years then—and I tell the man, "Sir, I want to buy a house."

He say, "Well, Mr. Bovell, what sort of house you want?"

I tell him just a little house since I ain't got much money. He asks about my job at George King Stephens Company. I tell him, "I earn seven to eight pounds a week" but that I do plenty overtime and that me wife work too.

He say, "Mr. Bovell, you will have to look for a two-bedroom house. He then give me a slip to take away, and I walk around looking at the houses. There do be some big, nice houses, but I ain't got the income for them. But then I see a house I could buy. The agent lend me some money, so I buy it. It got four rooms in all, but I took the basement and made a sitting room, and we all have enough space.

And I pay back the money so quick that he lend me more money to furnish the house, and I pay back that money so quick that you won't believe it. Well, then I asked the agent to lend me some more money to send for our oldest girl, to bring her up to England from Barbados. Me wife and I work a lot of overtime, and we pay that back. Then I borrow more money to send for the other three kids. The man said to the cashier, "I want you to look up Mr. Bovell's account for me." After he look at my account the man said, "We can't turn back a man like you, Mr. Bovell." And he gave me whatever amount of money I wanted.

Ann Bovell

When we moved into our house in Hitchen we hear a knocking at the door, and we look down from the top window, and we see this white lady. I say, "Hello, do you want some person?"

She say, "Yes, I want to see who my neighbor is." So I come down from upstairs, and I open the kitchen door, and she come in, and she say, "What is your name?" Just like that. I called my husband out from upstairs, and he come down. And she say again, "What is your name?"

I say, "My name is Bovell, and this is my husband, Mr. Bovell."

She say, "My name is Mrs. Collarbone." I laugh, because I never heard that name before.

She ask if we'd like some tea. My husband say yes, so she brought over a pot of tea and a jug of milk and a bowl of sugar and bread too. We had no table yet, so she had to rest it on the kitchen sink. We drink it, and it all right. She come back to see how we settle in. And soon we got very friendly. She would call for us, and we would call for her. After my children came from Barbados they would play out on the pasture [lawn] at the back of the house with her children. The lady on the other side was white too. There was white ladies on both sides of us. Well, she was nice too, and her children do be at our house all the time playing with my children. But it is a curious thing that she never have my children to their house to play. I never know the truth to that, but I think it because we are colored.

Many families left some or all of their children at home in Barbados while they were working abroad. Separations of ten years and more were not uncommon, though those who could afford it tried to return to Barbados every few years to see their children. Yet even separations of a few years could be stressful, and I often wondered how well the parents coped. The subject usually did not come up until late in the interviews. Even after many years at home it was an issue that some parents could not discuss comfortably. Ann Bovell left her four children behind when she emigrated in 1960; it was not until four years later that she could afford to bring over the first child.

Ann Bovell

I don't know how to tell you about being away from my children. It was so terrible. One time I keep going to the doctor—I feeling so sick over them. The doctor, his name was Dr. Haynes, he look me all over and tell me that he can't find what make me sick. Then he ask me many questions. Questions about how I get along with me husband, does me husband give me money, does I get along with the people in the factory where I work? I tell him, "Yes, I get along alright with all the people."

He then ask me about my children back home. He say, "Who look after them?" "Do you send money for them?" "Would you like to get them over here with you?" I tell him how badly I want my children here but that I don't have a home yet.

He say, "When you get a home will you bring them over?" And I tell him that I'm worried about the children living with my father.

You see, my father was not nice to me when I was a child. He made us work very hard, and he sometimes hit me, and I think he won't be nice to my children. My mummy will do her best, but I worried about how my father treat them.

The doctor say, "Mrs. Bovell, there nothing at all wrong with you except that you is worried. You is worried over the children. If you don't stop worrying over them there isn't anything that I, nor no other doctor, can do for you. So stop worrying and work as fast as you can to get them a home and bring them over to England."

I tried to stop the worry, but then I see pictures on the television of South Africa and pictures on Vietnam and pictures on the slums in America. When I see children in those pictures I'd say, "Oh Lord, I wonder if my children look like them." I'd remember my little girl, and I'd wonder how she is. She was two when I left, and now she going on five years. When her father leave Barbados she was just a baby, so she don't know him at all. Then I'd think it strange that me mother and father never send me pictures of her. And I wonder if she alright.

Well, we work real hard, and we save every shilling we can. Save, save, save. We send for the children, and they come on the airplane. When we go to the airport [Heathrow] I see the children come off the plane, and the littlest one begin to vomit. Then I don't see them no more [the children were being escorted into the customs area]. While I am out there [in the arrival lounge] waiting for them, through the loudspeaker a man say, "Is Mrs. Bovell out there? If Mrs. Bovell out there, please come to the second door."

I shout, "Yes, I am here." I don't know the speaker can't hear me. And the people out there laugh and look at me. Then I go to the second door, and there are the girls. The one that I worry over is stretched out on the beds [customs table] where they searches things. She has cotton up her nose. "Oh God, she dead," I say. I have a terrible fright.

Then the woman tell me, "No, she ain't dead, she ain't dead." I took up my child in me arms. She not saying a word. I slap her and shake her to bring her out of it. [Ann imitates slapping and shaking a child, and then the child giving a big sigh, coming out of a faint.] Then my girl Annie open her eyes, and she sees me. The room is full of people watching me bring this child to life. They tell you not to worry, not to worry. Well, that little thing could have gone dead. I had needed to worry.

The next week I had to carry the children down to the doctor for an injection. Polio or something. When I see the doctor I say to him, "I want you to see why I be so worried. This child, my eldest boy, should be a big young man, but he ain't but a little chalk. And that one there, I said about my eldest girl, I leave her big and fat, and now she be thin. And this one here, the youngest, I had to bring home in my arms. She nine years old, and I had to carry her home like a baby, and all the way I looking in her face to see if she be dead.

The doctor tell me, "I see why you worry, but you are not supposed to worry so deeply that you make yourself sick."

I felt better then, having all the children around me, and I start thinking about how I got to work on them to fatten them up and make them strong.

Well, the children was very happy to be with us in England, but they in a puzzle too. The little one always wanted to see her daddy. You see, her daddy left Barbados when she was just six months, so she had only seen a picture of him. She used to say, "Where is my daddy? Where is my daddy?" I wrote to him and told him to send some pictures over. He did. Then I could say to her, "This is your daddy, this one here in the picture." And every night she would huggy up the picture. When she got to sleep I would take the picture from her and put it down. But now when she got to England she didn't want to believe that Norman was her daddy.

And the big girl and the big boy wanted to know how their daddy got so dark skinned. He would say to them, "England make some people clear and some people dark." I'd say to the children, "He no darker than you, and he clearer than me." Then I say, "England make some people dark and some clear." After that they'd have no more questions.

After I got the children down to England, the boy learned to drive, and he'd take us for a ride on Sunday out to Luton and Bedford and places in the country. We didn't go too far because I'd want to be back in time for church [evening service]. I never like to miss church.

In 1973 Ann Bovell returned to Barbados to visit her elderly parents, but

*before she arrived her mother died. Her father wanted her to stay with him
and remain home for good. She refused but promised him that should he
ever become seriously ill and need her help she would return. Several
months later Ann received several urgent letters from her father. He claimed
to be gravely ill, and he beseeched her to return. She was not convinced
her father was telling the truth and did not want to leave England,
but Norman insisted that she keep her word. They argued, and he repeated
over and over, "If you promise, you got to go; if you promise, you got
to go."*

*Ann gave in, and they sold the house in England and returned home.
The youngest child returned with them, while the older children, already
grown and out of the house, chose to remain in England. When the Bovells
arrived home in Barbados they found Ann's father had tricked them.
Today, thirteen years later, he is still alive and well.*

*Once again Norman and Ann were separated from their children,
except one—but now it was the parents who were in Barbados and the
children who were abroad. At the time of his return Norman had not seen
Barbados in eighteen years, not since 1956, and Ann had been back only
once in thirteen years.*

Norman Bovell

When I got here I had a good rest for two days. Then I put up my
workbench and started fixing up the house. We stayed over there
[he points across the road to a ramshackle board house that had
been vacant for many years]. The chap that owned the house was
in the Virgin Islands working. We paid him money to let us live in
it while I fixed up our house.

I bought a cow, and I planted my fields with onions, okras,
pumpkins, cucumbers, cabbage, beans, and tomatoes. And I liked
being in the countryside again where you are surrounded by
various scenes. In the city you are too tucked in—a house here,
there, here, there; you all tucked in. There ain't much breathing
space, and that is no good for you. But I never regret going to
England, and I never regret coming back.

But to tell the truth, Barbados was a lot different when I came
back here. When I leave here people was very strict. In my boy days
you wouldn't come to school late. When you heard the bell ring
the teacher close the door, and if you come late you would not get
through the door without getting lashes. The teacher would knock

the smoke out of you. Now when I came back here the young ones want to fight the schoolmaster.

And the young ones don't want no work, and they smoking a lot of dope. Well, these changes make my blood boil. Make my blood boil. I proud of the world, but I not proud of how the people in it carry on.

And the people here are not so mannerly. In England when you go out in the bus there is nobody pushing you, nobody screaming. When the bus come they all walk on, and when the bus stop they all walk out. When you go to church and you don't know the hymns they take your book and they show you. In England they live mannerly. Sometimes I cannot get myself adjusted to the way these people here carry on.

When my wife gets upset she says she wishes we'd never come back. But I never say that. I was comfortable in England, and I is comfortable here. I think I was always a satisfied person. Money is not all that I want. I want to know that I am living fair. I want to know that I am living at the start of an Almighty God. I don't intend to rob no person or endanger no person, and, if I have anything to offer you, I'll give it to you from my heart. That is how I live.

Ann Bovell

When I first came back here I would be thinking a lot about my working at the factory in England and how I miss that. But then all that thinking go away from me. And now I think I did right coming home, because, if I was still over there, I wouldn't be working anymore because of my age. I'd be retired, and I'd just have to sit in the house all day with the fire burning, and that ain't going to make me feel good. Here I can run in and out of the house, and I don't have to put on all kinds of coats to go outside.

But it's not all good. When I come back the people look like they gone darker and dry out. They look so poor. But my friend say to me, "Annie, they look so black to you because you seeing all those white people all those years." I think she right. It was seeing all those white people that make me see me own people different.

Plus, I was working in those factories in England under white lights all the time that make me see my people different.

The younger women here don't know me, because when I leave Barbados they was just babies. But the older ones know me, and I try to speak to them and be as friendly as before I went away. But some of them gets cocky up against me. They do be very jealous. When the lorry come to our house with three big crates with all our things from England everybody in the village standing around, saying, "What you got there?" That's when the licks began. Colored people can be very jealous.

And when we fix up our house the people say, "What you ever going to do with that big house? Why you need live in that big house?" Grudge, grudge, grudge. The people say that I don't want friends. They say I don't want to share. Them that do the talking [gossiping] are the same ones that I brought goods for. I give them rice, I give them coffee, I give them dinner plates. I give all around, and I try to keep friendship with them. They took my things, but then they cut me up.

Some of them think that if you been over to England or America or Canada, that you have brought back a fortune. Some of them get very long faced when they see you bring back things they don't have. Norman say the men adopt the principle that, if you be near a rum shop, you should go in there and treat them all.

This morning I was telling Norman that I don't know what I came back here for. I would rather be up there in England. Never mind the cold and all the coats. The white people is so loving, and they talk with me so nice. And, to tell the truth, I feel real bad about the children being over there and me being here.

Chapter 5

Roy Campbell

Roy Campbell emigrated to England in 1962 at the height of the final rush before the ban on immigration went into effect. He had a sister and a brother already in London and therefore a place to go and family to help him get settled. He was just nineteen, had never been away from home, and had only a vague notion of what life in England would be like for a young West Indian. He planned to be abroad for about five years, just long enough to "make his fortune." But once he arrived in London he was so cold and unhappy that he wanted to return to Barbados, as soon as he could save enough money for the return fare. Nearly two decades passed before Roy finally went home for good. As with so many immigrants, the inertia of being settled, a larger salary than could be earned in the Caribbean, and a marriage and children were obstacles to returning sooner than he did.

In the beginning of his narrative he talks about growing up in a village in Barbados, where the life of young boys revolved around the game of cricket. When I learned that Roy had also played cricket in England, I was interested in learning more. I wondered how West Indians, the most talented players in the world, might fit into the local cricket scene and what role, if any, sports played in their adjustment. Roy did not say much about his own playing days; he agreed, however, to bring along some of his mementos to our next interview. A week later he showed up with a scrapbook and a bag full of trophies that he had won in England. He lined up the trophies on my desk and explained the meaning of each one. From the team's souvenir program I learned that he had been a star batsman: in 1972 he had averaged more than eighty runs per game, and by the time Roy left England he had become the third highest run producer in the history of the Trinity team.

Roy's narrative comes from three interviews; all were done in a marine

Roy Campbell at his home near Bridgetown, 1988. (Photo by Ellen Frankenstein.)

biology lab at Bellairs Research Institute, where I sometimes worked. Roy was a bus inspector on a route that ran by the institute, which made it easier for him to stop by than for me to drive to his home in Bridgetown. He was always an eager narrator; I needed only to raise a question, and he would take off with it, talking for many minutes with nothing more than occasional nods and raised eyebrows from me as encouragement to keep on going. Roy was concerned that his narrative be entirely accurate; if he couldn't remember some place or name, he would mull it over until it came back to him.

Roy is a handsome man and resembles a major league baseball catcher with his thick chest and muscled arms. He is energetic, likes to be busy, and has no patience for passing time on the street corner or in the neighborhood rum shop. Roy talks exuberantly and has a friendly, outgoing manner.

Today the Campbells live in a respectable wall house on the outskirts of Bridgetown. Wall-to-wall shag carpeting, patterned wall paper, plastic sofa covers, a bronze-colored replica of Big Ben, and an ashtray with a picture of the boardwalk at Brighton all speak of their time abroad.

I grew up in the villages of Josey Hill and Rockfield, in St. Lucy, on the northern end of the island.[1] It's called Rockfield because it's

---

1. St. Lucy is one of Barbados' eleven parishes.

Traditional chattel house near Rockfield where Roy was raised. (Photo by George Gmelch.)

flat and rocky, a good place to play cricket because you always had a nice flat surface. Cricket was just about the most important thing we had; we couldn't afford footballs. Cricket was not like what you see today with proper hardball and pads. You played with anything that was round, and the bats were made from a cherry tree, coconut limb, or any old piece of wood that you could cut into the shape of a bat. We'd play cricket every day, even on Sunday, when your mother might ban you from playing it. On Sunday, if your mother wouldn't let you play near home, you'd go to the beach and play in the sand. I'd play anywhere and anytime, and that was probably what made us so good at cricket.

The sea was pretty near to the village, so we used to always go there.[2] We'd be in the sea four or five days a week. Before you'd go to school you'd always have a dip in the sea. Weekends, you'd spend your whole day at the sea. You'd find yourself looking

---

2. The nearby coastline is rocky with sheer cliffs but indented with small bays, where it is possible to swim. Here and there are small caverns that have blow holes, which throw up great plumes of water when the sea surges into them.

around for sea coconuts, which are hard, small coconuts just like golf balls.[3] You'd see them floating on the sea and washed up on the sand. We never knew where they came from. We'd put them in a piece of cloth and make it round and then knit it so that you'd have a hardball that was good for cricket. We couldn't afford to buy cricket balls, so we made our own.

We had a small beach at Little Bay, and there was a nice white hole for swimming. That's a hole in the reef where you can see the white sand bottom. You'd go in and swim around. It was a good place for youngsters because it'd be safe. When you came home from the beach you'd wash off under the stand pipe because most houses didn't have piped water.[4] But you'd want to make sure the constable didn't see you because you weren't allowed to bathe under the stand pipe. If he saw you, he'd run after you. He'd always say he was going to arrest you, but he never did.

When I started school a normal day for me was to get up early in the morning. Mother wakes you up about five o'clock; you were never allowed to stay in bed after six o'clock. The first thing you did was get the bucket and go to the stand pipe and fetch the water. You'd take along your soap and toothbrush. My mother wouldn't allow you to come back dirty faced. "Don't bring the water until you've cleaned your face," she'd say. You'd bring about a half-dozen buckets of water.

Then you'd take the sheep or goats out into the field or pasture. Most people didn't have enough land of their own, so you'd have to take the animals out to the grass and stake them with a rope and an iron stake. Then you'd sweep the yard and prepare yourself for breakfast. Breakfast was four biscuits and a cup of tea. The tea might be green tea or bush tea made from pear, apple, or soursop leaves. You'd drink tea to cool the body so that you'd perspire, and then you'd feel free and cool during the day. Grownups reckoned that it would keep you from getting colds or

---

3. Commonly found on the beaches, these are seeds from a South American palm that have been carried to Barbados on ocean currents (E. Gooding, *The Plant Communities of Barbados*, 102).

4. A stand pipe is a government-supplied water tap found on the wayside in every village. It is a source of water for those who do not have water piped into their homes.

getting sick. It must have worked because I don't remember being sick much.

You went to school barefoot in those days, but you wore a uniform like the kids wear today. You had an hour off for lunch. Most kids had to go home for lunch and do chores. When you got home you had to take some water out to where the goats and sheep were and then move them to a greener spot. If your mother washed clothes in the morning, you'd take them in if the rain was coming. If they was white clothes, you'd spread them out on large stones in the sun and splash water all over to bleach them. I used to do all the chores as fast as I could so to get back to school and get in a game of cricket or pitching marbles before the bell rang at one o'clock. You could do a lot in that hour.

When school finished your mother wanted you to come straight home so that you would stay away from trouble. But we used to go to the hills first and pick dunks [a small round fruit], mammy apples, and cherries. You'd fill your belly. You wouldn't take them home because then your mother would know that you didn't come straight home like you were supposed to. She didn't want you getting onto somebody's land. When you got home you did your chores as quick as you could so you could have a game of cricket before the sun went down. When you finished cricket you'd go fetch the sheep, and sometimes you'd take them along the road and graze them there. In the crop time, during the sugarcane harvest, you'd go in the fields and pick up the cane tops and take them home to the sheep.

After your dinner you could go out for a bit. All the boys would assemble in one place and all the girls in a different place. You'd play games like "puss in a corner" or "hide and seek" or "outman [outlaw] and police." Your mother would say be home by ten o'clock, or nine o'clock if you were younger. And, if you didn't, she wouldn't let you out the next night. Now you didn't have a watch, but you were a pretty good judge of time. People used to be very accurate at telling the time.

When you got back your mother would send you back to the stand pipe for a wash. You couldn't go to bed with your face or feet being dirty. We didn't have electricity, so there were no electric lights, but people had kerosene or oil lamps, and some people had tilly lamps.[5] When you had homework you did it by the kerosene lamp.

I had two brothers and one sister, but we never grew up together. Being the youngest, I had to stay with my great-aunt, who wanted someone with her. Her children were grownup and gone out of the house, so I used to go and sleep with her. My eldest brother lived with his girlfriend. My second brother had a different father than me, and he lived with his father's mother. And my sister lived with grandmother part of the time. So, although we were all pretty close, we never actually lived together much. But we'd all spend Sunday at my mother's house.

I got my school-leaving certificate and left school at fifteen. From there my dad sent me to do a trade, to be a mechanic. I was at the same place working as an apprentice for four years, and all that time the boss was only paying me seven dollars a week. It was then that the British army came down here recruiting people for their army.

My mate said to me, "Campbell, let's go down to Fontabelle and put down our names for the British army and see if we can get to England." So at lunchtime we rushed down there. Two days later I got a letter that said to come take an exam. I took the exam and passed, and then I was sent to the clinic for a blood test and X rays of the chest. The next week they called me and said everything was okay and that I was to come into Bridgetown and have my pictures taken for a passport and that I should be ready to leave Barbados on the ninth of June 1962.

I went home and told my dad that I was going to England in two weeks. He was shocked. He said, "Where are you going to get the money from?" I told him that I didn't need any money for what I was doing. He said, "I don't want you to go in the British army. If you want to go to England, I'll give you the money, but I don't want you to go in the army." He was afraid I'd get into a war, and I was his only son. My brothers had a different father. So my dad gave me some money to pay my passage and more money to buy a suit of clothes and a suitcase. I went back to the headquarters and told the recruiting fellow that I wasn't going in the army. The next week I left on a boat for England.

5. A pressurized kerosene lamp.

I went to England because I wasn't getting anywhere in Barbados and because I wanted to see what England was like after hearing so much about it in school—you know, the "mother country." I was nineteen, and many of my friends had gone over already. My eldest brother was there. He'd gone over in 1955, but he left it to go to Canada in 1963. And my sister and her husband were there too. Plus, I felt that by going there I could learn a trade better than being here.

So I left Barbados on the sixteenth of June 1962. My suitcase was full of warm underclothing, rice, sugar, rum, peppers, pepper sauce, flour, yams, potatoes, and other foods I thought would be hard to get there. When I got there I found that the English shops had plenty of those foods. In the sixties you thought the foods that Bajans [Barbadians] liked here they wouldn't have over there in England, so you filled your suitcase up with them.

I went by sea on the ship called the *Serrienta*. An Italian ship. I was seasick for about three days, but that was because I had never traveled on the sea before. After I recovered and started to eat the days started going by too quickly. The food was good, and at night you could go down to the cinema and watch a movie or to the lounge, where you could listen to the news or read some comics if you wanted, and they had a nice little bar where you could have a drink. The ship had an Italian band, but they mostly played samba music so that both the Italians and the West Indians could dance to it. You had all the entertainment you wanted. I had such a good time, I didn't want to come off the ship.

I was sharing a room with a Barbadian who was living in England and had come back down to Barbados to take his son up to England. So it was myself, him, and his son. Since he had traveled before, he was giving me a few lineups about England, about what to expect, what not to expect. He said he would look after me.

After seven days on the sea we stopped at Tenerife in the Canary islands, then Barcelona, then Naples, and then Genoa. I was seeing places I'd never seen, places I'd never heard of. In Tenerife and Barcelona I saw policemen walking with guns. You said to yourself, these people are not as free as our people back home. I'd never seen a policeman with a gun back home. You were terrified; you were afraid if you said something bad you might be shot. In Barbados you could say anything at all to a policeman, and most would just laugh.

In Tenerife and Barcelona you saw for the first time white people begging. I never knew of such things. And then you'd see white people working as refuse collectors, and you'd say to yourself that you'd never consider doing that job yourself and here are whites doing it. And then you'd see white taxi drivers. Then you'd say to yourself, is it going to be like this in England? Your whole attitude begins to change, because you are going to England thinking of only picking the jobs that you want. Seeing white people doing those bad jobs, collecting refuse and so on, you start thinking you might have to do bad jobs too.

In Genoa, Italy, we got off the ship and took the train across the Continent to France and the English Channel. We got on the train in Italy about five o'clock in the evening; they gave us a ration for the trip, which was a couple of rolls and sardines, two apples, and a drink. Twice emigration men came onto the train to check our passports and stamp them. We changed trains in Paris, and from there we went to the English Channel, where we got the ferry over to the English side and then the train to Waterloo Station in London, where my sister met me.

The first week I stayed with my sister, her husband, and their kid. Then she got me a room in the same house. I shared it with a Barbadian who worked for London Transport. The room was three pounds a week, so we each paid one pound fifty. He did his own cooking, and sometimes he'd cook for me. But mostly I'd only sleep there because I'd go up to my sister's to eat and watch television. Later the landlord sold the house, and we all had to move. My sister and her husband got a flat with three rooms: two bedrooms and a kitchen. She gave me one of the rooms, while she and her husband and the kid lived in the other room and the kitchen. The first few years in England were rough because it was hard to find rooms. There were rooms that were vacant, but you'd see signs that would say No Blacks, No Coloureds, No Irish.[6] Or you might see English Only. And when you did get a room the

---

6. The Race Relations Act of 1968 outlawed discriminatory advertisements for rooms and flats. Within a short time the No Coloured signs, which were once common, were no longer seen (N. Foner, *Jamaica Farewell: Jamaican Migrants in London*, 47).

landlord would put restrictions on you, like all visitors must be out of your place by ten o'clock.

England was rough in the beginning; it wasn't what I expected. It looked gray and dreary. I thought it was going to be green and beautiful. The first morning I was in England my sister and I walked down to the bus stop. My sister doesn't say "good morning" or "hello" to the people there, and I am thinking this is strange because, if you go anywhere in Barbados, you say "good morning" and "hello" to people. The next morning I go to fetch the milk off the stoop, and when I get there the lady next door was there to pick up her milk as well. I said, "Good morning." She looked surprised and didn't answer. When I got upstairs I told my sister what happened, and I asked her why the woman didn't answer. Then she told me that was the custom in England, that nobody says "good morning" or "hello," at least not to black people.

When I first saw all the houses joined together with all their chimneys up in the air I wondered where the people lived. I thought the buildings that were really houses were all factories. I had never heard of people making fires in their houses, and they all looked the same—every building, every street, all the same way. I said to a man, "How do you know which is your house?" He said, "By the numbers." That alone put me off, only knowing your house by the number.

And, if you wanted to go for a walk, the park might be some distance away. When you got to the park you might sit down, and no one would say anything to you. You missed all the friendliness that you have here in Barbados.

The first winter I really wanted to go back home. It was so cold, the worst winter they'd had in many years. But I remembered that before I left Barbados my father told me that this was the last money he was going to spend on me and that I was on my own from then on. That was the only thing that stopped me from writing and asking him to send for me.

It was really, really cold. I remember going to the cinema on Boxing Day and watching this film with Elvis Presley. When I came down the stairs to go out I saw through the glass doors that the outside was all white. It was the first time I'd seen snow. Walking home, everything was so white and pretty. People told me that the snow would melt in a day or two, but that snow didn't melt; it just turned to ice. I think it was there on the ground for two months. You had to be careful when you walked. You couldn't walk in a hurry because of the ice. All the house steps turned to ice, and the water in the toilet cisterns froze up. Even in our house the water pipes freeze up. I really wished I was home, but, since I had no money and I couldn't ask my father for any, I planned to work just long enough to earn my passage back home.

On the way over to England my thinking was that I'd be away no more than five years. I had a goal of saving a certain amount of money and then coming back to Barbados and getting a little house. At that time the pound was worth $4.80,[7] and I thought that if I could save $10,000 I would be able to buy enough building materials to build a home. Building material was pretty cheap then; you'd get a cement block for $.36, a board for about $.40, and labor was cheap. I thought, with the pound being strong, I'd be able to save the $10,000 for a house, plus have enough for my passage back home. I thought I could save that much and be back in Barbados in five years. I wasn't thinking about getting married, settling down, or anything like that. I only wanted to make some quick money, see the country, and come back home. But it took a long time to save any money at all, and by then I was starting to get settled down.

My first job in England was working at a bakery as a porter. It was a Jewish bakery in east London. The pay was £8 10s., per week. I had to load the van with the cakes, then I'd clean the bread trays, pack the fridge with the cakes for the next day, and sometimes I'd sweep up. In Barbados I wouldn't have done that kind of work, but, as I said, seeing white people doing those jobs, I knew I'd have to do them too. My whole attitude was to get money and get back home quick, so I didn't mind what work I did.

After about six months I asked for a raise, and they gave me an extra pound, so now I am making £9 10s. But in my opinion it wasn't enough for the work I was doing, and the hours were long, from seven to five during the week and eight to twelve on Saturdays. And the conditions weren't very good. I was working in the

---

7. All figures are in Barbados dollars. One Barbados dollar equals fifty U.S. cents.

basement; all you had were two electrical heaters. They were overhead, so you never got your body warm at all. Down there my feet and hands were always be cold. I could have gotten a job somewhere else, but I'd be further away from home, and I'd be paying more bus fare and spending more time getting to work. The bakery was walking distance from home, plus they let you have rolls or buns for lunch. You'd bring a piece of ham to work, and you could eat their rolls, and they'd give you free milk to put in your tea. So at the bakery you could save that extra ten shillings that you'd have to spend on lunch if you were working somewhere else. I guess that is why I didn't leave the bakery, at least not for a long time.

In the bakery there were a half-dozen Barbadians, a couple of Jamaicans, and a half-dozen Montserratans. The foreman, assistant foreman, oven man, and storekeeper were all Jewish. Only the cake maker was English. You had more West Indians there than anybody else, but I think that was because we were cheap labor and we did all the hard work.

The West Indians became very friendly. We'd go to each other's houses to have a drink and a party. There'd be a lot of mickey taking [poking fun] at each other, especially about the country you came from. Jamaicans would call you "small island" because Jamaica was so much bigger than our islands. Then we'd say: in Montserrat the island is so small that the cricket players can't bowl very fast because, if they take a long run, they'd land in the sea. Or we'd say they can't even grow pumpkins in Montserrat because to grow pumpkins the vines have to run, and with so little land they haven't got anywhere to go.

You'd make fun of each other's speech. We used to laugh at the way Jamaicans talk because they talk back to front. Bajans would say "the top of my head" is hurting me, where Jamaicans would say "my head top" is hurting me. I would say "bring me the bottle," but Jamaicans would say "go carry come the bottle." We laughed at them. But then they would say all small islanders are "fou fou" [foolish].

One day the boss asked me if I would work upstairs, to learn pastry making. I did, and I learned to make what was called Danish pastry, Danish buns, fruit buns, and puff pastry. That is what the

Jews liked to eat, and most of our customers were Jewish. Jews love sweet things, with lots of icing and sugar and a bit of spice. The English and West Indian customers would mostly buy the bread and rolls; the Jews bought the Danish pastry. I learned pretty well, and, being pretty fast at catching on, he gave me another small raise. So now I was making £10 10*s.*

About this time, in 1963, I met the woman that later became my wife. I met her when I went to visit a friend of mine. My friend wasn't home, but his girlfriend and her friend were there. His girlfriend said to stay until he comes. Well, I got talking to her and her girlfriend because she was a Barbadian too, and I spent the whole day there. I told her about my work, and she told me about her work at the Lyons Restaurant at the corner of Oxford Street and Tottenham Court Road. She had come to England on a contract with Lyons when they were recruiting girls in Barbados. When I finally went to leave the two girls walked me up the road. But we kept on walking and walking, and they had walked me all the way back to my home. I gave them bus fares to return home.

The following day my friend's girlfriend called me at work to tell me that this girl wanted to see me again and that she was off from work that day. So I told my boss that I had to go home. I went and caught the bus and went straight there. She made me a cup of tea and something to eat, and I stayed there until about nine o'clock that night.

After that I'd meet her every night after work and take her home. After two or three months courting I said to her, "It's not profitable for you paying rent and me paying rent. Why not live together?" So we moved in together, and she got pregnant. She lost the first baby but got pregnant again, and in November she had the baby.

When she got pregnant she said, "You know this is not Barbados. Here if you have children and you are not married they look down on you." I said I would try to get a job where I could make more money so that we could get married. So I looked in the post office to see what kind of jobs were advertised. At the time there were more colored immigrants working for London Transport than in the post office, so I decided to give Transport a try.

I went to a place called Manor House Recruitment Center and filled in a form. They gave me a little test, and I passed, and they sent me for an interview. The interviewer sent me out for a driving test the next morning. At the driving test there were a half-dozen of us, five white guys and me. We got in this old Routemaster double-decker bus. We all sat upstairs, except for the guy who was being tested on driving. Each guy drove for fifteen to twenty minutes. Well, I drove pretty well, and the guy said, "You drive damn good."

When all of us completed the driving he took us back to the depot. The inspector said to us, "You all let me down, this black boy here drove better than any of you." So then I figured that everything was going to be okay, that I was going to get the job. But then he called me to one side. "What I advise you to do," he says, "is take a conductor's job, and maybe later you'll get to drive the bus."[8] Back in the room I talked to the five white guys, and they told me that they all got through, that they were all going to be bus drivers. When I told them about me they said, "Blimey, you drive better than us." That really put me off. I didn't bother with the conductor's job, and I just started for home.

On the train on the way back home I got the midday paper, the *Midday Standard,* and I saw a position for a postman. So I sent in the form for the postman job. Two days later I got a reply asking me to come in for a test. There were two dozen of us that took the test, and after we finished we all went out in the room and waited. They called out eight of us, and then I heard him tell the others that they would have to try another time, that they hadn't made it. I really felt good. Man, I had made it!

In two weeks they said I'd have to go to postman's school and learn the towns and cities in England, Scotland, Ireland, and Wales. And then I'd have to learn the London districts, learn the whole of London from North 1 to North 22, EC [East Central] 1 to EC 4, WC [West Central] to WC 2, E 1 to E 18, Northwest 1 to Northwest 11, West 1 to West 14, Southeast 1 to Southeast 27.

At the school we'd test each other, "Where is Southeast 3?"
"Greenwich."

---

8. In a 1966 experiment researchers sent out individuals with identical qualifications but different nationalities (English, Hungarian, and West Indian or Asian) to apply for the same job in forty sample firms. The English applicant was offered the job or kept in mind in thirty cases, the Hungarian in seventeen, and the West Indian or Asian in only three (Foner, *Jamaica Farewell*, 44).

"Where is Tottenham?"

"North 17."

"Where is South Tottenham?"

"North 15."

You had three days to learn all that and nine days to learn all the towns and cities. They gave you a pack of cards to take home at night so that you could study. I would give my wife the cards, and she would test me, even when we were eating:

"Where is Wellingborough?"

"Northhampton."

"Yeah, you know that one. Okay, where is Limerick?"

"Ireland."

"Where is Selidge?"

"Kent." And so on.

I learned them all with two days to spare. There were three of us colored fellows in the class of eighteen, and we all passed the exam early. Some of the white guys said they couldn't understand how these black people come here and learn these places faster than them who was born here and who was here all the time. I'd think to myself, hey, I am doing great in this white man's country. We wanted to do well, so we really put our minds to it.

I started in the north London post office. There were about eight West Indians and a dozen Africans. At first they gave us black fellows the dirty jobs like sorting parcels. Every post office has letters, packets, and parcels. They're all sorted three different times from when they enter the post office. Well, sorting letters and packets was a clean job, but parcels come in mailbags, and it was very dusty and dirty, and you got your clothes all dirty. But, whatever they told you to do, you'd always try to do it to your best so that the governor [supervisor] couldn't come in and say that you, a black person, wasn't doing a good job.

You and the Englishman would be working together, and he would say, "Hell with this, I am going to have a cup of tea." When the governor came and saw you working alone he'd say, "Where is Mr. Boyce? Why is he always pissing off?" Well, after a while the governor saw that we were doing a better job than a lot of the English fellows.

My boss used to call me Sam. I asked why he called me Sam and not my real name, Roy. He said that in his school days they used to call all little black boys Sam—you know, Sambo. "So if I call you Sam," he said, "don't be annoyed."

One day the boss said to me, "Sam, go down to Brown Brothers with the van and pick up six oil heaters for me. It's awfully cold, and we need some more heaters in here." So I went down to Brown Brothers and told the receptionist that my boss had sent me down to pick up heaters. She got the heaters, and then she asked me my name so that she could write it down.

I said, "My name is Campbell."

She said, "How do you spell it?"

I said, "Like in Campbell soup, that is how you spell it."

She said, "Spell it out for me." She still couldn't spell it. So I took the pen, and I wrote it out for her.

She said, "Oh, I didn't know you could write, or I would have asked you to sign your own name." And do you know that my handwriting was even better than hers?

Another English guy at the post office told me that when he was in school he thought black boys had tails. And he and his friend had followed a black man into a public lavatory to see if it was true. When the black man went into the toilet stall they got up on the next toilet and looked over the top at him. The black guy pretended he didn't see them peeping on him, but then when he was done he rushed for them and banged their two heads together.

But we West Indians got on better with whites than with Africans. Most white workers wouldn't show their prejudice. The Africans thought we were inferior to them. They were very insulting, and they'd say, "You are only white man's slave," or "You got white blood in you." They would say that all West Indians were descended from slaves and that the slave masters were white people who had sex with our great grandmothers and their mothers. That is why we are much fairer in color than the Africans.

I got to like working in the post office—you never did the same thing every day. One day you might be in the inward sorting, one day in the outward sorting, and some days you be out delivering letters or loading the vans or in the bag room folding letter bags or out in the van delivering parcels. There was always something different to do, so you didn't get bored.

After six months I applied to be a "postman-driver," and I got through. You were better off being both postman and driver because, if you wanted some overtime and there was no overtime for drivers, you might get some as a postman. And if there wasn't any overtime posted on the postmen's sheet, which they put up on the board, you could check the sheet for the drivers. If I was going to save money to build our house in Barbados, I had to get all the overtime I could.

When I became a postman-driver I did a lot of what we called firms delivery. Firms that used to get a lot of mail would have it delivered by van instead of the postman carrying it on his shoulders. You used to look forward to Christmas because then all the firms would give you Christmas presents. Some gave you a pound, some gave you five pounds, some gave you a bottle of wine or whiskey, some just gave you a card. In all you might get thirty pounds from them at Christmastime. And at Christmastime you got lots of overtime due to what was called the Christmas pressure. From the first week in December right through Christmas you'd work twelve hours a day. You'd look forward to it because the boys would have a good drink together when they finished work at the end of the day, and you knew you were going to get your five hours overtime every day during the Christmas pressure. Some days you would do ten hours of overtime alone. Well, you'd make a lot of money in December.

On Christmas Eve all of us West Indians would get together, pool up some money, and buy drinks, and some guys would cook rotis and chickens.[9] We'd get a stereo and records, and with the wives and kids we'd stop by one house for food and drink and then go to another for more food and drink. We'd keep that up until after midnight.

After I was in England about five years I started playing cricket in a league for a team called Trinity in Surrey; I also played for the post office team in the London Post Office Cricket League. My friend Winston introduced me to the fellows from Trinity and got me on the team. They were all white, except Winston, his brother, and me. In the first match I did very badly. I made naught [didn't score any runs]. I felt bad for Winston because he told them what a

---

9. A common West Indian food in which a mixture of meat and potatoes is wrapped in a chapati.

good bat I was. But the second match I did a little better, and the third match I was still better, and so on, until I was eventually opening the batting [batting first in the order].

Playing on an English team was different from playing in the West Indies. If you did well, say you scored a century [one hundred runs in one match], you'd have to buy drinks. In the West Indies they'd buy you the drinks. Playing with the English fellows you always wanted to do well, but you also knew that, if you did well, it was going to cost you money.

The playing conditions were better in England than in Barbados. The pitches [the area in front of the wicket] were a bit slower, but the outfields were good and grassy and pretty level. In the West Indies you may get a better wicket, but the outfield is often rough and bumpy with a lot of stones. When you go to field the ball in the West Indies you have to be careful that it won't hit a stone and dive under your hands. You always have to be thinking of what the ball is going to do when it gets to you, whereas in England you can be confident the ball isn't going to take a bad bounce.

After the game you would take a shower, change into your civvies, and go to a bar for a few pints of beer. And even if you didn't play, if there was rain and the pitch was too wet, you'd still go to the bar with the boys and have a few pints of beer and a good chat, and you'd watch somebody else play cricket on the television. You'd go home almost the same time as if you had played. I always looked forward to playing cricket. I got a good feeling from it.

I came back to Barbados for the first time in 1968, after being away for six years. I could see great improvement—there were many more cars, the roads were much better, and the people were doing better. In the stores you'd see many of the same things that you'd see in England. After that trip I started thinking again about what it'd be like being home in Barbados. The next year, 1969, my wife got pregnant again and I said to her, "We have to be careful because you want to go back to Barbados and I want to go back to Barbados, and if we have more children we won't ever be able to afford to go back to Barbados. So let's quit, no more kids." I was seven years in England, and it was time to start preparing to go home.

Roy Campbell (top row, second from left) and the Nordis Cricket Club in Middlesex, England, before the London Postal Region Cup Match in 1972.

After we'd gotten married her mom wrote from Barbados and told us that there was some land being sold, and if we would like a house spot it would be a good place. We didn't have much money, but we withdrew what we had and sent it home to buy the spot. This was Reeces, in Bridgetown; the price for it was thirty-three hundred dollars. In 1973 my wife and I came back together and had a plan drawn up for a house, and then we went back to England to save money. We came back again in 1976 and got a contractor. But when he said it was going to cost twenty-six thousand dollars to build the house and that he'd have to do the job all at once, we knew we couldn't afford it. So we went to my wife's uncle and asked him to start building the house and to build until our money was gone, and then stop until we could save some more. He agreed, and he told me to open an account at Plantations Limited, the builders' store in Bridgetown, and leave my mother-in-law in charge of the account. When we left Barbados that time I said to my wife that the next time we came back it must be for good. There were the kids to think about.[10] We had left them with my wife's parents during our last visit so that we could save more money in England to get home to Barbados sooner. Plus, I said there is no way I can leave such a beautiful country as Barbados to live in England; I really wanted to get back here as quick as possible to enjoy my own country.

You hear so much about England, but when you go there it is not exactly what you expect. The countryside is nice, but the seaside is not like here. You don't have nice sand, the beaches are more gravel than sand, and the water is dark. Then you only get three or four months of what they call sunshine, in what they call summer. You always seem to be loaded down with lots of clothes— shoes and socks, T-shirt, shirt, vest, cardigan, coat, and whatnot. It was always a weight on you. In Barbados you can just put on a pair of shorts and walk outside barefoot. To be honest, in England I felt old wearing all those clothes.

We came home to stay in 1979. The way that it happened was that I hurt myself at the post office. I went in and collected some parcels from a firm and was carrying them into the post office when I stepped on the lace of my shoe and tripped. At first there was a little pain in my back and a burn down my leg, but I didn't think anything of it, and I finished working. The next morning my back was stiff, and I had pain. So I go to the doctor, and he says it's a slipped disk. He gives me some time at home and tells me to take a hot bath every night, lay on a hard bed, and take some medication. I did that but my back doesn't get any better; the pain is still there. They told me that one of the nerves got trapped outside the vertebrae and that there is no operation that can put the nerve back in place. They could only give me some therapy exercises.

After three months the post office sent me to their own doctor to make sure that what my doctor said was true. He too said I was ill. So the post office decided to retire me on medical grounds. I

---

10. The Campbells left their two children in Barbados with Wendy's parents when they returned to England in 1973. The children were in good hands, but the separation was difficult for the parents, and Roy had difficulty talking about it; in fact, it was not until our last interview that he revealed that their children had not always been with them.

didn't like it when they told me, but they said they would take care of me financially. I received a check from them for £3,300 and a check from the Giro Pension Fund with a letter that my pension would be £80 a month. I still get a check every month.

My wife and I talked over what to do. I said to her, "Since I am not working, it would be better to go home."

She said, "Yes, it is time that we be with the kids." The house wasn't finished yet, but we thought that we might be able to live in it anyway and complete it later.

My wife gave her firm notice that she was leaving. We then looked for a firm to send our things home to Barbados, and we found this Dominican guy who shipped them home on the Geese Shipping Lines from Wales. I wrote the post office and told them that I was going back to Barbados and would like my pension transferred to me there. We came home on the thirty-first of November, which was Independence Day. We stayed at my mother-in-law's until our things arrived, and just before Christmas we moved into our house.

Coming home made me a bit nervous. I wondered if I could get a job and what kind of work I would do. My first job was as a security guard. The pay was small, but I didn't have much choice. I had to make some money because the kids were in school, the wife didn't have a job, and the house wasn't finished yet. The pension was enough to pay some of the bills, but I couldn't support the family without getting a job.

Then I meet a friend from England who had come back to Barbados too, and he told me that he had gotten a job at the Transport Board. He said he'd try and get me on there, and he set up an appointment for me to see the manager. I went in, and the manager asked me what I'd like to do. I told him I wanted to be either an inspector or a bus driver. He gave me a job as a bus driver. First, though, I had to pass the eye test, get a certificate of character, a testimonial, and then take the driving test. I went out with the other trainee drivers, and we drove in the hills of the Scotland District. I did well, but then the instructor looked at my driver's license and said I wasn't back in Barbados long enough. You have to be living in Barbados for one year before you can drive an omnibus.

The instructor sent me to the manager. The manager told me to close the door and sit down. He said, "Mr. Campbell if I offer you an inspector's job, will you take it?"

I said, "Yes, but what would the other workers say, being that I have never worked on buses before and being that I am new here? Wouldn't the other workers resent you making me an inspector right off, without being a conductor first?" He told me to let him do the worrying about that, that over the years they had chosen their inspectors from within the work force and that hadn't proven very successful, and that he wanted to bring someone in from the outside. I took the job. This was March 1980, and the pay was $180 a week. Now it is $304 a week, and I still have my pension, which has gone up to $182 a month.

Getting the job as an inspector and being able to travel all around the island, riding on all the different bus routes, helped me to meet a lot of people. Hearing people on the buses or at the bus stops say "Good morning Mr. Campbell" or "Hello Roy," people knowing your name and wanting to speak to you, and you just being back from England—well, that made you feel pretty good. It made me feel glad to be back in Barbados. But, being away so long, sometimes I'd have a hard time remembering their names. I'd say "hello" and pretend that I knew them. Sometimes I'd have to say that I forgot who they were, that I had been away for sixteen years.

I adjusted to being home pretty quickly, mostly because I'd come home quite a few times before—1968, 1973, and 1976—so that when we came home for good I knew what to expect. If I had stayed away for all those years and then come back and tried to settle down, it would have been hard. Plus, getting a job pretty quick and being able to move into our home so that we didn't have to pay rent was really important. Your few pounds can go pretty quick if you have to pay rent while you are looking for a job and have nothing coming in.

The one thing that bothered me, though, is that people here are not good at time-keeping. If people agree to meet you at eight o'clock, they don't turn up until eight-thirty or maybe even nine o'clock, and they don't say they are sorry for being late. That makes me annoyed. The English were very punctual. If they say they will get here at nine o'clock, they will be here at nine o'clock.

Another thing that annoyed me is that people here aren't as mannerly. The English always say "please" and "thank you." In England when people buy something in the shop they say, "Could I have a bottle of milk or a pack of biscuits, please?" You always say "please." Here you say, "Man, give me a bottle of milk there." Bajans feel that, because they are paying for it, they don't have to say "please" or "thank you." And if the English want to get past you, they say, "Excuse me, please." Here in Barbados they say, "Man, move it up the road" or "Man, move and let me pass."

I wasn't able to adjust myself to the West Indian type of cricket. By the time I came home I was thirty-seven, and my reactions weren't as quick; plus, the boys here were young and fast, and the pitches were hard and really fast. I decided that I had played enough, and I packed it in. Plus, I was busy trying to finish the house.

But I still watch a lot of cricket. When a touring team comes to play Barbados I find time to watch most of it, even if I have to tell my wife a little lie. When I go out to see a match at Kensington Oval I see lots of the blokes who played for the post office teams in England and who are now back in Barbados.[11] I look around for them—Ralph Walker, Paul Franklin, Euclid Alleyne, and the others that played in England—and during the intervals, during the lunch and tea breaks, we talk about what we used to do in England and how we used to play over there. We have a few drinks, and we remember the old times.

---

11. Kensington Oval is Barbados' major cricket stadium.

Chapter 6
Valenza Griffith

Valenza Griffith is a vibrant personality, not unlike Tony Carter (chap. 10). She has the air of someone who knows who she is and what she wants out of life. Valenza enjoys talk and often strikes up conversations with people on the bus, patients at work, and almost anyone who catches her interest. Whether telling an anecdote or a story, she is able to assume the roles and accents of different characters. Her high cheekbones accentuate her mouth when she speaks, giving the effect that she is emphasizing her words. Being a practical woman, her stories often have a message, if not a moral.

Valenza grew up on the northern coast of Barbados, in the village of Coles Cave, named after the caverns in the nearby cliffs carved by Atlantic breakers. Her mother was a self-employed maid and her father a fisherman. Valenza emigrated to England in 1961 when she was twenty-two, first working in a textile mill, then as a nurse. Nursing had been her life ambition since her teens when, as a member of the Police Girls Club,[1] she listened to the district nurses talk about their work.

I didn't meet Valenza until 1990, well after I had finished the other interviews. She had heard from a coworker that I was looking for rural families with which to place students, and she called me to volunteer. During my weekly trips to her home to visit a student I got to know Valenza. When we talked about her experiences in England I noticed that not only was she very candid but she also had an excellent memory for detail, and she enjoyed reflecting on her past. An added benefit, from my perspective, was that she had gone abroad to do nursing, which was a primary occupation of West Indian women in England. At the time I had only one

---

1. Organized by the Barbados police force, the local clubs met twice a week after school. One of the activities was to expose the girls to different jobs by inviting people—parish priest, welfare officers, nurses, etc.—to talk about their work.

*narrator who had been a nurse overseas, Rose Thornhill, and I thought
there should be another. So, during my last month in the field, I began these
interviews, three in all and done at Valenza's dining table.*

*Throughout her life Valenza has volunteered her time to charities and
social causes. As a child, she collected door-to-door for her church's mission-
ary work in Africa; she always brought back more money than the other kids
in the village. In England she regularly sold tickets for dances and picnics
for the Barbados Overseas Friends Association, which paid the airfare for
Barbadians who needed to return home for an emergency. And when she
returned to Barbados she had a fund drive to buy a wheelchair for a boy
born without feet. Several times she has taken in people who were homeless
or in need of help. Shortly before I began my interviews with Valenza, she
had lodged for seven weeks an English girl—a friend of a friend—whom
she didn't know. I asked Valenza why, and she said:*

> *It's important that we all help strangers. You don't know where your
> relatives or kids are going to go and when they are going to need
> someone's help. The people in England were good to me, so I sort of owe
> it to them. . . . Besides, tourism is our [Barbados'] business, and you
> want to make someone's stay as nice as possible.*

*I once saw a letter of recommendation written by Valenza's superior at
the hospital where she now works in Bridgetown. "A hard worker," "depen-
dable," "efficient," "shows initiative," "kind," and "always willing to share
her knowledge with others" read the description of Valenza. The adjectives, I
thought, not only described Valenza but also many of the returnees in this
book. In Valenza's story, like that of the Thornhills and Allmans, we see
how some of these traits—particularly efficiency, taking the initiative, and
working hard—were nourished by her experiences in England.*

*While Valenza's narrative adds more detail to our picture of immi-
grant life in England, it also strongly conveys how experience in another
culture can change a young woman's attitudes and worldview. Some of
these changes are brought into relief in Valenza's adjustment to coming
home to Barbados.*

We'd only been married a few months when Randall, my husband,
went to America. That would be 1958. In those days lots of Barbadian men emigrated to America, either for the fruit or for the

sugarcane. Being that Randall was a shop clerk and that cutting cane was really hard work, he decided to put his name down for the fruit. They sent him to Wisconsin to do apples. He had a three-year contract, so I wasn't going to see him for a long time. There were quite a couple of boys from this area [St. Lucy] that went up to America with him.

We all went down to Queen's Park [Bridgetown] to see them off. They were taken from the park to the airport in a bus, but we followed them in a private car. I was nineteen, and I felt a bit upset over him leaving for such a time, and we just being married. But my grandmother and a lot of older people had this philosophy that if a husband was emigrating to better his position that you shouldn't cry. If you cried it would bring him bad luck. So, although I felt like crying and carrying on, I didn't. I told myself that I was married to him and that he couldn't marry anyone else out there or he'd be in trouble. I was wife number one, and I had signed up with the emigration scheme for an allowance from his wages. Because we were going to be better off, you could accept not having your husband with you.

Randall would write every other week. I'd keep him up to date on what was going in Barbados, and he'd keep me up to date on the latest fashions in America. My sisters sewed a lot, so he'd send down the latest fashion book with all the skirts and things, and we'd make them. And, since I liked to read, he'd send down these little novels about the screen stars in America and detective stories by James Hadley Chase. And he sent down the Sears catalog, so, if we wanted anything, we would write and tell him. Had there been phones in those days, all our money would have gone to the phone bill.

You counted the months until he'd come back, but there was plenty to occupy my mind here. I was kept so busy with my job, the Police Girls Club, church, and Sunday school that him being away didn't bother me much. And then at that time there was a very big murder trial here [in Barbados] that helped pass the time. A fellow called Hitler, from St. Andrew, had killed someone. Now today a murder case wouldn't interest you much because there are so many, but in those days [late 1950s] murder was a rare thing. The case took up nearly eighteen months before it was over. I would go over to the courts during my dinner break to get first-class knowledge of the case and then that night I'd write it all out in a letter to Randall.[2] And I'd post him the clippings from the newspapers too. The excitement of the trial helped pass the time.

He came back from America a year early because there were bad floods that ruined the crops. When he got home he wanted to go to England, but I said no. I was wanting to do nursing, and I had just put in my application to the hospital. Randall went off to Trinidad to visit his aunt and sister, and, while he was gone, I got a letter from Eulinda Archer, all about the nursing situation in England. It sounded really good. So I wrote to Randall in Trinidad, and he said go to England and that he would join me later. You see, he was all for traveling.

He said, "You'll see different once you get into the outside world. In Barbados you'll just mix with the same people and hear the same talk. . . . Get out, and you'll get some new ideas." My mother and father didn't mind me going to England: I already had two sisters down there, and they saw it as an opportunity for me to get out and study. So I signed on with the emigration scheme to work in a factory in northern England, but I was thinking that after I worked there for awhile I would try to get into nursing. I thought it would be better to get to England and go to a hospital and apply [in person] than to write them a letter from Barbados.

I was put into a group with eleven other Barbadians, all going to the same city in England under the emigration scheme. In 1961 you could only take forty-four pounds [of luggage]; those who went before us by boat could take a lot more. But we went up well prepared anyway: lots of flannelette things for cold, and I also took rum, Alcolda [cologne], Vicks, and Thermogene, all for the flu. And I took cake and chicken in case we got stuck somewhere on the way. And I took the presents that people gave me when they heard I was going: pen sets, towels, pajamas. Some gave me pound notes that their relatives in England had sent to them.

A lot of the old people gave me advice when I was getting ready to go. Louis Lynch's mother said,

---

2. While her husband was abroad, Valenza worked in the Royal Store on High Street in Bridgetown and lived with her parents in rural St. Lucy.

Put your best foot forward. While you are in that country don't go after the money, go after the study. Get a profession and establish yourself with the right people, and then everything will come natural. And keep away from the dance houses and the cinemas.

She gave me money to buy woolen pajamas.

Funny, my cousin Malcolm Slocumb, told me the same things. He said,

Make hay while the sun shine. Choose a profession and do it well. If you are going to sew down there, then sew like a designer.

And Handle Bowen, the chief sanitary inspector, a very important man and a friend of the family, gave me advice too. "Val," he said, "you are taking a very big step. Do you understand what you are going about?" He asked me if I'd read the book [pamphlet] about England that the emigration scheme put out, and I told him I had.[3] The book told you the proper clothing to wear, to always travel by bright light in case you didn't know where you were going, to ask a policeman if you were lost, and things like that. He said, "Well what would you do if someone up there come up and call you a black so-and-so?"

I said, "I'll call them a white so-and-so."

He said, "Suppose they hit you?"

I said, "I don't think they will, but, if they do, I'll hit 'em back."

He said, "Do you know anything about their customs besides what you read in the emigration book? Do you know you'll be living in just one room, with other people living in other rooms in the same house?"

I told him I knew that and that I knew that everyone's letters were just pushed in through a hole in the front door and that you could take another person's letters if you weren't honest. I wasn't worried. I think I was curious more than anything; I couldn't get there fast enough.

---

3. The "book" was actually a pamphlet given to intending emigrants by the Barbados Ministry of Labour.

Finally, he said, "If you land tomorrow, and you don't know where to go, and nobody is there to meet you, what are you going to do?"

I said, "I speak English, and I can read."

And then he said, "Alright, go."

This conversation was on a Thursday, and I landed in England, at Heathrow Airport, on Saturday, and, as I got off the plane, I remembered everything he had told me. There were twelve of us Barbadians.[4] My sisters in London couldn't come to the airport, but they sent someone to meet me and make sure I was alright. She brought a coat and cardigan in case I didn't have warm clothes.

The liaison officer, Mr. Harold Brewster, met us at the airport and took us, the twelve of us, to the train to Lancashire, to Oldham. It was night and winter, so you didn't see much from the train, but I remember Mr. Brewster being like a navigator telling us about the different stations we was passing through along the way. He showed us how the doors would open automatically, how to read the station and platform signs, and that, if we ever got lost, to look for a man in a uniform. As soon as I got to England, I started taking notes so that I could write it all down—the width of the roads and what stoplights were and so on—in letters to people at home.

When we got to Oldham Mr. Brewster took us to the different places where we were to live; it was all arranged. Some of us went to a big two-story house on Waterloo Street. There were ten rooms with three or four people in each room but only one bathroom and one kitchen for everybody to share. Everybody shared just one toilet. It wasn't like here in Barbados where everybody has their own house. There were three of us—Cynthia from St. George and Isalene from St. Michael and myself—in one room. There wasn't much room to move around, so we took out one of the beds, and two of us shared a bed. The landlady was English, and she was pretty alright. It was Sunday morning when we got up, and because all the shops was closed she prepared breakfast for us.

---

4. By 1990 Valenza was the only one of the twelve to have permanently returned home to Barbados. Two had died, five were still living in England, and four had emigrated to Canada.

The landlady told all the colored people [Barbadians] in the area that we were coming, and they prepared a Barbadian lunch [chicken, rice, and peas] for us. I went out and looked around, and I thought the whole street was one long house. I couldn't fathom why the house would be so long until someone told me the houses are built right up against one another with no gaps between them. I remember it was so cold that when you breathed it looked like smoke was coming out your mouth, just like you were smoking a cigarette.

The people that lived in the house were English and Irish. They were okay. They were popping in our rooms and asking if we wanted any help and telling us where to buy things and where not to go. Some of them were surprised that we spoke English. Some of them didn't know where Barbados was; they asked, "What part of Jamaica is Barbados?" or "What part of Africa is Barbados?" We laughed at it, but I thought they were so stupid, and it gave me second thoughts about England. With all the tales we'd heard about England we thought everybody would be brilliant.

On Monday we started work at Lilly Mills in the cotton and weaving industry, making cotton bedspreads. You saw big bales of cotton at one end of the room and then all these big machines in lines going right down the length of the room to the far end. Men would put up the bales, and they would unwrap into long strands. The strands would be wrapped onto bobbins, and then they go to another machine that would thin them down to thick thread. Then they'd take the thread on smaller bobbins upstairs to where it was made into bedspreads. We'd go through two or three big bales of cotton a day.

Our job was to make sure the bobbins didn't get all tangled up. That's all there was to it. It wasn't difficult: you put on your bobbin and made sure it was going okay. Most of the time you just stand there and watch; the bobbins didn't get tangled too often. The other girls would come around, and you could have a chat. We got paid every Friday in cash—£7 a week. We worked out how much it was in Barbados dollars; in those days one pound was worth $4.80 BDS. The wages came to a lot more than we had been making in Barbados. At home I was getting just $10 BDS a week as a shop assistant. Now I could send £3 or £4 home to my mother and still have enough left over for all my needs.[5] I felt good about the money, and I knew that I was going to go into nursing soon.

After work we'd get the bus home and prepare our meals. We organized it so that the girls cooked for the boys. The men weren't good cooks, and you didn't want too many people cooking at the stove at the same time, so the girls cooked for all. And whichever girl got in first would start the cooking. You could be rich, £20 in your purse, but if you didn't have a shilling coin, you couldn't get a cup of tea. To get gas or hot water you had to keep shillings and put them in the meter. In the evening we all watched TV— "Coronation Street," "Hawaii Eye," and "Sunday Night at the Palladium," where all the stars would be. Some of the Irish men had TVs in their rooms, so you could go in most any room and watch.

When I went to England I was very religious. Most Barbadians take their Bible with them, just like they take their passport, and I was no different. I expected the English to be very religious too, but it didn't work out that way. Many of them don't go near a church; some of them don't even get married in a church. I questioned some of them about it, and they'd say the war [World War II] started on a Sunday, and they believed that, if there was a God, he wouldn't have let that happen. He'd have let the war start on a Monday, maybe a Friday, but not on a Sunday.

The first winter was really cold. The English kept telling you to keep your chest and soles of your feet warm and to eat porridge. Cornflakes in summer, porridge in winter. Sometimes I would say, "Boy, could I do with Barbados now; I wouldn't have to draw a match or turn on the electric to get warm." But I never really pined for home.

You just didn't think about coming back to Barbados then. I was there to get something from Britain, and I hadn't gotten it yet. There was so much to occupy your mind that you really didn't think about when you'd be going to get home. Even if we wanted to leave England we knew that we wouldn't get back the jobs we had in Barbados, so you might as well stick it out and make some

---

5. Like many immigrants, Valenza sent money in postal orders to her parents. The amount she sent and the frequency, she said, depended on her mood and financial needs in England.

money in England. Many of the girls were thinking of marrying and settling down and only going home to Barbados on holidays. Most of them were pretty young, only nineteen or twenty, and they weren't too bothered by where they were going to settle. I suppose they sort of got colonized. A lot was due to the friendly attitude of the people in Lancashire. They were a lot friendlier than people in London, as they were accustomed to seeing blacks, because there had always been black people around the docks in Liverpool and Manchester. People in the heart of London weren't as accustomed to colored people, and so you didn't get on as well with them.

But, even though we weren't homesick, there was always a lot of talk about Barbados. I would get a letter that somebody had died in my district or that there was a heavy rainfall. And someone else would get a letter that somebody in their district was arrested or had lost their house or cow, and we'd exchange the news. We'd compare what was going on in each district. Or a chap would get a letter from Barbados saying that the deep-water harbor was finished, and then there'd be a whole lot of discussion about that. The Barbadians that got to England before us would come around to ask us questions about home. They'd say, "Have you got a road to such-and-such place yet?" "Is rediffusion down by you yet?"[6] "How are the buses?" "Do you know so-and-so from such-and-such?"

And we'd be telling the English and Irish people in the house what Barbados was like. It was the Irish and the Scots that was most interested in what you had to say. They would listen, and some of them would talk about coming to Barbados someday for a holiday. The English wanted the stamps off your letter, but otherwise they didn't strike up a conversation with you like the others did. The Irish and Scots were more outgoing and adventuresome than the English. Did you know some of the English have never traveled? I knew people in Lancashire who had never been to London.

---

6. "Rediffusion" refers to the wired radio broadcasting service provided by Barbados Rediffusion. Its network of subscribers expanded rapidly after it was first introduced in 1934; by the mid-1980s it had 26,000 connected speakers reaching nearly half the population of the island (G. Dann, *The Quality of Life in Barbados*, 133). Wireless radio did not begin until 1963, when the state-run Caribbean Broadcasting Corporation began transmissions.

Your main worry was if everybody at home [in Barbados] was alright. You'd get depressed if you didn't get a letter on time. I'd get a letter from home every other week. My mother started every letter with the same thing. First, she'd tell you to keep yourself well, to be careful, and that she was praying that the Lord would let you live to come back. Then she'd tell you all the village gossip—who drove a car, what family was home [from overseas] on holiday, who was doing fine in school, what your sister was doing, what your father was doing—she'd even say what clothes Miss Babb or someone wore to church. She'd write just like she was talking to us around the table. I'd contact my sister in London, and, it was funny, she'd be telling me the same news, because she'd gotten the same letter from my mother.

In February I left the Lilly factory to do nursing, to work toward my SRN [state-registered nurse certificate]. The factory nurse at Lilly gave me and my friend, Annie Christy, a good briefing. She worked out our wages and made sure we got the holiday pay from the factory before we left so that we'd have enough money to pull us through until we got our first paycheck from nursing. Annie and I got on with the Oldham Royal Infirmary; it was theory—physiology, bacteriology, anatomy—in the morning and practical nursing in the afternoon. It was to be three years of training, but after I was there a few months Randall came over to England.

Randall signed on with London Transport Board [in Barbados], and they assigned him to the West Ham garage, London, E13,[7] as a bus conductor. Every other weekend he'd come up to Oldham to see me, and then after my first year I moved down to London, to Leyton, E10. We lived in a house with two Jamaican families: £2 10s. for one large room. There were lots of Jamaicans down there. They were okay; they were willing to learn about Barbados, and we listened to their tales about Jamaica. Most Barbadians think Jamaicans are ignorant because many of them can't read and write, and they think we're from a small island. There was so many Jamaicans in England that in the early days everybody thought that if you are colored you must be from

---

7. In speech the English commonly identify different locations within the city of London by using the first part of its postal code.

Valenza Griffith, 1983.

Jamaica. But later they found out that we were from Barbados and other places.

When Andrew was born [1962; their first child] we moved to Ilford, into a flat. We didn't want to bring up Andrew in a Jamaican house where the grammar might not be right. Now don't get me wrong. The Jamaicans were very nice people, and they went to church, but their speech and their music—they played just blue beat and reggae—wasn't what we wanted for Andrew.[8] And we wanted more room too. It wasn't nice having three people, the bed, the cot, the dressing table, and everything all in one room. So we thought a flat would be the best thing, but the problem with flats is they cost more, and then you can't save as much money toward buying your own house.

8. Blue beat was a style of urban popular music and dance in Jamaica in the 1950s.

Valenza Griffith in London, 1969.

In Ilford you saw signs on the flats: No Irish, No Blacks, No Africans. And you'd say to yourself, "Wait a minute—what is the difference between a black and an African?" But we found a super flat, and it wasn't much more money than the room in the Jamaican house. It was super: you had your own bathroom, and you didn't have to share no kitchen. It belong to a Jewish chap, Mr. Barnett, who rented people flats for a living. He preferred to rent to men who worked for the transport board and women who were nurses because he knew you wouldn't be laid off and that he'd be sure to get his money. And he knew that with jobs like those you'd be doing plenty of overtime, and you wouldn't have no time for partying or for idle company, and police wouldn't be coming around to his flat. Soon as you met him, he asked you what kind of work you did.

When Andrew was born I stopped my nursing for a time.[9] I

9. In 1965 Valenza went back and completed her training as a state-enrolled nurse. She did two more years of training in 1971–72 to get her SRN degree. From the

could have sent him home to Barbados to the grandparents and continued working. A lot of people did that. But I wanted to bring him up my way rather than have him indoctrinated by his grandparents. They might make too much of a fuss over him and spoil him. When he got a bit older I saw a sign [notice] for a nanny [babysitter] in the shop where I collected my daily paper; they put up signs in the shops, like if you had a room for rent or a pram or furniture you wanted to sell. So, an English girl we called Auntie Flo took care of him.

In England you got to keep your money organized because you spend more on fuel in winter to keep yourself warm, and you spend more on going out in summer. Your different expenses change with the season. We had little tins, each marked electricity, telephone, gas, and whatnot. And each week we'd divide up the money and put so many shillings into each tin. Say if you were punching for gas [putting coins in a meter], you'd know that six shillings would take you through the week. Up there you learned to plan out your money, and you don't forget that when you come back; when you come back you are more careful [with money].

All the time we were saving money for a house. Buying a house was more economical than renting. If you were paying £5 per week for a flat, you could get a house of your own for the same price. And if you had a house you could sublet it, or you could have guests staying with you, which the landlords wouldn't let you do in a flat. Many people wanted to buy a big house so they could rent out rooms and make money. All I wanted was good value and that the house be in good condition and near a train station. And I wasn't particular about what area it was in, like most people were, because I had lived in different places—Oldham, Leyton, Ilford— and they were all alright.

After we had been in Ilford about a year we found out that, because Randall worked in the inner city of London, we could get a mortgage from the Greater London Council. So in 1964 we got a mortgage and a house in Forest Gate, London, E7. We paid less than £3000. Two bedrooms upstairs, toilet and bath downstairs, near to the main road, near to West Ham garage, where Randall

---

time she began nursing at the Oldham Royal Infirmary in 1962 until she returned to Barbados in 1981 her wages as a nurse increased from £20 to over £300 per month.

worked, near to Upton Park Market, near to Stratford Market, near to two or three cinemas, and near to a pub—The Whiteheart Pub—which would be a good description [landmark] for people to find their way to our house. We were the fourth colored house in the area; the others were English, and there were two Indians down the far end.

In 1975, while living in Forest Gate, Valenza was working two jobs as a nurse: full-time at a hospital in Ravenscourt and on her days off at a borstal [a reformatory for young adults] in Southend, an hour's train ride from London. The warden of the borstal offered her a full-time job—eight hours a day, seven days a week. She took it and for the next five years worked in English prisons.

There were about two hundred girls at Bullwood Hall, mostly young offenders, from thirteen to seventeen. They came in for all sorts of things, like breaking and entering, fraud, stealing, the bump and draw [pickpocketing]. When a girl is admitted to prison you give her a proper examination and a strip search for drugs. They have to take their clothes off, and we'd check in their hair, behind their ears, and then we'd send them on to the doctor. He'd check them further—that's why they nicknamed him "goldfinger." We treated them for warts, flu, whatever they had. If they behaved good, the doctor would take out their tattoos, for ones that wanted them out.

It was interesting being there. I'd lived in England all this time [fourteen years], and I'd never known England had this sort of people. It was like going to the cinema for the first time and seeing your first cowboy and Indian picture, and you discover people you didn't know anything about before. Working there, you not only saw a different kind of people, but you got to understand them from a different view, not as criminals but as people that really needed help, that needed affection, that needed a firm hand, a really firm hand. Many of them were there because their parents hadn't much time for them. Some of them were brilliant girls who nobody had cared for.

But you had to be very watchful there, always on your toes, especially with cigarettes, because some of them would try to burn the place down, just to get attention. Many of them were attention seekers—I suppose because no one had ever paid much attention to them. Some would try to put their head through the window if they had the chance. So you had to be watchful. And they was really aware of their rights. They'd say, "I know my rights. You can't lay a hand on me." They knew you couldn't touch them, and that was a lot different from Barbados. When I was thirteen I didn't have a clue what my rights were.

They called me "fly in the milk" because I was the only colored person there. The girls would ask me, "How do you feel being here with all these white sisters? You fly in milk." At Christmas and Easter the officers and nurses put on a show for the girls. I was dressed up as Bob Marley, with dark makeup, locks, and whatnot. We put a record player in the back of the guitar, and I mimed it. You should have seen them. The music really did something to them; they just went berserk, screaming and all. Now that surprised me—they knew more about Bob Marley than I did.

After a year at Bullwood I moved over to Wormwood Scrubs, the men's prison. Tight, tight security. That's a superprison. They got a hospital theater there just like in any hospital. They do operations on prisoners from other prisons. When you looking after a patient the prison officer is there side by side with you. The prisoners were really well looked after. It was more like home; they had color television, and, if they didn't get a good meal, they would complain and maybe go on strike and refuse to eat. I think the British prison service gives them more nourishment than punishment.

After a few years there I moved over to Holloway Prison, one of the most modern prisons in England. They have an isolation block for the really naughty. I was at Holloway when they brought in all those people that was arrested demonstrating for that Ayatollah fellow. They [demonstrators] had cloth on their faces— you could just see their two eyes. They didn't speak English, and the way they talked among themselves it seemed like they was always quarreling. It was a waste of time getting involved because you'd never know what was going on.

The most I ever thought about Barbados in my twenty-one years in England was when I turned on the TV one day and saw

Ronald Biggs, the great train robber, was in Barbados, and there with him was Sleepy Smith, the famous Bajan lawyer. Sleepy Smith was giving some big speeches, giving the British government fits, making it hard for them to get Ronald Biggs back. Then I started thinking how a Barbadian like Sleepy Smith could be tying the British government up in knots.

The first time I came back home was in 1972; I'd been away for eleven years then. Andrew was ten years old, and he'd never seen Barbados. A friend of mine's sister was getting married, so I thought I would come down for the wedding and visit. Fifty-seven of us came down on a DC 10, on a charter with the Barbados Overseas Friends Association. The changes in Barbados was really something to see. There was a new secondary school in St. Lucy; free education had come in, and all the kids were wearing school uniforms.[10] Everywhere you went you saw different color school uniforms. The kids were given hot school meals; in my day it was milk and biscuits at 11:00. There was much better bus service; minibuses had come in. There was a new supermarket in Speightstown [the nearest town]. When I left for England there was no supermarket, and things didn't come already packaged. You had to tell the shopkeeper what you wanted, and he got it out and weighed it for you.

And when I came back there was a minimart and a lumberyard right here in the village [Crab Hill]. You didn't have to go to Speightstown to get a board or a package of nails. There were lots more houses. When I left it was pretty much all fields; when I came back it was houses, and good ones with television and fridges. When I left here there was no electricity, and when I came back people was watching television in their home.

And in the banks and stores there were a lot more black faces behind the counter. In truth, I became aware of the black people in the stores more by people talking about it than actually seeing it. In England all the people in these positions in the bank and so on are white, and you just get to expect that in your country the

---

10. In 1962 education became free to all citizens attending government institutions. In recent years the benefits have been expanded to include free lunches at primary schools, a textbook loan scheme, and subsidized bus fares (Dann, *The Quality of Life in Barbados*, 88). At the time Valenza emigrated from Barbados only the children at the elite schools (e.g., Alexandra, Harrison, and Queens) had school uniforms.

people in those same positions are going to be black. So, when I came back I thought the people in the bank would be black. But then I heard all the talk, like the day I went to the Hilton Hotel to meet my friends. They say, "You see all the changes since you come back. Black people are in here [the hotel] now, black people are in the sailing club, black people are in this, black people are in that." You had to be pleased for your country to see all these changes.

When I got back to England I encouraged Randall to come down and see all the changes for himself. So he came down, and he quite liked what he saw. Seeing all the changes made him want to come home. And when he came back up [to England] he'd decided that we should all come down [to Barbados] for good. Now I don't have to think over a thing for a long time to make a decision, not like some people who think and think and think, and after six weeks of thinking they still aren't sure what they want to do. Soon as Randall said he wanted to go back to Barbados, I started packing and sending [mailing] things down that we would need to get going. Just three months after Randall came back we were home in Barbados. First we sent David down [five years old, second child] to stay with my cousins, then we sent Andrew down to stay with his grandparents, next I came, and later, after he sold the house in Forest Gate, Randall came.

I brought everything back—bed, chairs, wardrobe, cabinet, sheets, everything except the carpet on the floor and those things that were connected with snow and cold, like heavy clothes. People in England gave us a lot of presents to take with us—pillowcases, tea sets, towels, bath soap, beach bags. We shipped all the things back in one big container.

For the people at home I brought back watches, clothing, and material. But I gave money to most people. If you gave them a trunk of clothing, they would still be looking for a dollar. I knew from experience that it was better to cut down on the gifts and give them money. I gave to nearly all the people in Crab Hill—friend, family, and foe.[11] I made sure I gave to my mother's age group, the ones that knew me from growing up. I would go and visit them

---

11. Valenza estimated that she gave away $600 BDS during her first three years at home.

and give them something. I gave something like $200 to my cousin, who was responsible for my education. The younger ones I only gave to if they asked me. They'd say, "Hello, you get back, you enjoying Barbados, you got anything to give me?" I'd say, "What would you like?" Then I'd know whether they'd want money or a T-shirt. When I gave them money I'd say, "Here is $10, but it's not for rum." They will always remember that I gave them something when I returned from overseas. Those who come back and don't give don't last very long.

The people here think that money in England is easy, that you are picking it up off the street. And because of that they'll try to overcharge you, or they'll put tricks on you, like they'll borrow from you and then forget to pay it back. When I got back I was in Speightstown shopping; I wanted carrots, cucumbers, yams, and so on. I picked out my things [from the hawkers' trays] like is the custom, and I hand it to her [the hawker], and she tell me an enormous sum, like $40. I thought, that can't be right. She knew that I didn't sound like a Barbadian, being that I was just back from England. So I say, how much are the carrots, how much are the cucumbers, how much are the yams? She just ignore me. So I tap on her the shoulder, and I say, "Do you remember me?"

She say, "No."

I say, "Well, I am one of the Slocumbs from Crab Hill. Now how much for that [the vegetables], or should I throw them in the tray and walk off?" The hawkers don't want a scene if there are a lot of people around. If it's just you, they'll shout, but not if there is people about.

She say, "Which of the Slocumbs are you? You are not Joyce, you are not Marlene."

I tell her I am the one called Valenza, and she say, "Yes, the one that be the nurse. You are Joyce and Marlene's sister." She say, "Take the vegetables, that be $10." And she put another cucumber in my bag. Not $40 but $10.

Soon after returning to Barbados Valenza contracted a local carpenter and a mason to begin work on a new house. She built on a plot of land that had belonged to her grandmother. Meanwhile, she and her kids lived with her parents. In four months their 44-by-22-foot-square house, paid in cash with savings from England, was complete.

If you build your house in stages, if you take too long to finish it, the villagers will think you are poor; they'll say you brought back nothing. And if you complete it too quick, they'll say you must have robbed somebody. They gossip about how well you dress and how well you look and so on. They like to gossip about people who come back. They don't always mean it maliciously; a lot of it is just comparing how well off you are today compared to when you left.

I think everyone who comes back from overseas should be able to build a house. England is the land of opportunity. The English don't stand in your way; they do everything possible to show you where you can make a living—painting, sewing, decorating cakes. We have a friend who is back from England and who says he wants to build a house but that he doesn't have enough money. I said, "Man, what were you doing up there—you were up there before me? Were you picking your teeth, were you putting your money into a hairy bag [spending it on women]?" I say, any West Indian that didn't make it, didn't want to make it.

All that I have gotten in life since I left school—property, experience, motivation, the will to get ahead—I got in England. I owe England a lot. Just working in the prisons has made me more tolerant, more patient; it's made me understand the problems people have. It's made me understand how young people can fall into trouble. I am very proud of my English training. It's given me the confidence that I can tackle any situation. And I'll stand up to a doctor if I had to; I'll say what I believe is right, even if it cost me my job. I don't think I could do that had I not been in England. And I am not afraid of court. Most Barbadians would not be seen near a magistrate's court.

Valenza learned about litigation from working with prisoners and also as a witness in a case tried in the Old Bailey. Two years after she returned to Barbados she was wrongfully dismissed from her job as a nurse at the government-owned cement plant. Her firing was political: a local politician wanted one of his supporters to have her job. The boss of the plant told her that he could do without a nurse but not without the support of the local MP [member of parliament]. Valenza sued. Before the case was finally settled, in her favor, she marched into the prime minister's office to complain about how she was being treated.

In Barbados some of the nurses see you as a threat because you've been away. The standard of nursing in England is completely different than the standard of nursing here. Up there you are exposed to more equipment and teaching than here, and you have more different kinds of cases there. But you can't apply what you learned up there without being criticized. They'd as soon tell you you should've stayed up there. They form little groups against you. Some of them say I am a show-off, and they look for silly little things to report me, to complain to the superior. When they give me trouble I speak to them in parables, and that shuts them up because they don't know what I am saying. I tell them things like, "Who the horse like it lick, and who it hate it kick." Or, "When I weed the ground took my hoe." Or, "When I left the army I brought my stripes." They [enemies] say, "She talking in them old-time sayings. I don't know what she talking about." My grand-mother was a great one for using the old sayings, and I learned them from her.

But, while some picks on me, if the governor-general or some special people coming to the hospital, they [her superiors] push me up to the front. First, they tell me to come properly dressed, with my proper cap and badges on. They push me up to the front because most of the nurses want to stay in the background; they are shy, scared of somebody asking them something, afraid they'll panic before they can find the answer. But they is good nurses; they know their nursing.

To fit back in here [Barbados] you must give up a lot of the customs that you acquired up there [England]. In London no-body wants to know who you are; what you do is your own business. But here it is different. Here people want to know your everything about you—how many outside women you have and so on. In England no one cares. You can go out with six different women, and no one really cares. Up there people mind their own business. Being up there made me more broad-minded; Barbadians who have never traveled are really very narrow-minded. If they see a boy and girl talking, they think they must be up to something. They wouldn't think they might be having a normal conversation. And when you come back to Barbados you had better have done well or they will fault you. They will pass sly remarks, saying you should have done better. And if you done well, if you have bypassed them [done better], some of them will try to pull you down. I tried not to let that happen. When I came back and I met people I didn't know I would say, "Who is your mother and who is your father?" and I would get to know them. But if I wasn't an outgoing person, I don't think they would have saved me a glass of water.

When I was a child the people that came back from overseas were accepted back into the community. We were eager to learn things from them—what the houses were like, what the education was like, do they write like us. I remember when Granville [a neighbor] came back from America when I was just young. Granville would always have a group around listening to him. He'd be telling us about the [sugar] canes in America, and he'd really enlarge on it. He'd tell us the canes was as long from Crab Hill Police Station to here [about two miles]. Now we all knew that wasn't true, but you'd let on that you believed him because you wanted to hear more of his stories. We'd all have a good laugh. Today people know a lot more about America and England than they did in my time. But some people still asked me some weird questions, like if you get false teeth for free in England or if they really bury three and four people in the same grave or if people's toes drop off in England from the cold.

One thing that's hard about coming back is that people here move so slow. So slow! There are two speeds in Barbados, slow and dead stop. The shop assistants and the bank clerks are the slowest; they're not interested in helping you. Maybe the heat makes them that way. The only time I see people really pushing themselves is to get on the bus to get home.

Living in England you become fast paced. In England there is efficiency. In Barbados people are laid back. If the bus doesn't come for four hours they say, "Ah, well, that's the transport [board]." But in England you wouldn't put up with that. Here I don't wait around to see if the bus is going to come. I go in the bus stand [in Speightstown], and I ask, "When the bus to Connell Town?" And if one isn't coming, they will tell me, and I'll have an hour of shopping. The average Barbadian won't go ask. They'll just stand on the corner and grumble and get nothing done. They'll just stand there while they could be off doing something useful. And they'll blame the politicians. It's not them that is responsible, though they is to blame for a lot of things, but they not the ones that make the bus not come. It's the bus administration. The average Barbadian blames the wrong people. You got to know who is responsible, and you got to speak out, or it will never get better.

I believe those who've traveled have more regard for time. At work I have eighteen patients that I have to get bathed and all that. I plan it all out on a schedule: I get eighteen pairs of pajamas, eighteen bath towels, eighteen washcloths, the soap, alcohol, the Alcolada, the Savlon, and I put it all out on the trolley, so that it's all ready to go. Now, if something happen and I have to run off and someone else come in to take over, it will be all planned out for them. People ask how I can do nursing and have time left over for all these other things. Well, the answer is that I plan.

Another thing you notice when you come back is that Barbadians are not punctual people. Here if you are to meet someone at nine o'clock you don't start getting dressed until nine o'clock. In England it's not like that. I remember there was a big funeral in England—the wife of a Barbadian cricketer died—and all the cars were booked up so we had to get taxis. We told the taximen to come at three o'clock. Well, they were all there ten minutes before three, waiting for us. I try never to keep people waiting because I don't like waiting.

But for all the good in England I wouldn't go back. Here you have an easier life, and you have safety. You can walk anywhere at any time of night and not be in fear of someone mugging you. And, although you don't make as much money here, you have a better standard of living. Look at all the Barbadians who own cars here who didn't have cars in England. Here everybody has their own house. Plus, you don't have to buy a winter coat.

Sure, sometimes you think about going back, wishing you were in England. I hear myself saying, "Oh, I could have stayed up there," but I say it as a phrase on the spur of the moment; it isn't said from the heart. I can go back anytime, and when you know that being here in Barbados don't bother you. If things got really bad here, I wouldn't hang around and pine and lament. I'd wake up one morning, and I'd say, "That's it. I am gone."

Today Valenza works as a nurse, caring for geriatric patients in a hospital in Bridgetown. She still has many contacts in England and a half-dozen times a year prepares a meal for friends and friends of friends visiting from England. Valenza and Randall are separated: angered over an infidelity, she asked him to leave. Randall now runs a beauty salon on the south coast. Their eldest son, Andrew, is college educated and has a white-collar job with the Department of Trade and Industry, and their youngest son, David, is a student at Combermere School, one of Barbados' elite high schools.

Chapter 7
John Wickham

John Wickham, one of Barbados' most respected citizens, is a widely read columnist, author of several books, editor of a literary magazine, and member of the Barbadian Senate. He began his working life at age seventeen collecting meteorological information at the Seawell airport on the island's south coast. Although he spent most of his professional life in meteorology, his ambition all along was to write. His father, Clennell Wickham, had been a leading journalist.

John spent more than twenty years living abroad. His career took him to Trinidad, England, and Switzerland before he finally returned to Barbados in 1967. But, while many working Barbadians emigrated primarily to earn a better livelihood, John was equally motivated by a desire to see the people and places he knew from books. As he put it, "I wanted to compare the world I knew from literature with the real thing." All three interviews I did with John were in his office at the Nation, *Barbados' most widely circulated newspaper. One wall of his office has a large window that looks into the newsroom, where columns of reporters, feature and sportswriters, assignment editors, and clerks busily put together the day's news.*

John was a thoughtful narrator. My questions were often followed by silences as he ruminated before beginning his response. He was often more interested in telling about culture and society than his own personal experiences. He would prefer, for instance, to compare the character of Trinidadians with that of other islanders than talk about his own experiences in Trinidad. In reading over the transcripts of our first two interviews I worried that I might never learn enough of the particulars of John's life for the reader to care about his story. At the start of our third interview I told him about my concern, and, as I went back over the thin areas in the transcripts, he fleshed them out in considerable detail. Also, he had given me a copy of his novel, World without End, *and his collection of short*

John Wickham in his home study, 1988. (Photo by Ellen Frankenstein.)

stories, Casuarina Row, *and, because some of the material was auto-biographical, it helped me to compose more specific questions about his life.*

John lives on the south coast of Barbados; at the edge of his backyard is the sea. Today he is in his middle sixties, though he looks to be closer to fifty. Tall, soft spoken, and of gentle manner, he carries the dignity of an elder statesman, which he is.

My life has really been an effort to justify the faith that my father had in me. He died when I was fifteen, but I am still in many ways under his influence, as he was of enormous importance to me. Through him I learned what it was to love and respect someone in a total kind of way. He was a newspaperman, a journalist, and a great believer in books—Fenimore Cooper, Thackeray, Scott, and the great classics. I can remember clearly the books that were on his shelves; we were surrounded by books. He didn't have to tell me to read. I just had to look at him and see the immense enjoyment that he got from reading. Books became central to my concept of myself and the world around me, and that comes from my father.

From an early age I enjoyed reading, especially books like Conan Doyle's stories of Sherlock Holmes and Greek, Roman, and Norse mythology. My mother, who didn't share my father's passion for books, would get annoyed over the things that I read. She would say, "Why don't you read something that will teach you how to do something, how to repair something. You are wasting your time reading about things that never really happened." I was at a loss to understand how she could fail to see their importance, and my father, without any quarreling, would simply say, "Let the boy read what he wants." I tell you this because I am sure that my father had a vision of the world beyond Barbados, which I didn't yet know, and which made the outside world attractive to me, and which later made me want to go out and see it for myself. When I was young I used to go to town with my father on Saturdays when he went to the newspaper office. I'd go to the library for the morning, and then I'd come back to his office and sit while he and his cronies talked and drank and argued about politics and cricket. He never told me to go away and play; he never discouraged me from sitting in and listening, and what I didn't understand of the conversation I would ask him about afterwards. So from a very early age he would talk to me as an adult, without condescension or babytalk.

There were four of us in the family, and all four emigrated. One brother went to Puerto Rico and did a degree in Spanish; my sister went to Washington, married an American, and worked in an office recruiting West Indian farm labor to the United States; and my other brother went to England to study chemistry and married a Barbadian girl there who was doing nursing. All of us are now back in Barbados.

We were not well off, and I had to get a scholarship in order to go to Harrison College.[1] I remember the first lunch break at Harrison, wandering around like a new lost boy and watching a group of white boys playing with snowballs. They were buying snowballs of shaved ice [snow cones], compressing them, and throwing them at each other. I remember that vividly and thinking, My God, how can they do that? and thinking that I was going

---

1. Harrison College is Barbados' most prestigious secondary school.

to school with people who can afford to throw away money. Money for us was not easy to come by.

My experiences at Harrison were not totally happy. I wasn't the victim of any overt racial prejudice, and there were enough black boys there, probably more black than white. But nearly all the black boys were there on scholarships, while the white boys were fee-paying students. That was the great distinction, and from that flowed another disparity: white boys were all assured of jobs when they left school, in the stores in Bridgetown or wherever their parents worked. Hence, they never had to work as hard as the black students. The black students were expected to do better because we were exhibitioners [on scholarships]. The headmaster, an Englishman, made us exhibitioners feel really inferior, that if we weren't doing really well we were keeping other boys from being in the school.

I played a good deal of cricket in school with white boys. We played and batted with the school team as if we were one. However, none of the white boys ever acknowledged my existence outside of school. You would see them on the street, and they wouldn't speak to you. You were left wondering, what kind of people they were who would deny a fraternity which did in fact exist. I now see some of these same people in the shops and in offices in town, but we pretend that we don't know each other. At this adult stage that seems to me very silly.

I left Harrison College in 1941 when I was seventeen. I left because my father had died, and, with me being the eldest child, I had to help support the family. I did a training course in meteorology, which was just beginning as a new field in Barbados due to the war [World War II]. Aircraft were coming down here from Canada and then crossing the Atlantic to Dakar to join the fight in the desert. Since Barbados was one of the four staging points, they needed weather observations. It was a good job for me because it gave me lots of time between observations to read and to write. I was an observer at first, and then later I did climatology, compiling data from different stations in the Caribbean. I found it relatively easy and decided to make my living in it, but my real interests were in writing. Early on I was writing short stories, contributing some to the BBC [British Broadcasting Corporation] and *Bim* magazine.[2] All my energy was spent on writing. That is not to say that I did my meteorology job badly; in fact, I became quite proficient at it.

In 1946 the meteorological service I worked for became a regional one, and I was transferred to Trinidad, where I was responsible for setting up and managing different weather stations. I was glad to go. A small island does press on you if you are young and reasonably educated. Knowing about the world through books makes you want to go outside and see it for yourself. Also, Barbados for black people didn't offer the kinds of opportunities which your education had prepared you for; emigration has always been our hope. So I went off to Trinidad, and I stayed there for a long time—sixteen years—and I married a Trinidadian. In fact, I had no thought of ever returning to Barbados.

Migration among the islands is usually not traumatic because, whatever the differences between Barbados and Trinidad, we are similar kind of people. Besides, I had friends there. A boy I went to school with lived there, so when I knew I was going to Trinidad I wrote to him and asked if he could find a place for me to live, a modest boarding house. I fell in among compatible spirits, people interested in books and music and art.

The house I lived in was near Victoria Square in Port of Spain. As it stood at the corner of two streets, it had two numbers, one for each street, so that it was either No. 31 or No. 11, depending upon which street name was used. I was told that the property was subject to two tax assessments, but this may have been only a calypso joke. I used to think of the house as "the house of the hanging baskets" because it had a tiny porch with a rail of wooden fretwork and hanging from the eaves a row of wire baskets. The baskets were so close together and the green ferns so abundant that when you sat down you couldn't see out into the street.

I think life often resolves itself into little chunks of time, each with its own personality, so that it becomes possible to describe events or experiences with reference to a particular time and place. The house of hanging baskets was kind of landmark for me,

---

2. *Bim* is a Caribbean literary magazine published in Barbados.

of people I met when I lived there and insights gained. I have passed the house since that time, and it is now a completely different place. A new owner has done up the front porch, removed the hanging baskets, and the house is now just like all the other houses on the street.

At first I had difficulty getting adjusted to the Trinidadians' casualness. *Carnival* is an expression in Trinidad which means "to enjoy and to play." For somebody brought up in the solemn and puritan environment of Barbados Trinidad didn't seem serious enough. I couldn't understand its Gothic panache. But after a while I began to feel that it was good to be like that. Also, Trinidadians are rather spendthrift, not frugal like Barbadians, but that is only because they never had to be as frugal. The island is bigger, and they didn't have slavery to the same extent as Barbados, and therefore they haven't had to watch every penny as we did. Maybe that's why they don't worry as much; they have a faith something will come tomorrow.

One of the things that interested me was the Trinidadian phrase "for so." If you ask a Trinidadian "Why did you go to the country today?" he is likely to say "For so." He means "there is no reason." For a Barbadian there must be a reason for doing something, but not so for Trinidadians. You do it "for so." At first this was quite annoying, but then you begin to see it as being an admirable quality. Last year we had an idea here at the newspaper [the *Nation*] to do a series of articles on the Barbados-Trinidad connection. We agreed with the *Trinidad Express* that each paper would do a series of articles on local perceptions of the other country, and then we would exchange the articles and publish them. Well, we went ahead and did ours, but they never kept their word. That is typically Trinidadian; it was "for so."

Trinidad was extremely exciting for me. I knew freedom in a real way—freedom of movement, freedom from restrictions, and freedom from race. As you know, Barbados is very English and very class-conscious, so the chances of somebody like me meeting and talking with somebody like the chief justice in those days were dim. Whereas in Trinidad there was that opportunity because there wasn't a rigid separation of people. People who knock it say that relationships in Trinidad are thinner and more superficial, but never mind. Superficial or not, they were possible. There was an ease of commerce in social traffic; also you met people from all races, such as Portuguese, Chinese, Indian, and all the permutations.

In 1958 Trinidad became the capital of the federation,[3] and that was another beautiful experience, absolutely great. Eric Williams had come into power, and he articulated a notion of a unified Caribbean. He gave us a political drive and the image of all the Caribbean working together. Unfortunately, the confederation collapsed in 1962.

My first stay outside the Caribbean was to England in 1956. I enrolled for a semester in a program of English literature at a Cadbury college, Fincroft, on the outskirts of Birmingham. The Cadburys—the chocolate people—are Quakers and had set up several colleges for adults who never had a chance to go to university. Under the terms of my service in Trinidad I was entitled to a long leave for which the government was to pay my passage. At that time I was good friends with an Englishman, Norman Booth, who was living in Trinidad and who was very interested in literature. In Trinidad we'd often meet to talk and drink. When he heard that I was going on leave he said that Cadbury had a college that would just suit me, where I could spend six months reading, going to lectures, going to the library, writing essays, talking to students, and so on. He put me onto them, and they accepted me.

When I landed in London I was already late for the term, so I had to immediately catch a train for Birmingham. The train made many stops, and, by the time it got to Coventry, Stafford, and all those mining and industrial towns, it was already dark. At each station the doors to the carriage would open, and in from the dark would come three or four grimy men with their little cloth caps and scarves, and with their rich accents. They would plop themselves down and take out a pack of grimy cards and play them silently until the next stop, where they would all get out only to be replaced by others, and so on. It was pure D. H. Lawrence. I didn't have to be introduced to it; I knew exactly what I was seeing.

---

3. The Federation of the West Indies was made up of ten British colonies, including Antigua, Barbados, Dominica, Grenada, Montserratt, St. Lucia, and Trinidad and Tobago. It came into being on 3 January 1958 and was dissolved on 31 May 1962.

I had a glorious time. England was beautiful, but it was also very dark for somebody who was accustomed to the light and bright of the Caribbean. I have strong memories of cold mutton and cold cabbage. But, oddly enough, even those memories are nostalgic, and often I feel that, tasteless as the food was, I would like to have some just to recapture that time. From the college it was not far to the Evesham, the garden of England, and to the Forest of Arden, Shakespeare country. That landscape, for me, said all there was to say about England. What was most affecting about the landscape was the order that stemmed from a long occupation. The land had not only been lived on for hundreds and hundreds of years, but it had been loved. There was nothing disorderly about it.

We went to Stratford and saw Shakespeare, and I found that I knew more of the Arden and that whole Shakespeare thing than many of the English boys. In England I felt I had arrived at the cultural center which my education had prepared me for. Remember, the school I went to in Barbados was just like an English public school, with Latin and Greek and the same paraphernalia of cricket and colors. That background made it easier for me to fit in in England, although the attitudes you encountered on the streets and buses made you wonder a bit.

Because I was Barbadian and had played a lot of cricket, it was natural that I would play cricket for the college, though my introduction was somewhat bewildering. I had just arrived—this is the first Saturday—and I turn up to play. The captain of the cricket team is white and has never seen me play before, but, like most Englishmen, he has this stereotype in his mind that anybody tall, big, and black is bound to be a fast bowler. He doesn't know whether I am a bowler or a batsman or what; all he knows is that I am a tall West Indian, so he assigns me to the role of opening bowler, because I am just a stereotype.

At the end of that term I went on a bicycle tour of Holland and Belgium with a group of students. I shared a tandem with my tutor in English literature. He was a very ineffectual Englishman, quite at home with English poetry between Gerard Manley Hopkins and T. S. Eliot, but he knew precious little else. He lived in this world of poetry. He was from the Oxford system where you know everything about a little period, and you know it from its guts, but precious little else. Mind you, since these people have very good brains, it's not very difficult for them to absorb the rest afterwards. Anyway, there are some things you can only do when you are young, and this trip was one.

In advance we had mapped out our journey and booked a series of hostels so that, once on the Continent, we had to cycle so far each day to be sure to get to our night's lodgings. Well, in planning our route we had made some of our distances too long, so there was never any time to see things. We would pass through Amsterdam and just have time for a quick look at a museum, a meal, and then off again. The whole four weeks was a memory of my head down, looking at the paving stones and the bicycle path and the patterns of the road surface. Riding, riding, riding every day.

The first evening, when we landed, we took our bikes off the boat and rode to Bruges. When we arrived there was a gigantic street fair in progress, and walking along the pavement was not easy. Wherever I went I was the object of the most unashamed stares. I had noticed them earlier but hadn't thought much about it. Now it was unmistakable. Three of us were sitting outside a cafe drinking beer when a little boy came along with his mother. He just stared and stared at me. As his mother is dragging him along, he is saying "*Schwarte, schwarte,*" which means "black" in Dutch. My friends were embarrassed for me. One broke an icy silence with, "What do you say to charging a fee for all this show?" We all laughed.

At the end of the summer I went home to Trinidad and to the meteorological service, but within a few years I was back in England. In 1961 I was transferred out of meteorology and into the Student Affairs section of the West Indies High Commission. The work was purely administrative, processing West Indian students for entry into British universities and training colleges. The students would send us all the information on what they wanted to do and where they wanted to go, and we would see that their qualifications matched. It was an advisory job, and I enjoyed seeing how well the students' qualifications matched their ambitions. That job was a beautiful experience because I dealt with West Indians on the basis of being West Indian. The insularity of Barbados, St. Lucia, Trinidad, the Grenadines, whatever, didn't for our purposes exist. That was great.

When we got to London we were lucky because somebody at the High Commission had a flat for us in Chiswick, and we went straight into that. We got on well with the landlord, who lived upstairs. He was Australian, and his wife was English, an editor of a women's magazine.

But my wife didn't really like living in England, and that was understandable. She had two small children and was confined to the house, and the weather was cold and wet and miserable. I used to come home and find her in tears. The children were alright, but she was miserable most of the time and was anxious to come home. What she did like was the opera and dance; she still talks about Covent Garden and taking the children to see *The Wind in the Willows* and so on.

I enjoyed the bookshops and the art galleries, especially on Saturday mornings, but otherwise very little else. We had my meteorological friends, but mostly I was only meeting West Indians. The immigration bill had come along and had hardened race attitudes.[4] I'll tell you what I mean. While at Fincroft College, I shared a room and became good friends with a little Cockney boy named Harry. He was lively and witty and everything good you hear of Cockneys. When I got back to England in 1961 we picked up again. He had married, and we got on well with his wife. Then the immigration bill passed, and West Indians who had always thought of Britain as the "mother country" discovered that they were, after all, only citizens of a colony. They discovered that they couldn't come to England without special visas, which were very hard to get. We weren't wanted anymore. Anyway, Harry, who was my good friend and with whom I had lived, said to me one day after this bill was passed, "John, you know of course that this legislation is not going to alter our relationship—that I don't agree with it." Well, I thanked him, but I realized that it already had altered our relationship. The fact that he mentioned it at all suggested that things had changed.

---

4. The 1962 Commonwealth Immigrants Act. Some of its effects are described in chapter 3.

I remember one evening in particular. Part of my job was to work with the Public Relations section of the High Commission, and we used to have to respond to invitations to come and talk about the Caribbean and tell people what our country was like and so forth. Well, I was sent to this place in the north of London to respond to an invitation from a little political party group of liberals. It was a small meeting in a private house. The first people to turn up were two sisters, who were very well-bred and educated. This was my first assignment, and I didn't know exactly what reception to expect because this was at the height of the debate over the immigration bill. I was really nervous about what I was going to say, and I feared there would be hostility. One of the sisters asked me, "Why do you come here? Why do you leave the sun and all that?" Time and time again I came across that. I said, "We came because we were misled into believing that here is where we belong." Then one of these middle-aged women offered me a glass of sherry, and we began to chat, and the atmosphere warmed. It became a delightful evening because I could talk to them as I am talking to you, and I could see that the impression of West Indians that they started the evening with was not confirmed by my presence.

We had only been in London a year when the federation collapsed in 1962 and my job disappeared. My wife was so unhappy there that eventually I probably would have left anyway. But when it was clear that we were going to leave I wasn't sure where to go—Barbados or Trinidad? I was raised in Barbados, but I had lived in Trinidad for sixteen years. My wife was Trinidadian, my two children were born there, I had a house there, and I had friends there. Whereas in Barbados all the boys and girls I had gone to school with had gone away themselves or had forgotten me. The friendships that I had made between the ages of nineteen and thirty-five were my most important friendships, and they were in Trinidad. And I felt that I hadn't exhausted Trinidad, that it still had much to offer. So we went there.

However, soon after returning to Trinidad, I took a job with a former colleague, a South African who was a meteorologist. He wanted somebody to accompany him on trips up the Caribbean. He could speak no French and wanted somebody to go to Guadeloupe and Martinique. I really didn't want the job—I didn't want any job—as I was thinking about writing. I had two novels in my head, and I thought this was the chance to see if I had any qualities as a writer. But I allowed myself to be seduced by the notion of traveling up and down the islands because some of them I hadn't seen. I took the job. It was very nice, and it was a good education; we went to Martinique, Antigua, and so on.

When I got to Barbados, where the center of the operation was, there was a letter from a friend about a job for a meteorologist in Geneva, Switzerland. I really didn't want to apply, but I was staying with my mother, and, like all Barbadian mothers, she was very strict on protocol. Even if I wasn't interested in that job, she said I had to reply to the man and tell him so. And, of course, one thing led to another. I replied and said, "Well, send me the form." He didn't have any more forms and instead sent a cable telling me there was a man from Geneva who, coincidentally, was in Barbados and that he would interview me.

I was interviewed, it went very well, and by Christmas I had taken the job and was off to Geneva in the middle of the cold. I went early, before the family came, so as to get a house. I enjoyed it immensely. I suppose it was largely the challenge of a new language. Our children, who were very young, nine and twelve, went to grade school and were at first totally bewildered by the language, but they did very well for themselves. I found the Swiss interesting. They are so precise, prim, and clean—antiseptically clean. They're so clinical and meticulous that I figured they must be bad poets. The British have a different kind of tidiness and order; it's more in their imprint on the landscape than in the person.

For the first time in my life I was earning enough money to be comfortable enough so that I didn't have to think about what the new year would bring. And I enjoyed the work. I got a fairly rapid promotion and ended up as personal assistant to the deputy secretary-general of the World Meteorological Organization. Another benefit was that Geneva, being the center of Europe, offered all types of opportunities to travel, which we did.

But after four years I began to have doubts. I began to wonder what I was doing there. I couldn't put my finger on anything in particular; I wasn't discriminated against, and we had all the creature comforts. Then one day I looked out of our apartment window onto the park below to where the children were playing with other kids, and I saw my daughter standing apart. The boys were playing fine. My son was a gregarious kind of animal, full of life; he spoke beautiful French, was popular, and did well at school. But my daughter was alone, and that really got at me. I wondered what she would be like if she were to grow up in Geneva. Was that the kind of separateness that she had to look forward to? And that started me thinking. Things that you didn't notice before you started to notice, such as how the Swiss were always referring to the *étrangers*. You knew that you would never be one of them.

Even though I had a permanent appointment and was secure for the rest of my life, I'd get the feeling that I would never belong. Then I noticed that I took no real interest in Swiss civil life. There was always a referendum on something, whether a certain beach should be open in the summer or on the price of milk, and it occurred to me that I didn't care. How could I live in a place where nothing mattered? That annoyed me. Then I began to notice that none of my colleagues and friends, all international civil servants, belonged either. The conversations were mostly about where you were going for the winter, where you were going for the summer, your next home leave, the cost of living, how much you were paying for your apartment, and promotions. Nothing that connected with the place you were living in.

One morning I was walking to work, and there was a man that I met on the road every morning, the same man at the same spot walking in the same direction every morning, like clockwork. This day, just as I was passing him, a car backfired, there was a loud report, and I jumped. The man turned to me and said, "Ah, Monsieur, we haven't had a shot fired in anger here in four hundred years." He thought that was very funny. It was funny, but then I thought, What the hell is he saying to me—that where I come from there are shots fired all the time?

You know how things happen, you go on with life, with these concerns bubbling in your mind, and you don't say anything to anybody about them. Then suddenly something happens, and you make a decision, and for people who don't know how you've been thinking it looks as if you are making a hasty, impulsive decision. But the truth is that it was there all the time. And for me that moment came in March of 1967. I said to my wife, quite suddenly, without having consulted anyone, "We're going home."

She said, "What are you going to do? You are not going home to a job."

I said, "I don't know, the first decision is that we are going home. Having made that decision, we will see."

I put in my letter of resignation with adequate notice. My chief, who was a Frenchman, was baffled. He said, "Monsieur Wickman"—he could never say my name right—"what nonsense is this? *où est la Barbade?* You are a madman. What are you going to do there? Listen, I'll put your letter of resignation in this drawer, and when you change your mind I'll destroy it."

While I was serving out my last month I learned that the United Nations was setting up a regional institute for the teaching of meteorology in Barbados. It was a training institute, and that suited me to the ground, just the right thing. I thought I'd come back and try to get the post, as I had several connections with that organization. I got the post as senior administrative officer. And that is how we came back. By this time the children had changed schools three times, from Trinidad to London to Geneva, and now Barbados. My daughter said she hoped never to be a "new girl" again.

I think all these experiences that I have described to you have contributed to making us very happy. I don't mean happy in any material sense but happy in the sense that we have seen the world, and now we have no illusions. For example, we know now that Barbados is the best place for us. That is not to say I am uncritical of Barbados; there are many things that annoy me. Mind you, when I left here Barbados was still a colony, and when I returned it was independent. I came back to find a rampant nationalism, a chauvinism, a praise of things simply because they are Barbadian, and I don't like that. That is not patriotism, that is not love for country, it is nonsense! But I am not going to rush off to New York or London or Paris thinking that people are any different or any better there, because I know that they're not.

I think, too, that having lived abroad made me more efficient in dealing with life. You are not so fazed with simple things as you would be if you had stayed in the Caribbean all your life. And, having tested what you read in books against the actuality of life, you are not so satisfied with generalities—generalities like "All Cockneys are so and so." You say to yourself, Harry, whom you shared a room with in Birmingham, was a Cockney, and he is not like that.

John worked at the meteorological training institute in Barbados for ten years, until 1978. He quit in order to write his memoirs, World without End, *which was published in 1982. A year after he left meteorology he was offered and accepted a job as a columnist with the* Nation, *Barbados' largest newspaper. About that he said, "My job here at the* Nation *is another happy accident. Perhaps there is a way in which everything you do young in life is preparation for what you are going to do later on. As long as I was in meteorology, there was never any hope that I might become a writer, but it gave me experience to do what I do now. Yes, now I find myself in a job for which my whole life has been a preparation."*

Chapter 8
Cleveland and Rose Thornhill

In 1983 I was driving in the northern part of Barbados in the parish of St. Lucy, just outside the village of Checker Hall, when I noticed an imposing two-story wall house under construction. It was twice the size of any other house and had an unusual second-floor balcony. I stopped the car, thinking the owner might be a return migrant. A young workman told me the house was being built for a Barbadian family still living in London. He said the family had "made a fortune" and that they were planning to come home when the house was finished. I left the site thinking that the owners had to be arrogant to build such an oversized house in a rural village.

A year later when I was back in Barbados I stopped by to meet the owners—Cleveland and Rose Thornhill. I liked them instantly. They were warm and humble people, not at all what I had expected. They had worked extremely hard, often holding three jobs between them, for nearly thirty years in England. They had deferred many of life's pleasures in order to buy a home in London and later to send their three children to college. By returning to Barbados, they hoped to take life easy, to buy a small boat and spend time fishing.

Cleve had also lived in the United States. He went there to work as a seasonal farm laborer during and just following World War II, as part of a U.S. government program that recruited farm workers from the Bahamas and the British-controlled West Indies. Cleve and other West Indians replaced American workers, predominantly black, who had moved north to work in war-related industries.

Although Cleve spent under two years in the United States, compared to more than twenty years in England, they occurred when he was still in his teens, at a formative time in his development. In the Florida sugarcane fields he showed he could cut cane with the fastest of men in the migrant labor camps, and he became an adult. Cleve fell in love with America, but

Cleve and Rose Thornhill on the porch of their home
in rural St. Lucy, 1988. (Photo by George Gmelch.)

*he once declined a transfer back to cutting cane and after that was unable
to get back into the United States. He finally emigrated to England in the
hope that he could enter the States from there.*

*Cleve, as he prefers to be called, is short, brawny, and taciturn. When
in company he prefers to let Rose speak for the family. Rose is tall and thin,
with fine facial features and teeth filled with gold that glints when she
smiles and laughs, as she often does. In the five years they have been back in
Barbados they have not yet taken life easy. Cleve has not yet been out in his
boat, as all his time is taken up running the two buses they bought before
leaving England and had shipped home. They had planned to hire others
to operate the buses between rural St. Lucy and Bridgetown, eleven miles
away. Two young men do the driving, but Rose keeps the books, and Cleve
makes all the repairs. Before even finishing decorating their new home—the*

concrete floors are still bare, the walls unpainted, and many of their furnishings still in shipping boxes—they have laid a foundation for an addition on their kitchen.

I interviewed the Thornhills three times, all in their home. I had more difficulty scheduling interviews with the Thornhills than with any other subjects: they always seemed busy and perhaps not as committed to the project as others. Like the Bovells, they had a difficult time understanding why the reader might be interested in their lives.

Getting into their house for the interviews was nerve-racking, as they had four Dobermans chained to the front porch. The mere sight of me set them barking, teeth bared, and tugging at their chains; on each visit I had to wait in the driveway while the dogs were moved to the backyard. The Thornhills, having spent a lifetime working for what they have, are very protective of it.

Part of one interview, concerning their return migration, was lost when the electrical power went out without our knowing it. When, with the power back on, I later repeated the questions, Rose and Cleve did not have the same spontaneity and gave abbreviated versions, lacking the detail of the first telling. For whatever reasons I was never able to fully replace the information we had lost.

Cleve Thornhill

I was seventeen years old when I went into the immigration office in Bridgetown. It was in 1944, and at that time you needed a slip to get to America. When you went into the immigration office you had to look fit. If you looked fit, then you'd have a chance to go in and see the doctor. The doctor was the man who could let you into America. He was a Yankee doctor. He asked me if my mother knew that I am leaving home. I said, "Of course, she do." When I was a kid I did a lot of wrestling on the sand, and I developed muscles all over. When the Yankee doctor was talking to me he took his hand and punched me here, in the stomach. I figured if his hand had went in he wouldn't want me, but when his hand bounced off I figured I was as good as on my way to America.

Me and the other fellows they picked went to America on the sea. We landed in Miami, Florida. Then we went on a trail [road] that went north near the seaside. The scenery was beautiful. It was

Cleve and Rose Thornhill's passport photographs, 1971.

a pity that I didn't have a movie camera where I could take pictures all the time. They took us to a big camp. We were there for two days, while they put us into different groups. Then they put us on trains to different places in America, all according to where you were wanted for work.

They sent me to Minnesota. My job was to pitch peas. This machine cut the peas, and then you would pitch them with a fork [pitchfork] up onto the truck. The work was a bit hard. You see, I was the youngest of the men, and, being that I had just left school, I didn't have any experience of work. But I soon catched up. Most of the men were much older than me, and some of them used to call me their son.

Being that I was young and they was older, I used to watch what they'd do, and then I'd do the same thing. They would write a letter home on Thursday night and have it all ready so that, when they got paid on Friday, they would put the money—a money order—straight into the envelope and post it home to Barbados. We was getting seven American dollars every week. That was a lot of money in Barbados dollars. I'd post half my pay to my mother, and the other half I'd keep to buy my feed and digs [accommodations], and now and again I'd want to go to a show.

You'd work on a farm until they was finished with you, until they didn't need you no more. Then they'd turn you over to another farmer. When they were done with us in Minnesota they sent us out to the West. I did love that because you could see different parts of America. One of the places we passed through was Idaho. There I saw the real cowboys. We was on a train, and we pulled into a station, and out the windows you could see real cowboys all dressed up in the gear—long skirt [chaps], pointy boots with big heels and spurs on the back, and cowboy hats on their heads. They rode up near the train where we could see them good. I think they were putting on a show for us, being that a lot of us had never seen cowboys before and being that we were real curious, all looking out the windows. I was always a cowboy fan, so to me seeing them was out of this world.

Another place we worked was Chicago, in a place where they made canned pork [ham]. My job was to push a wagon loaded with the bones and scraps of the pig over to a furnace that boiled it up and made it into glue. I worked ten hours a day doing that. But it was nice there because they let us eat their meat. We would bring our own bread and have lunch in the factory with their meat. You could eat what you wanted, but you couldn't take any away.

The last place I worked was Corn Products, just outside Chicago. Corn from all over the country would come into this big factory, and with that corn we'd make sixty-four different products—whiskey, rum, beer, starch, sugar, seltzer, and all kinds of things. The job was pretty good, but the camp we lived in was pretty bad. The food tasted so bad that you couldn't get enough to eat. And we couldn't get proper sleep because some nights there'd be a lot of noise, especially when the fellows would be up in the night gambling. Some of us complained to the camp relations officer. He said that, if we could find proper digs somewhere else and if we'd give him the address, that we could live outside the camp. So this friend and me moved out. We found a private home [boarding house] where the man and woman rented out all the rooms in the house to different people. I still remember the address. It was 2717 Indiana Street in Chicago. My friend and me shared one room. We bought our own food and cooked it on a hotplate in the room.

Being young and stupid, I didn't know the real danger of living in Chicago. I used to go out and walk around at night and look at all the things on my own. Not being really tied down, you wanted to get out and live a bit of life, and, being in a big country, nothing at all like Barbados, there was lots of things to see.

Nowadays people tell me that Chicago is real dangerous and that they wouldn't live there. But would you believe that I never had no trouble? It's when you are afraid that you get trouble.

I was in America about a year and a half before they sent me home. The next time I came back to America was 1947. They sent me to Florida. I was in Belglade, Southgate, and Runyon, moving around from place to place cutting cane. Each day they'd give you two rows of cane to cut. The rows would be about from here to Speightstown [two miles], and they'd pay you $13 for the row.[1] The trick was to pick a row that had a lot of bad cane in it, where the cane was real thin, so that you wouldn't have to cut as much for your $13. A fellow can cut a thinned-out row in less than no time and go back to the camp and be done for the day. The people who lived down there the year-round knew where the bad rows were. Before the work was to begin they'd have gone out into the fields, in and out through the canes, looking for the thin place. When they'd find them they'd go back to the head of the field and mark the spot. Then, when the scratch woman came around and the men had to line up with the rows they wanted to cut, these fellows would be sure to stand by the rows that were thinned out. I used to watch these fellows who knew the fields, and when I'd see where they'd line up I'd go line up next to them.

We'd get up around three o'clock and go to the kitchen to eat. You'd be anxious to start early because the earlier you start the earlier you're done. We'd ride on a truck to the fields; sometimes the fields would be an hour from the camp. We'd start to work around sunup. There was always a truck coming back and forward to take you to the camp when you were done.

The fellows that could really cut cane fast were called "ginny gogs." These were fellows who would go from here to there without stopping for a breath or to stretch themselves. Being young and fit, I said to myself that I could be like them. So, one of the first days in the field I lined up next to a ginny gog. He was the fastest fellow in our camp. He started cutting right down through the cane and I right next to him. Every foot he made I made the foot after him. At one time I had a couple of dead holes [empty

---

1. The length of the row was probably much less than he remembers. In the 1980s a standard row was 1,240 feet. Cutters are still assigned two rows each day, called "a task," which contain approximately eight tons of cane.

spaces in the cane], so I jumped four or five feet ahead of him. I worked as fast as I could, not wanting to let him get ahead of me. When we get halfway down the field, he says to me, "Greenhorn, you give me some trouble." He cut and he cut, but when I got to the end of my row he was still behind me. Well, when the foreman come around he was pleased to see that I had beat him. He checked the cane to see how low it was cut, to make sure I was doing a proper job, and then he said, "You've done very well today."

I said, "Yes, I think so."

He said, "Do you want another half row?"

I said, "I don't mind." And I finished that extra half row before some fellows had finished their first row. Well, from that time onwards I had my name printed on me: I was always among the fast fellows.

Some of the ginny gogs were soft hands fellows who had only done office work at home [in the West Indies]. They were called "soft hands" because, if you pressed their hands, you could see the blood under the skin. They hadn't done much work before with their hands. But some of them became the fastest cane cutters in Florida because they had determination. They had a goal, and they set about learning how to cut cane the fastest way a man could.[2]

The fellows who had learned to cut cane at home had a more difficult time cutting in Florida. The way you cut cane is different in Florida, and it was hard for the fellows to unlearn the way they knew from before. The main difference is that in Barbados you use a cane bill—a broad knife with a long peak on the end for removing the trash [leaves] from the cane. It's all steel, and it's very heavy. The soft hands fellows learned the Florida way from fresh, where the old cane cutters kept falling back on their old habits.

But being one of the fast fellows, one of the ginny gogs, was real hard in the heat in Florida. Sometimes you'd really want to go to the water truck for a sip of water, but you didn't want to leave

2. Today sugar growers prefer cane cutters that come from small farms over urban workers because of their physical stamina and their previous work experience (C. H. Wood and T. McCoy, "Migration, Remittances, and Development: A Study of Caribbean Cane Cutters in Florida," 264–65).

the field because you knew that some other guys would catch you up. You worked so hard that sometimes you could taste blood in your mouth. The only time you'd stop is when the food truck came and they sounded the gong. Then everybody would stop to get food.

But being one of the fast fellows was important because you'd want the foreman to know that you could handle your job. If you did well in the cane fields, you might get chosen to go north when the cane cutting jobs finished. They pick the good men and send them up north to pluck corn, to pick tobacco, to pick cherries or apples, and these kinds of things. If you were no good, they'd put you in the ship and send you back home.

In the evening, when we wasn't in the cane field, we'd go into these little towns where they have taverns and jukeboxes. We'd have a drink and dance with some of the girls. We'd buy them all beer. The fellows would be out for a good time. I was a shy person, so I'd drink my beer and sit down and watch the other fellows. Sometimes the law would come in and give one of our fellows a hard time and carry him away and lock him up in the station. Then the sheriff would call our camp manager, and we'd have to take up a collection to get bail to get the fellow out. I think the sheriffs were just looking for pocket money for themselves, because sometimes there wasn't any bad behavior. I knew that for sure. I've seen the sheriff drive up with the siren, come inside the tavern, and just grab one of the fellows. There was no bad behavior. After we'd pay the bail that would be the end of it, no court or nothing. We figured that, if the fellow had really done bad, they'd have taken him to court.

After the cane cutting was over I got a kind of promotion. They sent me up north to Connecticut, where they had me topping beets. When I finished there they wanted to send me back down to Florida to cut canes again. Some of the other fellows who weren't so good were getting jobs picking apples and such. I was very upset that these fellows were getting the good jobs, picking apples. I wanted to pick apples and not cut cane, because you could make $16 or $17 a day picking apples, and the conditions were better. I didn't want to go back to Florida cutting canes for less money, so I told them, "No, I'd rather go home before I go back to Florida." So they sent me home. That was 1947, and I have never been back to America since.

Had they not sent me home, I might still be in there now, because a lot of the fellows stayed on, moving from north to south, backward and forward, up and down. Some married and became American citizens. I might have been able to do that. Looking back on it, I think going to America, being young and having had all that experience, made me grow up for my future life.

Before I came home I bought some cowboy shirts and a Zenith radio to bring back. The radio doesn't work anymore, but I keep it as a souvenir to remember America by. And, being that I was thinking of becoming a mechanic, I bought a book, *The Mechanical Encyclopedia,* that showed how everything worked, even airplanes and steamships. I brought back a big dictionary, so big that you have to put it on a table to use it. It has every word you'd ever want to know. I doubt that you could find one like it in America today.

Coming back to Barbados was alright, but when you get back here you find that there isn't much to do. And you find that you don't want to go back to the stage [economic level] that you were at before you left. You want to go a bit higher. So, when I got back I decided to learn a trade, to be a mechanic. I got on as an apprentice with Charles McEnearney's garage in Bridgetown. There was a very smart fellow there. He used to say to me, "Cleve, learn what you can from here, do it quick, and then move on because, no matter how long you stay, you'll never get proper pay here." It was true, there were fellows that had been working at Charles McEnearney for five years, and they were only getting pocket money. So, after I did my apprenticeship there—I was getting just $5 a week—I moved on to another job with a big garage, where I got $30 a week. I worked there for ten months, and then I went over to Dean's Garage where I got on for $32 a week. I worked there for a time, and then I started looking around to go a bit higher. So, I went over to Linton Garage and asked about a job. The boss said he didn't have a mechanic's shop but that he had lots of customers who wanted their cars fixed. He said that he could get me customers and that I could pay him a percentage. I said yes. He got the work coming in and soon I was getting good

money. Some weeks I'd make $75. I did that for a year, until the
Gulf Oil Company came to Barbados to do some drilling. I went
up and had a chat with the fellow at Gulf Oil and asked him if he
had a job for a mechanic. I wore my best shirt, one that I had
brought home from America with all the cherries on it. It said
Cherry Grove. He said, "I see that you've been to America." And I
told him about my times up there.

After we chatted awhile he said, "We are just starting up in
Barbados, so we don't need a mechanic just now, but we can use a
man like you." I helped them make the roads and prepare the sites
where they were going to drill for oil. We'd dig out the big rocks
with a tractor and lay down concrete. Later I became their mechanic. I worked for them for four years, but all during that time I
made applications to get back to America. I even tried to get to
Canada, thinking that from there I could get into America. I
applied to the Canadian government as a mechanic, and my
application was all accepted—they even told me what date I could
come. But they wanted me to send a photograph. This was in the
early years when they weren't accepting so many colored people,
like they did later on. Well, after they got my photograph they said,
"Sorry, your application was not successful." When I first put in my
application they must have thought I was white.

Then I thought, Well, if I could get to England, I could go to
America from there. You see, my main ambition was to get back to
America. I was seeing in the papers in Barbados that in England
there were lots of jobs vacant, and some were for mechanics. I
knew that I'd have no trouble getting into England, so I gave up
my job at Gulf Oil, which was a good job, and got together the fare
for the boat to England.

When I got to London I found things were completely
different from what I'd thought they would be. I thought it would
be something like what I'd seen in America. But it wasn't like that
at all, and I couldn't get mechanic's work because I didn't have my
tools. I had to write home and have my tools sent over, and the
people back home didn't really know how to go about sending
them. While I was waiting for them—it was a year before I finally
got them—I did ordinary laboring jobs in factories, packing bags
and lifting things in order to get money. Mostly, I drove a van for a
furniture company, delivering and picking up sofas and things. I'd

make four or five trips a week to different places, like Birmingham, Leeds, Liverpool, and Stockport. You'd leave early in the morning in the van with a pack lunch, and you'd push on all the way to Leeds or wherever, unload the stuff, and drive straight back to London, to get back home as soon as you could. The only time you'd stop was to pass water. You'd carry along your eats [meals] in the van and eat and drink your tea while you were driving.

All I was making was five pounds a week, and that was a lot less than I'd been making in Barbados. I really wanted to go home. I was told that I could have my old job back with Gulf Oil. But I didn't have the fare for the passage. So, I decided that I'd work on until I could save enough for the fare. I tried to make myself homely [comfortable], thinking it was going to be awhile before I had the money, and before long I met Rose.

Rose Thornhill

What happened to me was that I'd finished my secondary education in Barbados in 1953, and there was no work. Work was very hard to get then. Some of my friends went out to England to be trained as nurses. A good friend of mine went to Strickland Hospital, a mental hospital in York. She wrote to me and said it was quite good out there and asked me to come over and start my nursing. I'd already applied to do nursing at the mental hospital here in Blackrock, but they didn't take me. So, I told my friend that I would try for England.

I wrote a letter to the matron at the hospital in York. The matron wrote back and gave me permission to come, since they were looking for help. But my parents didn't have money for the fare. It was $320, and that was a terrific lot of money for a family to find. I wrote to my aunt in America to ask for her help, and she sent the passage. But we still had to have twenty dollars in English money for me to travel with. We borrowed that from a good friend of the family, who lent it to my mother until she reaped her cane crop. After the harvest she paid him back with no delay.

So, I went to England. I was pretty young at the time, about twenty. And I'd never been a person that went around a lot in Barbados, so traveling was new to me. But I had a fantastic experience on the boat to England, mixing with all different na-

tionalities of people. All the way over I was thinking, Oh, I am on
my own now—this is it—I've got to make my own decisions, my
own everything. My mother, who was a careful woman and traveled
a lot, must have taught me how to mix with the different nationalities, because I got along just fine.

It was 1956, the month of February, and very cold and gray and
lots of fog when I got to England. Everything seemed so strange
coming from a little country like this and going into a big country
like that. When I arrived at Victoria Station I sat very frightened,
but the people from the hospital that came to meet me were very
nice English people. They, being of a bigger country and having a
bigger experience than we did, knew what it was like for us. We
were taken on the train from Victoria Station up north to York, to
the mental hospital where we were going to work. It was four-thirty
on the Monday morning when I arrived at the hospital. And I was
sent to work at seven o'clock the same morning. I was sent right
into "strong ward," where they keep the real violent patients.

On the trip over [to England] my thinking was to get back to
Barbados at the end of three years. But it didn't work out that way.
Life began to change after I got to York, and I decided that I
wasn't ready to go back yet. When I finished my training at
Strickland Hospital in 1957 I decided to come down to London to
work. My sister was living there, and she asked me to come stay
with her for awhile. That's where I met Cleve. I was cooking the
evening meal when I saw him out the window, coming up the walk.
I said to my sister, "Who is that?"

She said, "He is a friend."

I said, "He may be a friend, but he can't have any of this food
because there isn't enough."

She said, "But he is a good friend." So, I made an extra share
for him.

I didn't like him at first. But he was such a gentleman that I
thought if he asked me out I'd better go with him. At first I used to
tell him that I liked a fellow here in Barbados and that I planned
to go back home to be with this chap. But, gradually, we got to
know each other, and I forgot about this other fellow. We've been
together twenty-five years now.

After we got married [1958] we had children very quickly—
three of them, one after another. We had a flat in Stoke New-

ington, and it wasn't enough room for a family. I wanted a larger home for the kids. And Cleve didn't want to raise the kids in Stoke Newington because there was a lot of colored people there, and, where there are a lot of colored people, one or two may make a scene of themselves and then everybody will be painted as one. We wanted to move to a white area where we knew that we could gain some respect. It's sad to say that, but it's true. We then worked very hard to buy a house.

Cleve Thornhill

I was working for the post office in London as a mechanic. From seven in the morning to three-thirty in the afternoon, or to six if I could get overtime, I'd be at the post office. Then I'd go home and get my dinner. After dinner I'd do private mechanic work— repairing cars in the street where we lived. I'd work till eleven or twelve o'clock at night under the street lights. Most of the people around the neighborhood knew that I was a mechanic and that I was a good one. So, they wanted me to fix their cars. They'd tell other people, and those people would bring me their cars too. News of a good mechanic spreads like fire, and I had more work than I could manage. There was times that I'd work right through the night, until six o'clock in the morning. Then I'd wash up, get my breakfast, and go off to my job at the post office. Sometimes at the post office you'd go on a repair job that was classed to take a certain number of hours. If you could do the job in less, you could have the extra time off and be paid for a full day. I used to do those jobs in a couple of hours because I was young and very fast and keen to get on. Then I'd leave the post office, maybe before noon, and go on home to do my private repair work.

Rose Thornhill

The children often wouldn't really see him until Sundays because he was working all the time. But on Sundays he used to sit indoors all day with one child on each side and the youngest in the middle and play with them. They'd be so glad to see him.

For a long time we were both working two jobs, and after we had saved enough we bought a real nice home in Stanmore,

Middlesex, near London. It was a semidetached house with three bedrooms and a lovely garden front and back. The area was real nice with shops nearby, and the railway station was just ten minutes' walk. We were the only colored people in the neighborhood. I wasn't frightened because I'd been living in London for quite awhile by then, and I knew what I should do and what I shouldn't do.

The neighbor next to us, he was English, came over the very first day and ringed the doorbell. He said, "My name is Jack Phillip." He and his wife became the two closest friends we could ever have. He was a builder, and he would give us any help we needed on the house. Sometimes he would take us out for a meal. But some of the neighbors were a bit funny, being that we were black, they kept asking Jack what it was like living next to black folks. Jack would tell them that it was really nice living next to black folks. You know the English people—they are a race that will never come out and tell you things to your face. The neighbors watched us closely to see what style of living we would have. Eventually, I think everybody on the street came to like us. Being black never bothered me on the street because everybody treated me nicely. If they had bad things in their mind, they never told me them. And I never bothered myself over what might be in their minds, so we got along nicely. We lived there twenty-one years.

The people on the street had money and could really pay to have their cars done. They all brought their cars to Cleve for fixing, and he became famous. Everybody knew him, and they all called him Cleve. Now these are all white people I am speaking of, not colored people. They'd come around and have a cup of tea with us—you know how the English like their tea. And our children played with their children like one family. They was into everybody's homes. The neighbors used to treat our children and take them out all around. You see, they didn't class us as colored; we were part of the neighborhood, no different from anybody else. Not once did we have any kind of quarrel or ill treatment from them. Not once.

When our two girls went to high school I started thinking about doing more nursing training. I'd done my mental nursing training in the north, but I hadn't done general training. So I said to Cleve, "I would like to do my registered nursing, my SRN."

He said, "We still have the children to look after, do you think you can manage?"

He wasn't ever a person that would stop me from doing what I wanted, not even from buying clothes. So I went. He guided me, studied with me, through the entire three years at Edgeware General Hospital in London where I got my SRN. It was rough, really rough. We were both doing shift work and I was training as well. He'd have to come home to look after the children in the evening. But we were both happy. We managed—we really managed good—and I passed my exam the first time. After that I got a job as a nurse at Scotland Yard, but I can't tell you about that because I had to take an oath not to talk about anything I did there.

But things were really rolling our way. We was working hard, but you don't mind that when you see the money rolling in. We never had time to go out on the town, but you didn't mind that either when you're bettering yourself. What really drove us in those years, after we had gotten the house, was the desire to give the children a proper education. I wanted both girls to be doctors. That was my ambition. We had a private teacher come to the house to help them with their school lessons. Today my eldest daughter is the supervisor of the casualty and outpatient department at a big hospital in London. My second girl is doing her masters degree in chemistry at London University. And my son is a car spray painter for a large firm in London. He has ambition to start up his own firm.

In 1971 we decided that we'd like to bring the children back to Barbados to see their grandparents. When we got here Cleve really liked it. He said to me, "We've been away from our own country for fifteen years; it's time to come back here and live." I didn't want to come back, not really. I had a good job in London, we had a nice home, we had nice friends, we had a car, and the children were in a good high school. To that Cleve would say, "But we're not going to remain young all the time."

I said, "Yes, when we get older we can live in the countryside in England. We can get a home there."

He'd say, "No, Barbados would be better place to live, especially when you are old." He often talked about how beautiful Barbados was, that the country was doing much better, that there were better homes, and now they had a deep-water harbor which would bring more commerce. So, I finally said, "Okay, we will do it." We started to save up our money to come back. We really pushed hard then. I worked two nursing jobs, and on my days off I'd do more work at a private hospital in Stanmore. Cleve did two jobs as well. We did that for seven years, till we felt it was the right time to come home. But before we came back for good we made two trips here to have our house built. We paid for the house with cash; we never borrowed a penny. What people here don't understand is how hard we worked to have all this. They think you just pick money up off the street. They can't begin to know how hard we've worked over the last twenty years.

We hope the children will come back someday. They've been here four times to visit. They think Barbados is nice, but it's a different style of living than they're used to in England. In England people mind their own affairs; in Barbados the children found that the people, especially the women, can be nosy and telling you what to do. You never get that in England, not in Stanmore, so my daughters don't understand it. But I like it here. I like the peacefulness, and though there are nosy ones here I just try to get on with my business.

I visited the Thornhills in the winter of 1990, three years after the last of the oral history interviews with them. They were working as hard as ever. Cleve was operating three minibuses and was soon to get a "maxi-taxi"; Rose was keeping the books and doing private nursing on the side. The interior of their house was still not decorated, and some things were still in their shipping boxes. Their three married children, raised in London, had come to Barbados for a six-week holiday. And, although Rose and Cleve were hopeful they would come "home" for good, the two daughters were still unsure. But their son had made plans to leave his spray-painting business in London and try Barbados for a year, while working with Cleve. He was to arrive within a few days.

Chapter 9

Janice Whittle

Janice Whittle arrived in England in 1975 to study art at the University of Newcastle-upon-Tyne, her education paid for by a prestigious Barbados Scholarship. She was the first person in four years to win the award. Her father, an architect, and her mother, a nurse, had always stressed the importance of doing well in school. To give Janice and her sister more time for their studies the parents excused them from almost all household chores. Janice became an avid reader at an early age, and throughout her childhood made regular trips to the local library with her sister, who today is an English teacher. At Christmastime their mother escorted the two girls to Bridgetown's bookstores for them to choose their presents, as it was mainly books that they wanted.

Janice spent five years in Newcastle, an industrial and ship-building city in the north of England. She met and later married Nick, another art student, and gave birth to Rose, the eldest of her two daughters. Her adjustments to the cold and to living in a new culture were like those of many other West Indian student migrants in England. But there were also differences because Janice was in a region where there were not many blacks.

Janice kept a diary during her stay abroad. During one of my visits to Janice's home she read aloud an excerpt from it, written during her train ride from London to Newcastle on 9 October 1975, just a few days after she had landed in England:

> *I'm now on the eleven o'clock train bound for Newcastle. The train is going by lots of scenic areas, occasionally trees about to change color. It certainly doesn't impress me with its beauty. My intent is to make the most of the opportunity of studying here, but then I'm going home. I don't think I'd ever want to live here. Even America would be better. There are rows and rows of houses all the same. Is this the glory of the*

Janice Whittle, 1988. (Photo by Ellen Frankenstein.)

Empire? Now we're passing more ugly houses on one side and plains on the other. It's a good thing I'm not a landscape artist. Maybe Newcastle will be nice.

Today Janice is an art teacher at Queens College in Bridgetown. She lives with her husband, who is also an art teacher, and two children in an old and weathered house with large overhanging eaves at the end of a narrow lane not far from the sea in Bridgetown. The interior is spacious as the ceiling is open. Books, paints, beads, and other crafts clutter the main living area. Next to the chair where I always sat while interviewing Janice is a large aquarium with a loud bubbling filter system and three overfed goldfish.

The train journey to Newcastle was quite exciting for me. I'd never been on a long-distance train before, and, of course, I'd never been to England. My only knowledge of British life came from books and from my father, who had studied architecture there. But he had lived in London. Nobody I knew had ever been to Newcastle or knew anything about the place. But I guessed it wasn't going to be like London.

I was anticipating what it would be like to be confronted with racial prejudice. That was my biggest fear. I had no strategy in mind for dealing with it because I had never encountered it. In Barbados there were black and white students in my school, and we all mixed together. It's true that outside of school my friends were of the same color, but I didn't think it was anything deliberate. In England I expected racial prejudice to be manifested in far more obvious ways, like the terrible things that you read about in the newspapers. I was really quite fearful, but I was also very excited. And I was looking forward to devoting all of my days to my painting and the study of art history.

I lived in a hall of residence my first year. It was an old Victorian house, the smallest of all the residence halls, with just twenty girls. A little further down the street was the men's hall, with about a hundred students. We all ate together in the same dining room in the men's hall, and that was quite exciting. Because there were only twenty girls, we got to know each other very well. A lot of the girls were from small towns in Yorkshire and northern England. I had somehow imagined—I suppose from reading and films—that anyone living in a large country like England would be extremely sophisticated, just as we from the West Indies all dreamed of someday becoming. But they were actually very provincial, and I found that strange.

They were very kind to me; I suppose because they knew it must be especially difficult for me being so far from home. I think, too, they were interested in me because most of them had never met a black person before. Very few black people chose to live in the northeast. So they were interested in what my life was like. And they were intrigued to discover how similar my Barbadian education was to theirs, and even that I spoke English. Not having met black people before, they just assumed that we were something exotic.

There were no other black students in the art department and none in the residence hall where I lived, though there were a few in the men's hall. So, naturally, I stood out. But really everyone was very kind, and I began to think all my fears of racial prejudice were groundless.

However, after a time it struck me that, while the students that I'd gotten to know well accepted me as an individual, they still

made comments and observations that revealed a certain prejudice. While I personally got on well with them, their attitudes
about black people included me. But this was quite a subtle thing,
and it wasn't until after about a year there that I began to feel this.
You expect prejudice to be something that is very blatant, but it
really isn't. And, as I said, a lot of these people had been very kind
to me personally. I simply tried to accept their limitations, just as
I'm forced here in Barbados, even among people I like as individuals, to realize their limitations and prejudices against white people.
I've seen it from both sides.

My days in Newcastle were quite pleasant. After I'd eaten my
breakfast in the hall I'd walk into the university, sometimes with a
friend. At the art department I'd sign in. You were supposed to be
there from eight to four each day. So I'd arrive, sign in, and then
go over to where all the first-year students worked. Then I'd
agonize over whatever the day's project was. The whole first year,
doing the foundation courses, was quite difficult at Newcastle. In
the States and at some other places in Britain they let first-year
students explore things—like jewelry making—that they haven't
done before. The idea was to expose them to different art forms.
That way, if a person has a talent for something, say sculpture, but
hasn't done it before, they can discover themselves. Then in your
second year the student would choose a few of these options to
work at, and then in the final years they would concentrate on
one.

But at Newcastle they didn't do that. Instead, the foundation
courses were based on the Bauhaus, the design school of Walter
Gropius and Mies van der Rohe. So we did a lot of exploratory
experiments on color, space, and line—all very broad topics,
which you could interpret any way you liked. It was very threatening, because you felt that you had to produce something clever or
witty. That year caused me a total loss of confidence. But a lot of
other students also felt lost, so I wasn't alone. We'd agonize over a
project, and then the tutor would come around and probe a bit to
see if we were doing anything vaguely intelligent.

I had a good friend who was Polish, and she and I would have
lunch together in the student commons room. And then we would
go back to class and labor some more. Some days, especially
toward the end of the year, we would work until quite late. The

university had a wonderful library, with endless periodicals on art, and I spent lots of time there just reading and making notes because I enjoyed it so much.

The cold and long, dark evenings in winter were very strange and difficult for me to get used to. I don't think in all my years there I ever really got used to the climate. I dealt with the cold by staying in. Once I'd come back from dinner I would stay in my room and write endless letters and keep the radiator on as hot as it could go. I would buy flowers, loads of flowers. I'd put them outside my window at night because it was so hot inside that they'd wilt.

Sometimes people would drag me out. I remember the first Guy Fawkes Day,[1] being dragged out quite unwillingly because it was so cold. And I remember traveling to London and it seeming so warm compared to Newcastle. The letters I wrote were really my way of keeping in touch with people in Barbados. You see, my whole life-style growing up in Barbados was centered on talking for hours on the phone to friends. In England I did it through letters. I was very diligent about it. When I got a letter I would write back instantly.

The second year all this changed because I moved into a flat with some other students. In that flat there was more social life. I gave a lot of meals, especially Sunday lunches, for friends. I tried to cook Bajan, but at that time I couldn't get many of the ingredients, like fresh spinach. The Indian shops carried certain things, and later I discovered other shops that had things like sweet potatoes and coconuts. Once I tried to make coconut bread, but it was a disaster.

On the weekends I'd wander about the neighborhood and go down to a huge park, Jesmond Dene, with a giant wood. Sometimes I would take a bus to the sea at Whitley Bay. I first went there with our art class to paint the sea and the changing clouds. While we were painting the clouds, sitting on this beach freezing, there were rats running around among the rocks. As the summer came, things did improve. I often went to antique fairs, and I'd buy bits and pieces, like old lace, which I started to collect.

---

1. A day of public thanksgiving in Britain, observed annually on 5 November. It is held in celebration of the foiling of Guy Fawkes's plot in 1605 to blow up the British Parliament and kill King James I, who was in attendance.

I had to plan my budget, which I had never done before. When I look back on it middle-class children in Barbados like myself really lived a very sheltered life. You were taken everywhere—taken to school, picked up from school, taken to the library, picked up from the library. Very seldom did you have to walk anywhere on your own. To suddenly go from that to being totally on my own was quite a change for me.

Newcastle was very different from anything I'd ever known before. The river was the focal point of everything, and there were old streets with beautiful old Tudor buildings with exposed wood of which I became very fond. I was struck by the terraces of houses, as they were a complete contrast to the individuality of houses in the West Indies. The terraces were built entirely of exposed bricks. Many of the bricks had weathered and changed into many subtle variations of colors. Later I did a series of paintings with brick patterns and hung them up in the corner of my studio to create a "brick environment."

But it was the people that really made Newcastle for me. Most of them led a hard life, either working in the street or on the sea, fishing. In general, they are not well-off. They are the kind of people that you would describe as the salt of the earth. They're very tough; you'd see little children sitting on the ground or on the front steps in winter just wearing a vest. But I think the hard life they live makes them a very direct and sincere people. They are something like Barbadians in that they think of themselves as being hard working and stoic, not effusive like Trinidadians. They aren't outgoing, and they don't have that polite superficiality that most British people have. A lot of people expect the British to be cold, but you don't find that in Newcastle.

The cleaners in the halls looked after the students like children. They were particularly kind to the foreign students. They always asked me how I was and how I was surviving the cold. I liked that and the fact that Newcastle was a town that you could get to know. But it was very provincial, and at times I was quite wicked in my humor about the place. A few students seemed to be unaware that the [British] empire had been lost, and I couldn't resist being wicked to them. But, usually, my sarcasm would be lost on them.

Before going to England I had become a vegetarian. But,

because I never really expected to get accepted to the university, I didn't bother to mention it in my application. So, when I arrived there I was given meat meals. I didn't want to make waves, so I just ate them. Then one day I was out exploring Newcastle, and I came upon this enclosed market. Down one of the aisles I came across these huge carcasses hanging up everywhere. I literally felt like screaming. I hurried to get out, but every aisle I ran into there were more of them. It was one of the most horrifying sights I'd ever seen. It shocked me, and I've never had any flesh food since that day. It really stopped me from eating meat forever. I tried to do an art project about my experience with the carcasses, but it really didn't work out. None of my paintings really conveyed the horror of being among all those dead animals.

During my first year I went to Paris with a university group. I think it's my favorite place on earth next to Barbados. My art teacher had studied in the Ecole de Beaux Arts. She was a great Francophile, always going on about how wonderful Paris was, so I think I was biased before even getting there. But what I found strange was that there seemed to be a greater division between the races in France than in England. The only visible black people that I could see were North Africans, from France's former colonies. I saw many sitting on street corners with huge lovely mats, selling ivory jewelry. There seemed to be no contact between them and the French. I didn't see any mixed-race couples or children who were of mixed race, and I found that quite strange because I'd figured colonial systems were the same everywhere—that, whatever mother country was perpetuating it, whether it be England, France, Spain, Holland, or whoever, it would be basically the same. But in Paris it obviously wasn't.

I was even more acutely aware of this when I went back several years later, this time with Nick, a white person. Everywhere we went people stared at us just because we were a mixed-race couple. Some people would literally stop what they were doing to look; they just couldn't get over it. We were especially a sensation in the restaurants.

I was also shocked by the contrast in Paris between the opulence—the fancy boutiques and all those other signs of wealth—and the poverty. Next to the fancy boutiques were beggars sitting on the streets and stray dogs all over the place. I had a feeling that people were quite uncaring about the plight of other people, and that was something I didn't feel in England. In Paris you literally thought that if you dropped down dead in the street people would just walk on by. Being from Barbados, the evidence of poverty amidst so much wealth absolutely appalled me. But I admit that I did like Paris; I guess it fulfilled all my artistic expectations.

What was special for me was that, just before I went to Paris, I bought a Penguin paperback called *You Better Believe It,* a book of poetry by black writers—Caribbean, African, American, and British. I'd read quite a bit of the poetry before I went to Paris, and then while I was there, standing in this bookshop looking through the shelves, a black American man came up to me and my Polish girlfriend and complimented me on my straw hat. We got chatting, and I learned his name was Ted Joans, one of the poets featured in the book. I talked to him about the book, and he invited us to a poetry reading that night. The poetry reading made me feel a part of the Bohemian life—that was the highlight of the trip.

The summer of my first year in England I went back home to Barbados. I thoroughly enjoyed seeing all my friends again and reliving my experiences with them, but in some ways I also regretted it. I could have gone to the Continent and back to France instead. But I wasn't so adventurous then.

The following summer I stayed in Newcastle and worked as an usherette in a cinema. I decided that I needed to get a job where I could work at night and be free during the day to paint. Being an usherette also satisfied my interest in films. I could see all of them for free. The manager of the cinema took it all so seriously. During the intermission he made us wear these silly overalls while we sold ice lollies [ice cream bars] from little trays that hung from your neck. He'd say, "Wait till the lights go down and then quickly make your way down the center aisle so that when the lights come up you're there in front of the people."

In my second year I met Nick. He was one of the people I'd shared a flat with. But I really didn't go out with him until two years later, long after I'd moved out of the flat. When we were flat mates he had his own little gang of friends, and I had my Polish friend and a few others, so we really didn't mix that much. But we did become friends, and at times we had long conversations. And we also took an art course together. After marrying Nick I felt that people felt more threatened by me, sort of like I was marrying into the country. Maybe I was overreacting, but I felt that people acted like I was trying to take over.

I took a year off from school when I had Rose, our first daughter. Nick had graduated but was unemployed, so he would take Rose out every morning for four hours so that I could get on with my painting. I'd wash up, clean up the flat, sit down and try to do some painting. Nick would come back and scold me: "Why haven't you gotten further on this painting?" I didn't really produce many paintings that year.

The following year I went back to the university to finish up. Nick had gotten a fellowship, sort of an artist-in-residence, at the fine arts department at Sunderland Polytechnic, and I had become more confident in my own painting. I had my own studio at the university. I was doing huge paintings, eight-by-four feet, with collaged bits in them. I was also painting abstract portraits of my friends; I reduced things about them that I thought revealed their personality to just marks and colors. Nick had introduced me to jazz and blues, so I would sit there painting while listening to the music of Billie Holiday.

Rose was born in 1977, around the time Steve Biko was murdered. His death had a very traumatic effect on me. There had been a lot of reporting about Biko's incarceration, the Soweto riots, and the whole situation in South Africa. The news is very insular in the Caribbean, and I'd never heard much about South Africa before going to England. The Biko incident was a shock. I started reading a lot about South Africa then, and one of my final-year paintings was about Steve Biko. Just recently it occurred to me that there were certain subconscious links with my own childhood. When I was a child of six I remember hearing my mother talk about the assassination of Patrice Lumumba in the Belgian Congo. The memory is still very vivid.

I had a South African friend who went back home with her husband to participate in the struggle. I never heard anything from them again. I wrote to them through an address in London, but I never got a reply. I don't know if they are alive or dead.

Sometimes I was mistaken for a South African in Newcastle. Students from South Africa would tell me that I looked like

Janice and Nick Whittle on their wedding day.

someone they knew from home. I don't know why, since West Indians are supposed to look like people from Ghana, Sierra Leone, and other places in West Africa. No slaves were transported from South Africa.

Having Rose revolutionized our lives. We decided to devote our body and souls to seeing that this child had a good life. We read endlessly on child rearing and nutrition, and we based her upbringing on a book written by Suzuki of the Suzuki violin method. We thought she should never be left alone, that she should be taken everywhere, and that she should listen to music to calm her. We took her to endless exhibitions. She constantly had the attention of two adults every day, which I now think more than anything else has made her need the company of others.

The decision to come back to Barbados was Nick's. He'd

come to the end of his fellowship at Sunderland, and I'd come to the end of my degree. The situation with jobs for fine arts graduates in Britain was really bad. There weren't even possibilities for us to consider. So, we came here in the hope that at least Nick could get a job. I'd decided I would stay home to raise Rose and not look for work until she was school-aged. We also decided that we shouldn't have just one child, and, indeed, we later had Bertie. That meant that I'd be home for a little while longer.

Nick wrote to Barbados from Britain to apply for various jobs. He'd gotten no replies, but we came anyway. We came on hope alone; we even shipped all our stuff back here. It was quite a daring move. I think I needed to come back; I had really begun to feel isolated in Newcastle. My aunt who lived in London had returned to Barbados, so I had no connections in England except for Nick's family. As time went on, I became more and more aware of how different I was from everyone else.

Living abroad had given me a sense of being black, of having a black identity. I had never really thought of myself in racial terms before; rather, I had always thought the important thing was what kind of person I was and that what color I was didn't really matter. Seeing myself as a black person made me want to delve into my cultural heritage, and I read a lot of books about links between African customs and customs in the West Indies. I would compare the foods we ate, birth rituals, and other things to see how similar they were. I got interested in black culture generally, like black jazz, blues singers, and calypso. When growing up I'd associated calypso with my parents' generation, but then, after I came back to Barbados, I got into it myself. I think I saw coming home as a getting back to my roots.

My friends here were surprised that I'd married a white person. Before leaving Barbados I'd said that marriage itself was difficult enough, but if you married someone of another race you'd make it even more difficult. Then you'd have to work against the opposition of the outside world. My friends tried to get to know Nick because of their feelings for me. Some got on with him; others didn't. Nick is very blunt, and that is a very un-Barbadian thing. Barbadians find it hard to cope with people who are very outspoken. As you know, being outspoken is frowned upon here.

The summer we arrived back Nick filled out a form with the

Ministry of Education for work as a teacher. He was going to be offered a job at a teacher-training college, but it didn't work out because the commission decided they wanted to fill the position with a Barbadian. But Nick did get a one-term job filling in for somebody at the Barbados Community College. Then he filled in at Queens College for a term and then at Parkinsons Secondary School for a year.

He was full of bright ideas about bringing to the student population what seemed to him obvious African links, though it didn't always seem so obvious to the children. He would bring to school tapes of African music and have the children paint while listening.

But just getting to work was very stressful for Nick. We couldn't afford a car, and in order to get to school on time he had to take a 6:15 bus every morning. The minibuses then were just pickup trucks, and they'd be so full that Nick could never get a seat. Invariably, somebody would stare at him or make a comment like, "Why are you on this bus if you're white?" They just assumed that if you're white you must be rich. So he had all this aggravation to contend with on the journey to school. He developed stress-related physical reactions like an eye infection. The culmination of it all was when a student in a remedial class started acting up. Nick told the student to pack up [leave]. The student picked up a cutting knife and stabbed him. It wasn't a terrible cut, but still it was awful. When he came home from work with blood on his shirt I said jokingly, "What happened, one of your students stab you?" When he answered yes I couldn't believe it. The boy who'd stabbed Nick was allowed to continue coming to school, so Nick had to continue to teach him. Nick finally got a permanent job at Queens College, and that's where he is now.

For a number of years I was at home with the children, and I was severely criticized for that. People said, "We sent her off on a Barbados Scholarship, and she comes back spending time at home." It was ridiculous. But, undaunted, I stayed home with my kids. I took Bertie to the beach every day, and I talked to her endlessly. When she really needed the company of other children, at age two and a half, we sent her off to the Montessori School, and I accepted a job at St. Winifreds School, a mostly white girls' school. I opted for St. Winifreds because it was small and because I had no experience teaching boys.

At St. Winifreds I've encountered more white Barbadian students than I would've at most any other school. The children's reaction to me has been interesting. The students had never had a black art teacher before, although the teaching staff is mixed. I have strong views about what I consider acceptable work; I insist that students produce the finest quality that they're capable of, that they try and try again until they fulfill their potential. And that was a new experience for them; they weren't used to anyone making such demands or viewing art as actually important. There were great battles in the early stages, but we eventually grew to like one another.

Many of the white students were from families with money. They knew there would be jobs waiting for them after they finished school, no matter how well or poorly they did. There was one white student who was particularly lazy. I once asked her if she wasn't concerned about passing her O Levels.[2] I said, "What will you do if you don't pass them? How will you find a good job?"

"It doesn't matter," she said, "I'll get a job working with Daddy."

I said, "And what does he do?"

She said, "I have no idea what he does, but he's got a business of some sort."

Imagine at age sixteen she had no idea what her father did; all she knew was there was an endless supply of money. In that same class I had a black student whose mother cleaned toilets at a police station.

Coming back to Barbados and being in a mixed marriage, I saw the world very differently. Before coming home I had never known of the prejudice that exists here against white people. I remember the first summer Nick and I came back, we rented a "mini-moke," the typical tourist vehicle. We went driving in the country and stopped at various places to take pictures, and, at some point in St. Andrew,[3] this guy comes up and spits on us because we are a mixed-race couple. Right there I began to wonder what the future would hold for Nick in Barbados, and for us as a couple.

---

2. After five years of secondary education students may take the general certificate of education (Ordinary Level) examinations. Students choose the subjects in which they wish to take the exams.

3. A rural parish on Barbados' east coast.

In his teaching, Nick had found that students were quick to take offense. Nick is a demanding teacher and quite strict in his grading, and students sometimes interpreted this as prejudice— Nick being white and they being black. For whites in Barbados any sort of conflict or criticism often gets twisted into an issue of prejudice, and the real issue becomes obscured. If you get into a quarrel with a person of the other race, you always fear that it's going to turn nasty. A lot of white expatriates here feel that way. They might not openly admit it, but that's what they're thinking. And many white Barbadians feel that somehow they have to justify themselves just for being white and living in Barbados. Unfortunately, racial prejudice is getting worse. The young white students that Nick and I teach don't think there is any future for them here. They feel very much outsiders, and they look to the States or Canada for their future. Some of them actually hate living in Barbados. It's really quite sad to see the races growing further apart and so many young people wanting to leave.

Some black kids want to leave Barbados too, and a lot of that is because their aspirations today come from what they see on American TV programs. It makes them want to get out and go live in the States. But it's not just TV. A lot of the blame also lies with the tourist industry. The average Barbadian sees all these wealthy North Americans on holiday spending loads of money, not realizing that many of the tourists who came here have to scrimp and save and work at their jobs for the majority of the year to enjoy their three-week vacation. They think white people are so rich that they can come here on a whim, just take up the phone and book a ticket and come down here and live the good life. Then in the local department stores they see that the white tourists are treated better than they are, and that causes resentment.

All this is a great conflict for me because I feel very committed to doing something good in Barbados. I suppose it would be easier to opt out and go live abroad like so many others, but I strongly feel that this is my home. Unfortunately, Nick can't share this feeling. Even though Nick has taught at many schools and participated on various committees, he still feels at the end of the day that he is an outsider. It's very sad but true, and I don't know what will ultimately happen to us. If we moved it would probably be to England, but leaving Barbados would mean starting all over again, and that we are very reluctant to do. Besides I want my children to know their culture, to know the positive things about Barbados. Their identity will come from both cultures, both countries of their parents. That will always be a dilemma for them, but there are things to be proud of in both.

Part 3
Barbadians in North America

Chapter 10
The Mighty Gabby

The Mighty Gabby is the stage name of Tony Carter, a major figure in the revival of Barbadian calypso. Gabby was raised in a poor neighborhood of Bridgetown. As a youth, he yearned to become a musician and, while still a teenager, managed to obtain work singing on cruise boats in Barbados. It was there that his curiosity about North America was first piqued by the tourists he met. In 1971 he emigrated and spent the next five years living as an illegal alien with relatives in Brooklyn and working in the garment district. His experiences in New York City radically changed Gabby's music, his politics, and his fortunes.

When he returned to Barbados in 1976 he helped establish calypso as the voice of the people. Gabby's calypsos like "Take Down Nelson," "Culture," "Jack," and "Bajan Yankee" are biting political and social commentaries, inspired by what he saw and learned as an emigrant in the United States. His performance tent, aptly named The Battleground, became famous for its criticism of the Barbadian government.

Gabby is an intense, vigorous man. He speaks with conviction and emotion, punctuating his thoughts with body and arm gestures. When making a point his voice rises and falls in the fashion of a fundamentalist preacher. He has the body of a long-distance runner, thin and sinewy. By choice he does not own a car and walks to and from his home on the outskirts of Bridgetown. Like many Barbadians who return from the States, Gabby has a fondness for gold jewelry—although, in his case, just a necklace. But, unlike other returnees, Gabby regards Western dress—socks, button-up shirts, coats, and ties—as unsuitable in the Tropics and dresses instead in sandals, loose-fitting pants, and a cotton dashiki.

Gabby, 1988. (Photo by Ellen Frankenstein.)

I grew up in Emerton, and I think that there is no child in Barbados who would have had a more interesting childhood. I do not say that in braggart fashion. The neighborhood where I grew up was next to the sea, five minutes' walk from the finest beaches, and ten minutes' walk when the tide is low from Pelican Island.[1] That island had atmosphere, the water was beautiful, and there were sea eggs and conchs to gather.[2] And there was a hospital on it too, for people off the boats who were put in quarantine. Then there were the fishing boats. You could wait for the fishermen to come in with their grub buckets, and they'd give you some fish. You would swim and fish and swim. It didn't matter if you were going to school: you'd swim in the morning before school and again when you came back in the evening. On Saturdays you had Princess Alice playing field,[3] where you played soccer, cricket, and

---

1. The island was joined to the land in the late 1950s when a deep-water harbor was constructed nearby.

2. Sea eggs are the roe of sea urchins. It was a popular food until the sea urchin population declined in the 1970s. In Barbadian folklore sea eggs are said to give virility and fertility.

3. Princess Alice Field no longer exists. The land was developed into a handicraft market called Pelican Village, an amalgam of art galleries and curio shops that cater primarily to tourists from the cruise ships that berth nearby.

lawn tennis. There were swings and slides and an indoor club where you played dominoes, draughts, table tennis, and all that. In terms of recreation, I had the finest.

Five minutes the other way is Bridgetown. The markets, lines of women hawkers selling fruit, vegetables, fish, and this and that. The color and excitement of the market was something I looked forward to on Saturdays.[4] My mother would send me for black pudding and souse[5]—I grew up on that. The market was a big part of my life, and that's why I later wrote the song "The Bridgetown Market."

Then when the rain was falling [summer and fall] it was crab season.[6] All the boys in the neighborhood made their own traps. We'd try to outdo each other. We used these big rubbers [rubber bands] so that when the crab pulled at the bait, the trap door will fly shut, and you'd catch him. You have to know the crabs' habits—some crabs won't go into the trap unless it's set in just the right place. You'd get to know a lot about the crabs' behavior; you could even tell what kind of crab you were hunting by examining the crab hole.

When I was in school my main hobby was playing road tennis.[7] I was Barbados' champion as a teenager. I used to play every day in the streets. I couldn't wait to get home to play. I'd play in my school clothes, then my mother would beat me. We didn't have a lot, so, if I tore my pants, I'd have to go to school with a patch, or I'd have to wear my Sunday school pants, and she didn't like that. I had just one pair of pants to go to school in. My mother made me take off the pants when I came home so she could wash them so

4. There were (and still are) two large public markets in Bridgetown: Fairchild and Cheapside. On Saturdays housewives from all over the island came to town to shop in the lively and colorful markets. In recent years supermarkets and mini-marts have eroded some of their appeal and clientele.

5. The pudding is made from grated sweet potato, which is stuffed into pig intestines and steamed. It looks like a dark sausage. It is cut into slices and served with souse, which is pickled pig's head, feet, and flesh. It is made at home and sold by hawkers in the markets.

6. The "rainy" season runs from June through November. An average of forty-two inches of rain falls during this six-month period versus eighteen inches during the "dry" season.

7. Road tennis is a popular game played with wooden paddles and a tennis ball. The court is marked on the road, and a plank is used in place of a net. Games are often interrupted to let traffic pass.

that they'd be clean every day. Pants and the shirt—wash them every day by hand.

When a neighbor cooks at night they would bring some of the food to my mother: "Hey, I got some extra yams, you take some." The next day maybe my mother got some food, and she would give it away. This happens constantly. And, if somebody didn't share, people say, "Oh, Irene has gone very selfish. I saw Irene bring home six or eight pounds of potatoes, and she only has two children. She don't need all those; she could at least come and give somebody two or three." This was a very strict thing; you understood that you had to share. That's the kind of environment I grew up in.

My father went away when I was six years old, and I haven't seen him since. But I was told that up until that time he was a very nice man. I don't know what happened; I have no animosity toward him.

My mother used to sell fish cakes, black pudding, and souse; she was also the neighborhood midwife. Sometimes a man would come on a bicycle to get her, or sometimes I would walk with her to the place where the woman was to have a baby. She'd say to me, "Wait here an hour; if I don't come, then walk back home." So, if the woman was near time to deliver, I'd wait for her, and we'd walk back home together. But, if she ain't near time to deliver, I'd walk back home, and my mother would be away until the woman had the baby. We were left alone a lot. But my mother was a great disciplinarian, and we were pretty much under control.

In the neighborhood you would watch people at work. There was a man caning chairs and a man rolling tobacco that he grew himself, and there was a man named Forbes, who raised goats, and I helped him milk the goats. He would tell me, "Tony, come for your milk first before the water goes in." You see, to make a little extra money he would put in water to stretch the milk. But he would always tell me to get my milk before the water went in.

Next to my neighborhood was Fontabelle, where the rich white people lived. That was a real paradox, because all the affluence you could think of existed in Fontabelle. Some of the biggest merchants lived there, and yet next door to them there we were, living in squalor.

When we'd go up to Fontabelle we'd walk very fast, and, if by chance we were stopped and a white person spoke to us, we felt honored. If a white woman said, "Good morning son, how are you?" I felt like a million dollars, and I'd run back and say to my mother, "Hey, a woman in Fontabelle just spoke to me, and she was real nice and everything." I used to feel it an achievement for them to speak to me.

My grandfather and uncle used to take fish to a white man called Tom Herbert, who owned the biggest lumber company in town. When I heard that Tom Herbert wanted my grandfather's fish, I felt honored. I used to brag to the boys, "Listen, man, do you know who supply Tom Herbert with fish? My grandfather." I felt big and important about that. That is the way the whites made you feel.

My mother also did servant-nursing for a white man. And when he used to drop my mother home in his car I used to feel honored. I'd say to my friends, "Listen, man, my mother just got dropped home in a car." It never occurred to me that I had a right to have exactly what that white man had. The majority of the people in my neighborhood never questioned it; they'd even root for the white team in cricket or soccer, if it was better than the black team they were playing.

The people in Fontabelle had dogs, and after six o'clock they let them loose. White kids didn't go out after six o'clock; they was inside studying, doing their homework. So, there was no problem with the dogs bothering white kids. But black people like to walk. They didn't have television; they didn't have things like books to keep them in. But because of the dogs you just couldn't go into Fontabelle or into Strathclyde or into Belleville or into the other rich white neighborhoods. If a black servant had to leave Fontabelle, the white people had to escort him out or give him a ride. When the dogs run at you they'd always run to a point and stop: they knew the boundaries of their neighborhood, and they never came into our neighborhood.

My whole family was into sports. We liked to think that we could do everything better than everybody else. My sister was the Barbados table tennis champion for awhile, and I was the road tennis champion, and my brother played soccer for Barbados for a while. We all had drive. But, although I played lots of sports as a child, I always wanted to be a musician. Always, always, always. I used to tell my mother that I was going to be a singer, and she'd say, "You'd better get an education. You'd better try and learn a trade." She'd say, "There is no black singers in Barbados who make money, not one. Name one. Tell me one." She broke up the guitar I had made. It's true there was none, but I was determined to be the first. But now that I look back on it, I must have been mad to think I could receive any kind of support from my mother, when the best singer and composer of the time, Shillingford Agard, earned no more than a few shillings per week. He was so rich in talent, yet he died poor, slumped over in his favorite chair in his little house.

I think what pushed me toward going abroad was the experience I had with tourists. I was young, just twenty years old, and I was singing on two yachts, the *Eoine* and the *Buccaneer*, for a guy named Captain Carlow Menduoy. You are on the water singing six days a week. You'd go out in the boat from eight o'clock in the morning, come back at two o'clock, then sail again from three-thirty until six-thirty. The first outing was called the "picnic cruise," and the second was the "cocktail cruise," and I'd get just one dollar for each cruise. Man, I can see the coastline of Barbados, every little point, in my sleep. There'd be thirty or forty people on the boat, people from all over the world, Europe and North America. I was doing this every day—meeting people—and it was fantastic.

People on the boats were very relaxed, and they'd talk to you. They'd talk about things that I had no experience of—fascinating things, like their countries, the size of them, the fastness of them, and the kind of things that you could do there. One man told me he lived in a small town, and then he told me that it had 250,000 people. I mean, gosh, that's the entire population of Barbados, and he says he lives in a small place. Well, I was a young man having all this information fed to me. A man from rural Saskatchewan talking to me about Canada, a man from Toronto talking about the same country as the man from Saskatchewan but with a completely different concept of what Canada is because he's from the big city. I was fascinated, and I wanted to go see for myself.

The tourists would say to me, "Why do you work here in Barbados? The money you are being paid is so little. Why don't you come to the States or to Canada where you will make a better living?" My mind was in conflict. I liked playing on the yachts, but finally I said, I'll go to the States and see for myself—I'll see if it is really better.

When I went in 1971 I said I'd stay away for no more than five years. That way when I'd get back to Barbados I'd still be in my twenties and I could build a house and start things going. My aspirations at the time were a house, a car, lots of money, and good clothes. I looked at the aim of life as being material gain. Art and the things that are important to me now never even ventured into my mind.

I took a plane to New York. Coming out from the airport was beautiful. I thought, I'm going to have a glamorous life. But then we got into Brooklyn, and I am thinking, Gosh, I'll be glad to get out of this area. Then we pulled up to a house, to my girlfriend's relatives, and I couldn't believe it. The neighborhood was worse than anything I'd ever seen in Barbados. Can this be America? Is this the same place the people talk about? That's what I thought to myself. That was Bed-Stuy [Bedford-Stuyevesant], one of the most depressed areas of Brooklyn.

The first two days were horrifying. My girlfriend's family kept saying to me, "Make sure that you lock the doors." There were three locks on one door. I thought, Nobody needs three locks on one door. I couldn't believe it. In Barbados we kept our front door open, and now in Brooklyn they're telling me that not only must I keep the door closed at all times, but I need three locks.

Everyone in the house went off to work each day. And there I was by myself. They told me, "If you need anything from the fridge, you can have it. And you can watch television." That was my day: television and something from the fridge. I did that for a week. "God," I'd say, "how can I deal with this?" I started watching television till late at night, so I'd be really sleepy and would sleep till midday. This way I wouldn't have to wait for the others to come home from work for so long.

The first few weeks I didn't look for a job. I was too scared to walk in the streets. I was thinking, If I have to put three locks on the door when I'm in the house, imagine what it must be like out there. So I didn't go out. Then one morning I got adventurous and left the house. I marked in my mind where the house was, the corner of Madison and Sumner streets, and walked right down the street. No left or right turn, I just walked down the block, so I wouldn't get lost. Then I walked back until I saw Madison and Sumner. But when I got there I saw a man coming out of our house. What is a strange man doing coming out of our house? I got scared, and I wouldn't go in the house. After awhile I saw a police car, and I stopped it. I said to them, "There's a strange man coming out of our house." So, the police came back with me. One of them told me, "Lots of people live here; this is just a common door. There are other people living in the building, and they use this door too." This is how I discovered there was a family on the first floor, a family above us, and a landlady in the basement. They all used the same front door. It was a shock to me. I never realized it. After that I began to get out more.

The first job I had was down on Graham Avenue in Brooklyn in a factory that made feather pillows. I didn't stay long. There were feathers all over the place, and the chemicals they put on the feathers gave off some terrible fumes. We had to wear masks at all times in order to breathe. The chemicals were so bad that I had to quit. I was thinking, too, that it would be nice to work in Manhattan where at lunchtime you could go out and see this and that. In the summer you could see these nice concerts, and in the winter you could go up 42nd Street and see some movie. So, I went and applied for a job in the garment district. I went to Starwood Fabrics; there were two Bajans working there and some Puerto Ricans, and I got the job. The shop, Starwood Fabrics, was one of the biggest sample shops in the garment district. We supplied big stores like J. C. Penney and Montgomery Ward with samples of material, and then they would order what they liked. They'd have to buy a minimum order of ten thousand yards of a fabric in a particular color.

I started off at $80 dollars a week. But the work wasn't easy: you had to lift huge pieces [bolts] of material for them to cut for customers. You might lift two hundred yards of canvas, and canvas is pretty heavy. And when a particular type of canvas got hot, when it was selling well, you'd be lifting that over and over for weeks. I was also delivering packages, taking samples of material to different companies in the garment center. Many a day I walked and delivered packages from the East River to the Hudson River.

That was a great experience for me. You got to know Manhattan better than any part of the Caribbean. You knew all the UPS [United Parcel Service] people; you knew all the truckers; you knew the whole garment district. And I got on well with the guys at the shop. We talked sports, how the Knicks were doing or, if it was baseball season, how the Yankees were doing. They could rap with me, and I could rap with them.

The garment district was my education. Here I was in the middle of the garment center, and I'd go into these men's offices, they were so fabulous, so plush. One had a huge bar right in the man's office. "Gosh," I'd say, "this is an amazing place." Here I was just two doors down from the freight elevator, and this guy has an office with fabulous things, a bar and the best in curtains. I'd think, If this guy's office is like this, imagine what his home is like. You'd read in the newspaper that some of these guys come in to work from Long Island by helicopter. You are impressed, and you start thinking that you'll work toward that, toward what these guys have.

And sometimes you'd hear the talk. You know, people designing things for people in Hollywood. You also learned about people stealing patterns from one another. It happened all the time. If somebody brought out something that had a black, blue, and yellow pattern with big flowers on it and it was selling hot, legally all you had to do was reduce the size of the flower, take out one of those colors, and you had a different product. But to the customer's eye it looks like the same thing. That happened all over the garment district.

One day when I came out of the shop there is this man standing there—Frank Cherry is his name—and he is from District 65 Garment Workers Union. He asks to talk to me, and he tells me that he wants to unionize the shop. He shows me a paper that shows that workers have a right to unionize, as long as 75 percent of the workers vote to join the union. Well, I went down to union headquarters then and learned more about the union— that they were the biggest garment union in New York and that they owned the whole block. I learned all that they could do for us—that they would raise our pay to $125 per week, that they had their own dentist right there in the union hall, that they paid 100 percent of hospital bills, and this and that.

I always had a drive in me that said, If it can be better, make it better. And I always liked to try to do things that people said were impossible to do. When the other workers said that our shop would never be unionized I accepted that as a challenge. I said, I'm going to unionize the shop. How I went about it wasn't really kosher, but it was the only way I knew. At first the Spanish-speaking guys at work didn't want to join, so I told them that, if they didn't join the union, the union was going to bring people in to replace them, and I read them an order from the union. The order didn't really say that, but the guys didn't understand; they didn't know much English, and, besides, they wanted better conditions at work too. They signed up, and we became a union shop.

Most bosses would have fired me when they saw me organizing, but we had a good boss. Mr. Warner called me into his office and said to me, "I understand that you are trying to get the fellows to join the union. Why would you do that? Don't we offer you good conditions here? Are you not happy here?" He said, "Unions try to break up the relationship between the workers and the bosses." I told him that I liked him and that I liked working for him but that the workers came first and that the union promised us more money and more benefits.

I worked hard, very hard. I don't mind working hard, but what I didn't like was the clock—having to be there nine to five, the same hours every day. The supervisor used to quarrel with me. "Man," he said to me, "you come in at nine-fifteen, you come in at eight, you come in at ten. I don't know when you're coming in. I'm going to have to put in a time clock."

I told him, "I can give you better work than anybody else in this shop, but you can't put a clock on me. You can't chain me." Then he starts telling me how 90 percent of the people in New York live by the clock. "I'm the other 10 percent," I say. "What do you really want from me? Do you want *time,* or do you want *production?*"

"Of course, I want production," he says.

"Fine," I say, "you watch me for two weeks and see what kind of production I give you."

"Alright," he says, and he tells everybody. Well, one Friday afternoon he calls everybody in. He has all the work orders there and tells each of them how much they have done. Then he points to my pile, which is bigger than all the others, and he says, "Tony, it amazes me what you can do in the time you are here."

I said, "I am a musician at heart, and a musician can work for sixteen hours or sixteen seconds, depending on inspiration." From then on he never bothered me. I could come in at noon, and I could work from then to eleven that night and lock up the place when I was done.

When I first saw those fabulous offices in the garment district I'd think to myself, If I work hard, I can do well too, and I can have these nice things. To improve myself I tried to absorb what I was seeing in New York, to learn from it and apply it in a positive way. Later what I came to want was to see my people develop, not just me as an individual. I realized that none of those bosses I saw in the garment district would be considered great men, because they were out for themselves.

It was meeting Paul Webster that changed my life in New York. He was a young Barbadian, about my age, but he was from a different background than I am. He was from the privileged class; he grew up in Belleville, an area in Bridgetown which was then almost totally white. He grew up as one of the bourgeoise. When I met him I couldn't understand why he'd want to live in New York, in poor conditions, when he didn't have to, when he came from Belleville. Through him I learned about other people who were also privileged and who were struggling against the unfairness in their societies, and I got involved in the Barbados Theatre Workshop that he was organizing. Through him I started to take things seriously, and I started to read.

I read James Baldwin's *If Beale Street Could Talk, The Autobiography of Malcolm X, The Muhammed Ali Story,* and books by W. E. B. Du Bois, Marcus Garvey, and Frederick Douglass. I followed the life of Adam Clayton Powell and Harry Belafonte. I read black history, which I wasn't aware of at all because my experience of anything black had come from reading schoolbooks in Barbados, and that was the British interpretation of history. When we went to school in Barbados we were told that we had no history—that our history was just the slave thing and that it wasn't worth knowing. I believed them. When I look back on it now I realize that the reason I didn't know anything about black history was because it was deliberate. I knew Henry VIII. I knew King Charles I. I knew Shakespeare. But I didn't know the history of my own people.

This man Paul Webster made me see how much there was to learn. Through Paul's connections some evenings I would sit in at classes at CUNY [City University of New York], and I'd take notes just like the students. On Saturdays, every Saturday for two years, I went to the Street University of Harlem. It was upstairs in Seamans Furniture Store; Alma John who worked for WPIX and who did a program called "Black Pride" ran it. She had college professors and experts come and talk about their fields. A fellow would come and say, "I am from Queens University, and I teach English," then he'd talk about his work. Then somebody else would come up and say, "My field is this and that and I go about it in such and such a way."

I started moving around New York, seeking information. I checked out the Muslims, I checked out the Italians, I checked out the Jews, I checked out other groups, and I found out what they were all about. I stored that information right up here in my head because I knew that one day I would use it, and that's what I'm doing right now. It comes out piece by piece in my music. When I write a song like "Boots" or "Jack" or "Culture" it almost always comes out of my experience.

One day I went downtown, and there was a West Indian boy playing the steel band, and I stayed and watched him. I went back several days in a row, and he called me over. He said to me, "Either you play music or you know a lot about music—I've seen you here for five straight days." I then asked him to play "Yellow Bird" and some songs that I used to do on the boats. And he played them well. He could play almost anything you asked him to play from classic to calypso. After that each time he'd see me coming he'd play those songs. I'd put my dollar down, and he'd give it back to me. "I'll get money from the other people," he would say. He was a great player, and he got me thinking about playing music again.

About that time Mr. Warner, the boss at the shop, heard that I could play and asked if I would play for the company's Christmas party. I didn't have an instrument, so he sent me to a place in Long Island called Syosset to buy a guitar. The deal was that I would pay him back $10 a week; the guitar was $200. But after I played that

Christmas he said to keep the guitar, that I didn't need to pay him back. He couldn't believe how I played; he didn't know that I could really play. The salesmen were shocked that not only could I sing but that I was singing impromptu about them, about things that happened in the shop, dealing and wheeling. This was the first time I played in public in the States, and from then on I got back the feeling. Yes, playing at that party got me back into music.

I loved New York. I loved the sports, the respect that they paid to artists; I loved the beautiful buildings. But there was a lot that I didn't like too. I used to live near a candy store, and the children would come there for the candy but also for marijuana and other drugs. You see, the candy store was just a front. The police closed it down a couple of times, but it always opened under a different name. I remember the very first time that I ever smelled marijuana being used openly. It was in Bryant Park in New York—Sixth Avenue around Forty-second Street. The shocking thing about it was that I saw a policeman pass by the guy who was smoking marijuana. The cop said to him, "Why don't you put that away? You don't have no respect for me, man."

I said to myself, Gosh, in Barbados they would throw this guy in jail, and here in the States was this cop saying to the guy, "Why don't you put away that joint? You don't have no respect for me." Wow, then I realized I am living in a totally different society.

The children going to school—I noticed that they tried to outdress each other. Many of the stores gear themselves to young people, and the children with more money were able to dress better, and that created a stigma for those who couldn't dress as well. The school kids didn't have uniforms like in Barbados. That was bad because it made a child from an early age think that he is better than another child just because he had better clothes, and it made the other child feel inferior. It creates the feeling that material things are what is important.

But it was the violence that really bothered me. I had an Arab friend who sold newspapers near the entrance to the Saratoga station on the IRT [Interboro Rapid Transit]. I used to say hello to him each morning. One day I talked to him in the morning, and then later in the day, on my way home, I saw the shop closed. I had never seen him closed at that time. I was thinking it might be an Arabic holiday. Then on the evening news I heard that this Arab guy, my friend, was killed. He was killed resisting the robber; the robber got something like $18. Okay, I know there are ten murders a day in New York, but that is just statistics to me. This guy I knew; he was no statistic. I knew him not as an Arab, not as a statistic; I knew him as an intelligent human being. I saw him in the morning, and he was dead in the afternoon.

New York is not like Barbados, where people trust other people. I suppose it's the size of the place, the masses of people, that make people fearful. When we moved to Rockway Parkway in Brooklyn there was this white woman living next door. It was snowing one day, and she had these two huge grocery bags in her car. Now, she never knew me, and I never knew her at that point. I said, "Can I help you with the bags?"

She said, real nervous, "No, no, it's fine, I can manage." She thought I was some mugger.

I said, "Look, I am a West Indian, and I am from an island called Barbados, and my name is Tony, and I want to help you. I live right here, next door."

After a pause she said, "Okay."

I carried the groceries, and, as I went to take them into the house, she said, "No, just leave them on the step." She was afraid to let me in the house.

But do you know that a few days later she came to my door with a cake—she had baked me a cake—and after we talked she asked me to come next door to her house. She said, "I have something to show you." She showed me the door that joined our apartments, and against it was a big chair and a big pile of books. A barricade. She said, "I have kept these here for years because I never knew if somebody from the other apartment would try to break into my place. And now I am going to ask you to help me move these things." She and I became friends.

I saw a lot of people living in very bad conditions. I saw some places with three people living in one room. The people were well-documented aliens with the right to work and the right to live in the States, but they still had to live in one room because they couldn't get benefits. When I saw that, I'd say to myself, God, if I ever get the opportunity, I will fight hard to make sure that my people will never have to go through this, never have to live like this.

People thought I was crazy—crazy that I couldn't accept those conditions. They would say to me, "What you see is the norm." They would say, "Lots of people start out like that, and they now live well; they now live in Flatbush, in Sheepside Bay, and nice places." But even hearing that didn't convince me; there are lots of people who never get out of those places in Bed-Stuy and the South Bronx.

It is true that many Barbadians have done well; many families have established nice homes off Kings Highway and over to Ralph Avenue, Tilden, Beverly, Clarendon, Foster, and that whole area. And a whole lot of other West Indians have bought houses. These people are well established now, and their children do not know what the conditions were like. And many did it in fifteen short years. I thought that was beautiful. But the children of others, especially black Americans, are still living in the same depressed areas as their parents grew up in.

I knew a girl from South Carolina who collected records of singers from the South, and she used to say that what amazed her was how West Indians would take any job and save and save their money to buy a house, while the black Americans would rent forevermore. The West Indians' way of life would annoy the black Americans. But now I see black Americans buying houses too. They're buying houses near the West Indians. Another thing I found strange was that black Americans would not paint their apartments. They'd say the landlord must do that, that it is the landlord's job. But West Indians would paint their apartments, and the landlords would take the cost of the paint off the rent.

When I first lived in New York I was an illegal alien. Not having the proper papers to work was hard on me. When I saw a policeman on the subway, I'd think he could come and arrest me right now. Once I laughed to myself at the thought, and the policeman looked right at me. Being illegal made me feel horrible, like an eighteenth-class citizen, not a second-class citizen but an eighteenth-class citizen—as low as you can go. I didn't want to live like this; I wanted to live as a respected human being. There were times when I packed up everything, saying, "I am going to leave; I'm going back to Barbados." And people would say, "Why you leave, what you going to do in Barbados, go back to playing on the boats? There is nothing to do there, man."

I'd say, "Alright I'll try New York for awhile longer."

But in 1976 I finally came home. I thought I would go home and get everything organized and then come back to New York. My friends in New York accepted me as Gabby, who had the ability to write songs but who never got the breaks. I wanted to go back as Gabby who went home and from scratch built himself up and goes back to New York, to Madison Square Garden. To them and to me the Garden is a prized thing. Moving from Brooklyn with little or nothing, playing in just small basement clubs, and then to the Garden—that is what I wanted to do. But when I got home and got in with my friends and other people I wanted to stay. It was really good to be in Barbados, and after awhile I stopped thinking about New York.

Having been away for five years, my attitude had changed dramatically—my food habits, my dress habits, everything about me had changed. Before, when I was singing on the yachts, my concern was to make as much money as I could from the tourists, get as much as I could out of them, and uplift myself. You know, to get a nice house and a big car—that was my concept of life. Today my concept of life is different. Now I think about doing what I can for the Caribbean, not just for myself.

At home I got in with some other musicians—Romeo, Viper, Destroyer, Grynner, and Sir Don—and we formed Calypso Enterprises. In 1976 calypso was down; it was in the gutter. Nobody cared about it. I joined them, and we started to work. We started on a grass roots level, playing all the little places around, places that hold just fifty people. We started to become popular. Word got out that "Hey, these fellas are worth going to." And by 1981 we were able to take the show to the National Stadium, and by 1982 we were able to fill the National Stadium. We're talking 15,000 people. In five years from 50 people to 15,000 people in an island that has a population of 250,000. And we would have sold more tickets if the stadium could have held more people.

I used Muhammed Ali's tactics; I had read his book in New York. Like Ali, I talked my way into the spotlight by constantly taunting and reminding people that I was the king. That did two things. It made them notice me, and it created a following for calypso that crossed the class barrier for the first time in Barbados. It also created an "I hate Gabby" section as well as a "Tell them

Gabby" section in the community. You were either my fan or not, but never again would you ignore me.

Gabby was voted folk singer of the year in Barbados for three consecutive years, 1977 to 1979. In 1982 his recording "Jack" became Barbados' biggest selling record ever; it was also an international success, earning him a platinum record. His success in the Caribbean led to invitations to perform at major venues in Europe and the United States and, ultimately, Madison Square Garden.

I felt really good going back to the garment center, seeing the people who were my bosses and being able to invite them to the Garden to see me perform. When I was delivering packages I used to pass the Garden. I even took pictures of it. My friend Les and I used to go to the Garden to watch hockey; I liked to watch Bobby Orr play, and I'd say to myself, Man, one of these days I am going to be down there. Then I'd say to Les, "I am going to sing here one of these days. This same Garden, Les—you are going to pay to come and see me sing." He would make fun. He didn't think it could ever happen.

I remember the first show I did at the Garden. This security guard came into the dressing room and said, "There is a guy out there who wants to see you." I told the guard to send the guy up. When the guy came in I recognized his face, but I'd never known his name. He used to be at parties with us when I lived in Brooklyn. He said, "I am so *proud* of you! I had to come back here to let you know that. I came to both shows. I want you to know that you are my hope. You are my hope that one of these days we will get out of the conditions we live in here." Well, I really felt good. Really good.

A lot of what I sing comes out of my experience of having lived in the States. I saw the conditions the people are living in, and I thought, If only I could bring out the story in my music, I could help do something about it. I think music can bring the message. But there aren't many Bob Dylans anymore whose music will bring the message. Marvin Gaye stopped his after awhile and the same with Joan Baez. So my aim is to paint a picture of my experience, of the West Indian experience. I want people to understand why they are the way they are. I try to lift people's awareness and let the people judge if my message is worth hearing.

Take my song "Take Down Nelson" [the song urges the removal of the statue of the English Lord Nelson from the center of Bridgetown]. Well, having lived in the States, I know that Americans have taken down a lot of Nelsons, or the likes of him, and established a lot of Abraham Lincolns in their place. You will also find that many streets in the States once had British names but that the Americans have changed them. In Barbados there is not one statue of a Barbadian. Not one. Can you tell me that Barbadians were all so unimportant that there wasn't one that could have become a statue? I can name dozens of men—sportsmen, artists, and others—who deserve a statue.

Many of Gabby's calypsos have been hard-hitting political commentaries in which the average citizen has been shortchanged or unwittingly exploited by his leaders or government. The song "Jack," named after a government director of tourism, attacked the director's plan to prohibit Barbadians from using the same beaches as the tourists.

> I grow up bathing in sea water;
> But nowadays that is bare horror;
> If I only venture down by the shore,
> Police telling me I can bathe no more,
> Jack tell dem kick me outta reach'
> Strengthen security, build barricade. . . .
> Tourism is vital, I cannot deny,
> But I want Jack to know that the beach belong to we . . .

Gabby followed "Jack" with other songs equally critical of the government. "Boots" flays the prime minister for spending the taxpayers' money to build an army.

> Is it necessary, to have so much soldiers?
> In this small country, is it necessary,
> to shine soldiers' boots with taxpayers' money?
> Unemployment high and the treasury low,
> And he buying boots, to cover soldier toe,
> I see dem boots, boots, and more boots,

on the feet of trigger happy recruits . . .

"Boots," released the same year as the American invasion of Grenada, was a huge success in Trinidad, where there was little support for the military action. But in Barbados, where the government supported the invasion, it was banned from radio.

In "West Indian Politician" Gabby excoriates elected officials for their narrow provincialism and their failure to promote cooperation between the islands.

West Indian politicians and their narrowest views
For me will always have to be on their P's and Q's
West Indian politician,
I check out your evil ploy
And de more I hear you,
de more you sound like West Minister choir boy
De people will rise,
with swollen pride
Your shackles will be loosened,
and then cast aside . . .

Also expressed in "West Indian Politician" is Gabby's fervent desire to see the Caribbean islands unified under one government. Like many of Gabby's other political beliefs, its origins are found in his experiences in the United States.

Just look at all these little islands in the Caribbean. Each one with its own little passport. You go 90 miles to St. Vincent, and you need another passport; 150 miles to Grenada, and you need another passport. It makes no sense: all these little islands struggling on their own trying to compete with big countries, when they could be cooperating with each other.

A unified Caribbean would give us power. Barbados or St. Lucia or Dominica have no power in the UN [United Nations]. It is like the newspaper editor of the *Plattsburgh Daily* compared to the editor of the *New York Times*. The Plattsburgh man has no influence.

In New York, when I said I was from Barbados, people would say, "What part of Jamaica is that?" Or they'd say, "Is that in

Trinidad?" They knew two places, Jamaica and Trinidad. And now
they know Grenada. Eighty percent of Americans don't know
where Barbados is. But they know there is a Caribbean. Barbados
by its tiny self doesn't have any clout, but if all the islands were
unified, one Caribbean, they would have clout. Tell me, would it
be good for California or New York or Texas to each be a separate
country? Of course not. The United States has clout because it is
big, because it is unified. It's the same with the Soviet Union. And
Canadians have one unified thing across their continent. The
people of Quebec know that they are French, but at the end of the
day they want to be part of Canada.

Take the West Indies cricket team. They are the most powerful
cricket team in the world; they beat everybody. When little islands
like these can beat England and Australia and India, we are talking
about something important. Now, if we could just do that in
government, all the people of the Caribbean would have better
lives.

Some people in Barbados don't like my ideas. They are afraid
of new ideas, of what changes they might bring. So, they don't
want to hear my songs. For a while I had a lot of trouble playing for
the hotels, and you need them if you are going to make money. I
wanted to choose what songs I would sing, but the hotels didn't
like that. They wanted me to sing "The Island Bird," "Island in the
Sun," "Barbados, the Island I Love." I said, "These songs are not in
my repertoire, please don't ask me to sing them. I cannot allow
you to tell me what to sing." One hotel manager said to me, "That
is outrageous. We always tell the bands what to play, and they must
play songs for the tourists. This is my hotel. I am paying you, and
you will just have to play what I want."

I said, "No, I am a creative artist, and you must give me a
chance to show my creativity."

He said, "But your songs are radical. You will ruin tourism.
You will make the tourist go away."

"No," I said, "most people who come to Barbados are working
people, and they understand what I am saying."

He fired me, and then I got the same thing at other hotels.
One hotelier told me that the hoteliers had a meeting, and they
had decided that I was too radical and that they had to do
something about it.

Gabby visiting in his old neighborhood of Emerton, 1985. (Photo courtesy of the *Nation*.)

The hoteliers didn't like my songs because they weren't the songs where everything was nice and wonderful. My songs are about struggle, about the development of Caribbean people, about what the politicians are doing, and about what colonialism has done to us. I believe tourists like my songs because they say something. Today the hoteliers say the tourists only like my songs because the beat is nice.

To that I say, Maybe, but the tourists also sing the lyrics.

Migrants often return home with lofty ideas about changes that they would like to see made in Barbados, but few are in a position to be innovators. Most of them simply lack the position or authority to put their ideas into practice, and some become discouraged by the resistance of local people to change. Gabby has been an exception in that he has used his popularity as an entertainer to lobby for change in a number of areas. Apart from the influence of his songs, he has transferred the idea of New York's neighborhood block party to Barbados. In 1980 he organized the island's first "Neighborhood Day" in Emerton, the community of his youth, and its success is now being imitated in other neighborhoods.

The idea came from watching block parties in New York. They really inspired me. I thought, Gosh, I would love to do something like that for Emerton, when I grew up. I thought I could expand on what I saw. In New York they had food and music and a little impromptu basketball. I thought we should have sports and activities right through the day. So, I got the top teams in Barbados to come and play, bag races for the children, artists and craftspeople to show their work, and others to cane chairs, and even a few grandmothers to wash clothes in the old tubs so the children today could see how it was done in the old days. All that, plus food. Many people came, and it was a big success, and now other neighborhoods are getting into it—Clapham Day, Davile Day, St. Thomas Day, and so on.

I've got other ideas, like how to cut Barbados' crime rate with a citizens' watch and how to beautify the island and attract more tourists at little cost by planting flowers. But government people say, "Who the hell is this guy telling us what we should do?" They object because these ideas are foreign and because they didn't think of them first. The truth is these ideas will someday be common sense.

Chapter 11
Siebert and Aileen Allman

Siebert and Aileen Allman are in their fifties, with five grown children. Siebert emigrated twice to England in the early 1960s, each time returning to Barbados within a year or two. England, he concluded, was neither the place for him to make his fortune nor to raise a family. In 1968 he took his wife and later his children to Canada, vowing not to return to Barbados in less than twenty years.

The Allmans returned to Barbados ten years later. They had devoted their lives abroad to hard work in order to save enough money to achieve their "plan" of building a comfortable home in Barbados and sending their children to college. Today their large, four-bedroom house, perched on a bluff overlooking the quiet fishing village of Half Moon Fort, is like a beacon, signaling to the surrounding community the Allmans' success as migrants. Inside the house the kitchen accessories, wall-to-wall carpeting, drapes, and sliding glass doors are pure North American. On the roof is a small deck from which one can look down the west coast of Barbados to Speightstown and beyond.

Their home and two automobiles belie the Allmans' humble beginnings. Siebert's father died when he was six, and his mother supported him and his older sister by working as a maid in the Blackrock mental asylum, with wages of just $16 per month. She stressed to her son that education was the only way to get ahead. Siebert did well, finishing secondary school, and today he is a supervisor for a construction firm in Bridgetown. Siebert is a modest, disciplined, and private man, who prefers his own company and television to a social gathering. Many of the villagers mistake his aloofness for snobbery.

Aileen Allman is less serious and more outgoing than her husband. But she is also inured to work. A self-employed seamstress, she rises before dawn to sew dresses and uniforms for maids, waitresses, and bartenders at

Siebert Allman, 1992. (Photo by George Gmelch.)

Sandy Lane, Barbados' poshest resort. Aileen sometimes regrets having come home to Barbados, as most of her children are still abroad. She works hard and saves her money for the airfares to periodically visit her three children who are scattered over England, Canada, and Belgium. She also returns occasionally to Montreal for short stints of work as a seamstress with her old employer. Her trips away, she believes, help her to cope with the social isolation of the village and satisfy her desire to be with her children.

As I mentioned in chapter 1, I met the Allmans while looking for families to house my students. I would drive around the countryside, and, whenever I came upon a village that looked large enough for a student researcher, I would ask in the rum shop and of passersby if they knew anyone who might be interested in taking in an American student for ten weeks. One morning, I entered a small general store in the village of Sutherland and found Siebert and Aileen Allman cleaning up after a break-in during the night. They had lost $900 in stock, all uninsured; Siebert was bitter and talked about leaving Barbados and going back to Canada. (Later he closed the business and took a salaried job instead.) We chatted for a long time about Montreal, among other things, where we had *both been immigrants (I had gone there to teach). As I left, they said they would consider taking one of my students themselves.*

When I began recording the Allmans story in 1987 I already knew them well, as over the years they had accommodated several of my students, and, therefore, I had visited their home often. Several times the Allmans had said they wished other Barbadians could know how hard they and other emigrants had worked overseas, that they had paid for their luxuries with the sweat of their brows. Despite these sentiments, they were initially reluctant to be interviewed on tape. Their concern was that the attention they might receive in being the subject of these interviews and having their lives published would cause jealousy and resentment among some people in their community. They didn't want to bring any attention to themselves. Their brief experience as shopkeepers, which they describe in this narrative, helps explain their hesitation. In any case, they agreed to the interviews, mostly I suppose, out of friendship and their belief that, if others knew what the lives of West Indians abroad were like, there would be greater understanding.

Siebert Allman

I first went to England in 1960. I thought there would be more opportunities there. Barbados was stagnant then, and, with all the people around here going to England, you had to think it must be good. We heard that jobs were vacant because English people were leaving their own country to go to Australia and New Zealand. At least that's what we heard. In those days you could just buy a ticket and go, since we were a colony belonging to Britain. The English had no objection to us at that time.

I didn't take my family. I wanted to see what it was like first. If it was something my family would benefit from, educationally and moneywise, then I'd send for them. When I got there I found out that it wasn't what I had perceived, so I didn't send for them.

I went on the *Ascania,* an Italian ship, mostly for tourists. It took us two weeks. In 1962 they didn't yet have a harbor in Barbados, so they took you out to the ship in a launch. The fare was three hundred Barbados dollars, and that gave you a cabin with three other fellows. All the way over, leaving a small country like Barbados to go to a big country, to the "mother country," you are anticipating what England is going to be like. You have funny feelings leaving your family behind and wondering what is ahead of you. You wonder if you'll fit in, what kind of environment you'll find yourself in. Will it be a bad environment, low-class housing, where there'll be plenty of criminals? All this is what was going through my mind. I prayed a lot, because I am a very religious person. You had to be because you didn't know what was going to be at the other end.

We got off in Genoa, Italy. Then we took a train down to Calais, France. At certain points policemen [customs agents] would get on the train and check the carriages, but they found everything alright. Then we took a ferry to Southampton and then a train up to Victoria Station.

When I got there I had no work lined up. I could've gotten a job with London Transport, on the buses, before I left. But, being a cabinetmaker, I wanted to continue my trade if I could. But I arrived in England when the cabinetmaking places were on their summer vacation, and, having a family to maintain at home, I had to look for other work. I applied at the Transport Board, at Manor House in north London, and took the tests to become a bus conductor. They were very difficult. You had to do fifteen sums in your head in five minutes. It's what they call "maths" and what we call "arithmetics." They'd give you a problem, like, say, you have a family of four traveling a certain distance, then you'd have to figure in your head the fare in shillings and pence and give the correct change from a pound note. We weren't used to shillings and pence in Barbados. You'd have to do five of those and then write an essay of fifty words on why you wanted to join London Transport. I wrote about how I wanted to support my family, that I needed a permanent job, and that I would find working on the buses challenging and exciting. After I did the five sums and the essay I was called into the office for an interview. But after it was over the man told me to call back again some other time.

The next day I applied to London Transport again, but this time at Griffiths House in Marlebone. They didn't take me either. So then I went to the transport recruitment office in Chiswick, and there I finally got my job as a conductor. By then I'd been in London ten days.

My routes were the 134 from Victoria Station and the 43 from

Freinbarnet to Londonbridge, about twenty kilometers out. It was upstairs and downstairs all the time. Very tiring. At the compulsory stops you have to be on the platform on the lower level of the bus, and that was really laborious during rush hour. With just two or three minutes between stops you'd have to keep people from getting on when it was overcrowded and then get all the new fares upstairs and downstairs. You'd always have to anticipate the next stop so that you could get back to the platform on time.

They didn't have a standard fare like the buses here in Barbados or in Canada. That would be easy. You had different fare stages—three pence from here to there, six pence from there to there, and like that. A fellow would come on and say, "One to the Green Man." That's a pub, and you'd have to know where it was to figure out the fare. For each fare you'd have to get the right combination on the machine before you rolled the crank. The machine was strapped around your waist. Sometimes people would see that you're new and that you're colored, and they would try to take advantage of you. They'd call for a certain destination, maybe the name of a pub in the back of a street that you wouldn't know. Then when you'd charge them two shillings they'd say, "Last time I only paid one shilling—what do you mean two shillings?" This is where you'd have to use your ingenuity to get the real truth from the people. There are plenty of English people who want a cheaper fare, if they can get it.

You'd have to deal with people who didn't like you just because you were colored. I remember this one lady who put her fare on the seat. She wouldn't hand it to me because she didn't want me, being a colored person, to touch her hands. You'd try to look past that. You'd say to yourself, This person has never traveled. Or you'd remind yourself that there are narrow-minded people in your own country like that woman.

I had a little problem with "teddy boys" and punks. These were weird-looking fellows with long hair and tight pants and boots. They'd go upstairs, and when you went up they'd say, real surly like, "Right, sir. Yes, sir. Goodnight, sir." There was one incident where they beat up a fellow Barbadian conductor. He lost his eye. After that I'd think, No way am I going to put my life on the line just for a few fares. If they looked like trouble, I didn't collect their fare.

Aileen Allman sent this picture of her and the
children to Siebert in England in 1962.

I worked a split shift—six-thirty to nine-thirty in the morning
and then two-thirty to seven in the evening. But I did all the
overtime I could get, as my purpose in going to England was to
improve my family's standard of living. I was always happy for the
extra work. My wage was £16 1*s.* 6*d.*, but with the overtime I was
getting about £30 a week. I'd leave £10 for me and send home the
rest.

At one point I started a night course in draftsmanship at City
and Guilds.[1] I thought I could improve myself, but with working
overtime, which I had to do to maintain the family in Barbados, I
didn't have time to finish the course. That was a mistake. If I had
continued with it, I'd be better off today.

---

1. City and Guild refers to a standard certificate that is usually earned at a
polytechnic or college of further education.

It was a very lonely time, that two years in London. I missed my family, and I'd have sent for them, but the conditions really weren't good. The rents and food were high, and there wasn't any organized babysitting. Some folks had to go miles for a sitter, and it was hard on the parents as well as the kids. I knew what the kids of immigrants had to face because I sometimes cared for a little boy and girl for an hour each day. Their mother had to leave for work early in the morning before the husband got home from the night shift on the railway. The husband and wife hardly saw each other. I remember one incident where a lady was taking her baby home in the dark after work and had to cross a small railway bridge. The weather was bad, and she fell down in the snow. She was so exhausted that she couldn't help herself. She couldn't get up. Luckily, an English lady saw her and the child lying in the snow and went for help. Things like that helped me decide not to send for my family.

To put away the loneliness I used to travel on the bus after I finished work. I'd go to Trafalgar Square, Hyde Park, and places like that—anything to distract me. When I was tired I'd go home, just to lay down and sleep. Otherwise, it was too lonely. Some of my friends got involved with other women and started families in England, but that wasn't for me.

Because I missed my family, I decided to go home to Barbados. That was 1962, right on two years. On the trip home on the boat there were many Trinidadians, and with them there was never a dull moment. Trinidadians make you laugh. They are lively people who always look on the brighter side of life. They were always telling jokes and mickey laughs from morning till night. They wouldn't leave the deck till one or two o'clock in the morning.

From England we sailed to Portugal, and we saw where Christopher Columbus was born. From there we went to Vigo, Spain, and from there to Madeira and from there to Barbados. We'd get off the ship and walk around, five or six of us in a gang for safety. The people in these places were much poorer than we were, so you'd want to stay together. You saw what life was about in these other countries, and you compared their lives with Barbadians. It made me realize that I really wasn't poor and that Barbadians really weren't so poor either.

After I came back I got word from the London Transport office in Bridgetown that not enough fellows were signing up to go to England, that the fellows were losing interest in England. At that time there was lots of talk that West Indians were not being treated properly over there. This officer from London Transport came to my house and told me that the English wanted Barbadians more than other islanders because we had more education and could speak better English. He asked if I could be interviewed on rediffusion [radio] to tell young fellows what the conditions were like in England, to encourage them to come in and sign up with London Transport. And they wanted me to go back to England as a kind of example, to impress the young fellows. They thought that I wouldn't be effective if I stayed down here in Barbados, that I should go back. They offered me passage and my old job, and so I went. That was late 1963.

To tell the truth, from the time I left my wife at the airport I regretted going. If the plane had circled back, I would have gotten off. Even on the flight over I was already sorry. When I got there I said to myself that I'd stay one year and no more, that I'd save a little money and then come home. I went back to my old routes, the 43 and the 134, and I moved back with the same landlord. I had one room, fourteen feet by ten feet, with a bed, a table, a chair, and a paraffin heater, which I had to buy. There was no toilet. Everybody used the one toilet. I cooked for myself in the kitchen with the others. To cook you'd have to put shillings into the meter to get gas, and there'd be arguments over how much each fellow had put in. The landlord was so cheap that when you showered there was so little hot water that, just as you got lathered up, the hot water would run out, and you'd have to put more money in. I was paying seven pounds rent per week for the one room.

Things had really deteriorated for colored people in England in 1963, while I was away. With all the emigrants coming in and jobs getting scarce the English people were thinking we were taking their jobs away. They started getting hostile and being more aggressive. They'd call you names like "nigger" and that kind of thing. You'd see signs up: No Colored People. No Irish. When I saw that I thought, No way would I raise my children here. You can't imagine how much England had deteriorated for colored people. Even some of the people that I'd known on the bus route had their attitudes changed. There was a lady who got on the bus every day at Franley Gardens. She worked in Highgate, and every day she used to say to me, "Well, how are you today?" There'd be a conversation between us, if I wasn't too busy. When I went back in 1963 I asked her how she was, and she didn't speak to me at all. Not one word.

And young people would make it difficult for you. And I am not just talking about teddy boys or punks but respectable young folks. They'd call for destinations that you wouldn't know. In Camden Town you'd have people on a Friday night, after they'd had a couple of beers, who wouldn't want to pay their fare. And when you'd want to take their fare they'd want to fight you; they might even cut you with a knife. This is the hostility that caused me to come back home. And that's what I did after my year was up.

I was home five years when I had the urge to travel again. And I was also thinking that my wife, Aileen, had never traveled before, and I wanted her to see how the other side of the world lives. At that time we had friends in Montreal, and they encouraged us to come to Canada. They told us that the newspapers had lots of advertisements for artisans. They said you could walk out of one job and into another. I was a cabinetmaker, and Aileen was a seamstress, so we felt there would be opportunity for us there. At that time, 1968, work wasn't so good here in Barbados. Money was hard to come by. So, I wrote to the Canadian government in Ottawa and asked if we could come.

Aileen Allman

He should have written to the Canadian High Commission in Trinidad, but he didn't know. The fellows in Ottawa sent our file down there. Then Mr. Rodgers interviewed us at the Hilton Hotel in Bridgetown. Lots of people were there, all hoping to get to Canada, but most of them didn't make it. We told Mr. Rodgers that we wanted to go to Quebec.

He said, "Why Quebec? It's French."

We said, "We have friends in Quebec, and we don't know anybody in any other part of Canada." Plus, seeing it was a French province, we thought it would be a great place for the children to learn another language. It worked well, because all the children today can speak French, and my son, because he is fluent, got a good job in the Barbados embassy in Belgium.

The interviewer told us that it would be best for me and my husband to go alone and see if we liked it—then, if it was good, to have the children follow. Before we left Barbados we made reservations for our two oldest ones to come in six weeks. They were thirteen and fifteen, and, being girls, we didn't want them to get into trouble. We figured that within six weeks we'd have a place to live. The other three kids came ten months later.

Siebert Allman

When we left Barbados it was 84° and when we got out of the plane in Montreal it was minus 8°. That's what sticks in my mind. We had coats to wear. I'd bought them from friends who'd returned from England. I'd gotten them just in case our friends in Montreal, who were to meet us at the airport and bring coats for us, were not there. It was a good thing we had the coats because the people that were to meet us at the airport weren't there. A friend of ours who was flying on the same plane knew where our friends lived and took us there. When we pulled up in the car and Aileen got out her foot went right down in the snow. And when she pulled her foot out her shoe was stuck down there in the bottom of the snow. I was anticipating that she would get a cold or the flu from that, but she didn't.

When I left Barbados my thinking was that I wouldn't be back in under twenty years. But when I got there and felt the cold and saw the conditions I asked myself why I'd left my own home, a home I didn't owe anything on, a home with three bedrooms. Why'd I come to this cold place, so cold that you couldn't move around? And I asked myself why I left my work. I had twelve cabinet jobs lined up at home, and I had to give everyone back their deposits. I said to Aileen, "What am I sacrificing myself for?"

Aileen used to cry every day over being away from the kids. We should have brought all the kids with us when we came. The Canadian government would have let us, but we didn't know that then. We thought we had to do just what the man [Mr. Rodgers] said. We made a mistake leaving the kids behind because they were treated badly. They were with a friend of ours, who had two daughters of her own. She didn't treat our kids as well as the others.

A friend wrote us a letter and told us that our kids were not as clean as we used to keep them, that there was some deterioration in the looks of them and in their apparel. We were sending this woman money every week for the kids, but she was putting it into something else. And we sent the kids clothes every month. We had wanted eventually to bring the woman to Canada to live with us. In Barbados we used to have her over for lunch and talk with her, and she projected a kind of love for the kids. I was heartbroken when we learned she was treating them badly. I wrote a letter to her son explaining it all, and he confronted her point-blank. She confessed to him that, yes, we were sending her money every week. When we came back home in 1977 she came over and said she was very sorry. We said, "It's happened already. We forgive you." We still speak to her.

When I got to Canada I found it was very difficult to get a job in my trade. They wanted you to have Canadian experience. They felt that West Indian artisans were not up to their level, that you weren't as competent. I had disciplined myself to work, so I said, "If I don't get work in my area, I'll look for other jobs." Instead of making cabinets, I started out on a conveyor line at Standard Desk Company, inspecting desks for scratches. After two months the old man who was in charge of the desktops retired, and they gave me his job. So, I was in charge of the tops. As the tops came from the machine shop, they'd have rough edges where the glue squeezed out; so, I'd use a router to smooth them off, then you'd turn the tops over and put little dowels in holes to attach the tops to the desk bottoms. I even handled big executive desks.

The pay was pretty good, about $125 a week. But I couldn't get along with the foreman. He was Austrian. I think he learned that I'd come from the Caribbean. Some people think that because you're black and from a small country that you're not as gifted, that you don't have the same potential as they do. The Austrian was always watching me, seeing if I could handle myself. I'd look around and see him looking for me to make a mistake, but he couldn't because I knew my job. You can tell how well people work by the way they position themselves at the workbench. A fellow who doesn't know the work has a funny way of standing at the bench.

One day, during the ten-minute morning break, a fellow came back a few minutes late. The canteen was about two hundred yards away, and, if there was a queue, it took a little time to get your cup of coffee or tea. Well, the foreman, the Austrian, really gave out to this fellow; this fellow had been working there for twenty-five years. I said, "Leave him alone, man." You should have seen the Austrian. He took me into his office and brought in the supervisor. I asked the Austrian point-blank, in front of the supervisor, "What is this? What is your complaint with me? Is it my work?"

He said, "No."

I said, "It must be something personal." He didn't like my saying that, and afterward he made it hard for me. One time he took me away from assembling the tops, which I was good at, and put two Greek guys on it. The Greek fellows couldn't read the instructions properly, and both were left-handed. He'd take me up to the supervisor for the slightest thing. The supervisor knew I was okay, but, with the things being out of hand, I decided it would be better to leave that job.

I got on with the Canadian Pittsburgh Glass Company, where my job was breaking the glass [into panes] and putting them into boxes. It was big, thick glass for shop windows and showcases. You had to be skillful, or you'd waste a lot, which I did when I started out. The company couldn't close at night because they had to keep the furnaces going continually, so there was lots of opportunity for overtime. I did all the overtime I could. With overtime I was making about $300 per week. During the Christmas period I'd make even more, since the guys wouldn't want to come in during a holiday. Some days, with the overtime, I'd get four days pay for just working one day. This is where I really made some dollars.

The only bad thing about the job was the heat. They had to keep the room hot to prevent the glass from cracking, so they had you working just above the furnace. You'd be sweating as soon as you stepped into the room. The conditions were not good, but I was thinking about what we had planned, how we were going to use the money to come back here and build a better house. I'd always say to myself that I was there to improve my family's standard of living. That was my goal.

Aileen Allman

As soon as we got to Canada, I went out looking for a job. I first tried the hospitals. I must have registered [applied] at every hospital in Montreal, but I didn't get anything. Then I got sick with the Hong Kong flu and couldn't go out looking for work. When I got better I tried looking for work in my field, as a seamstress, but every place I went wanted Canadian experience. Now I'd just come from Barbados, and they were asking for Canadian experience. The friends we were staying with told me to go to Canadian Manpower for help.[2] They promised to put me into a course on sewing and pay me the minimum wage while I was being trained. But they took a long time getting the course organized, and, while I was waiting, I got a job with the Jews clipping threads, cutting the ends and loose threads off the clothing for the Jews. In Barbados I was making my own dresses, and here I was in Montreal just clipping threads. It didn't seem right. And the Jews don't pay you a lot, only a dollar an hour—under the minimum wage. But they gave me a chance to get Canadian experience.

What I didn't understand at first was that, if you had to be at work at eight o'clock and if you got there at five past eight, you'd lose fifteen minutes' pay. Not five minutes' pay but fifteen minutes'. At first I thought, Well, if I got to work fifteen minutes earlier the next day I'd make it back, but that didn't matter to them. I worked there for eleven days until the Manpower course started.

When I finished with Manpower they sent me to a place where there was supposed to be a job for me. I waited a long time to see the boss. When he saw me he said he didn't ask Manpower to send anyone. I thought that was strange. I said, "I didn't go to Manpower asking for this job. They called me." I told him that Man-

---

2. The Department of Manpower and Immigration (1966–77) had responsibility for immigrants and immigration policies. It was superseded by the Canadian Employment and Immigration Commission in 1977.

power wouldn't send me there unless they'd received a request from his factory. Right then I realized that all the people I'd seen in the factory were white. There were no blacks in there. So, I figured that was the reason he didn't want me—just being black.

I went back to Manpower, and I told the man that the factory didn't accept me. He said, "Okay, I am going to send you to a different place. It's called Town and Country Uniform." He told me where the place was and who to ask for. I asked him, "Could you call them first and tell them I am black?" He said, "Why do I have to do that?" I told him that I thought that it was only because I was black that I didn't get the job this morning and that I didn't want to go to the new place and have the same thing happen again. In the United States you know where the prejudices go, but in Canada they don't want you to realize that it's there. They try to cover it up.

So, he called up the man at Town and Country Uniform and said that he was sending over a black woman. The man was Italian. He said that he didn't care what color she was, as long as she could work. So, I went, and he gave me the job. It was a small factory, a family thing run by four brothers. There were about twenty-five workers, and I was the only black. I got on great with them, but after five months things got slow. The boss called me in and told me that, since I was the last to come, I'd have to be the first to go. He said he'd help me get unemployment, and then, when things picked up, he'd call me back to work.

I didn't think I wanted to get unemployment, so I went and found a job in a different place. That was Dominion Lock in west Montreal, near the Bluebonnet Race Track. It was near to where we lived, so I could walk to work. I cut keys and assembled locks. I worked on straight pay, no bonus. But then one day there was going to be some bonus work available after we finished our regular allotment. All morning I did my locks as fast as I could, so I could get the bonus work after lunch. When lunchtime came I had just one box left. That was a mistake. When they saw how fast I'd done the locks they decided to give me all the locks and to give a new girl who'd just been employed the bonus work. She was white. I told the foreman that I didn't think it was fair. I told him I worked very hard to get the bonus work and the other girl had only just started on the job that day. I even said they could share the bonus work between us. He wouldn't listen. So, I went to the manager. He told me he couldn't do anything about it, that I would have to do the work the foreman had given me.

I said, "You can let me go then."

He said, "Okay, but you people will come back here begging for a job."

"That will never happen to me," I said, and I left.

That was Thursday, and on Friday I went to the street that had lots of the needle trade, and I got a job. I started work with them on Monday. It was section work, putting pockets on shirts. You had to work three months to get a paid holiday. When I was coming near to three months one of the floor ladies started to get very strange. Things that she never found fault about before she found fault about now. Then one of the workers told me that they don't let anybody reach three months, that they change their staff all the time so that they don't have to pay for your holiday. When I heard that I started looking for a new job. When I got off work the next day I took the Metro [subway] across to Town and Country Uniform in east Montreal, the place where I'd been laid off. When the manager saw me he said, "Where did you go? I've been trying to get you. I thought you'd gone back to Barbados. I want you to come back to work." He showed me my sewing machine and said to come to work on Monday. He gave me $1.60 an hour, 10¢ more than I had been getting. I worked there for nine years, until we came back to Barbados in 1977.

Siebert Allman

We saved most of the money we made in Montreal. We always sent our savings back to the bank in Barbados, and then every three months we'd send the passbook down to have them bring it up-to-date. If you kept the money in Montreal and you saw something in the stores, you might spend it. But with the money in Barbados it would take a long time to get it, so you'd forget about it, and you wouldn't buy things.

We also took out a PSP [Personal Savings Plan] to help us save. It was like having a debt, because, if you didn't pay in your $100 every month, they would send you a note. You couldn't draw from it until it had matured. When it matured, in fifteen months, we sent the money to Barbados and started a new plan. One time, when the Canadian dollar went up to $2.03 Barbados dollars, we borrowed $5000 from the bank in Canada to deposit in our bank in Barbados. We had to pay interest on the money we borrowed, but it worked out okay because it made us save even more money. And the Canadian dollar later went down as well.

For the first ten months in Montreal we had a one-bedroom apartment, in Mountainside, near NDG [Notre Dame de Grace]. Then we switched to a two-bedroom apartment on the same street. We had the five kids in one bedroom. When my son was getting big we needed a three-bedroom apartment. It was awkward for him to be sharing a room with the girls when he was getting dressed and when he had to go to the bathroom. We needed a room just for him, so we started to look for a new place. We called about a place, a duplex in NDG, and the man told us to come look at it. A friend took us in his car. We got there just half an hour after we had called, but the man said it was taken. You knew it really couldn't be taken that fast. Our friend called from the corner phone and asked about the apartment, and the man told him to come and see it. Our friend let the man know what kind of person he was. We could have gone to a government office and made a complaint, and the office would have made the man let us have the apartment. But we didn't. You see, the man lived right downstairs. He could have given us problems, and we didn't want any trouble, especially with the kids.

The next place I called I said to the lady who answered the phone, "We're black. If you don't want me, please tell me now because I don't want to waste my time coming for nothing." She said, "Oh, no, no, no, we have nothing against blacks," and we got the apartment. It was in L'acdie, and we were the first colored in the house. There was a Greek family underneath and Armenians above us. The kids used to play together, and the family used to bring up some of their supper for us, and we'd send some of our supper down to them. The Greek husband was weird, but apart from that we'd get along like family.

Aileen Allman

The cold didn't bother me. The first year it didn't affect me at all. I think the heat from Barbados was still in my body. When I first came to Canada I'd see people at the bus stop shivering. I couldn't understand it. I'd say to myself, Is these people sick? I guess I'd never seen people shiver before. Now after the first winter I did feel the cold; maybe it's your blood that changes. But I thought that, as long as you're dressed properly, you won't be cold—you're not cold at work, and you're not cold in the house, so you just make up your mind not to be cold in the street.

But Siebert used to complain a lot. Every evening at six o'clock he'd turn on the TV to see what the weather was in Barbados. He'd say, "What am I doing here? If I was home now, I could go to the beach." We had the most quarrels over that. It was always about Barbados. He used to annoy me so.

I'd say, "I'll never talk against Barbados; it's my country. But you are here now; you are in Canada, so stop talking about Barbados." Siebert could only think about Barbados. We lived there all those years, and we never went to Toronto, never went to Ottawa. He'd say all big cities are the same. Sure, we'd go on picnics outside of Montreal, but that was it.

I got along well with the people in Canada. There are some white ones that are not good, but there are black people that's not good too. So, it didn't really worry me. On the bus I'd meet black people that would avoid you, that didn't want to speak to you. I learned not to speak to people. In Barbados you speak to everybody, but not in Canada. Sometimes I found myself scratching my head when someone talked my way, and I wasn't sure if they were really speaking to me.

It finally came to a point where I just didn't say anything. That was a problem when I came home to Barbados on holiday because I was into the habit of not speaking to people. When you do that here people say, "Look at her now—she thinks she's so great. She thinks she's so proud."

When people at the bus stop in Montreal did speak to you they'd sometimes ask where you come from. Because you're black, they'd think you couldn't be a Canadian. I'd say, "I am from Barbados." Some would say, "What are you doing here?" Lots of people don't know anything about Barbados. They'd say, "Is that part of Jamaica?" or "Is that the Bahamas?" They'd say, "What kind of language do you speak there?" It was frustrating because in Barbados we knew so much about Canada, and they didn't even know who we are.

Siebert Allman

We came home on a vacation in 1974, and we brought along a friend of ours, a French Canadian lady from a poor place in Montreal. When she came here and saw our home and all our family she said, "What are you living in Montreal for?" She loved the climate here, the sea bathing, and all the different foods. She'd say, "What are you trying to achieve? You have everything here, even a home of your own." Well, hearing that made you think different. It was then that we really decided to come home.

People in Barbados have a way of thinking that the grass is greener on the other side. They think England or Canada or America will have more to offer them. But when you go there you see there's really no difference, because in those places you still have to work, you still have to pay your rent, prepare your meals, take up the paper—just like you do in Barbados.

Aileen Allman

It was my husband that really wanted to come back. I was happy in Montreal. I would have stayed. The two eldest girls had graduated and become registered nurses at St. Mary's Hospital. The third daughter wanted to come home. She was just starting at Vanier College in Montreal when she got a letter saying that she was accepted at Barbados Community College. My husband used that as an excuse for us all to come home. He said we should all go home together. So in 1977 we got ready to move. My second daughter then decided that she also wanted to come, but my son wasn't sure. He had all his papers tied up to go into the Canadian Air Force. Daddy [Siebert] kept asking him why he wanted to go into the air force. He said that he would decide within two weeks whether or not he was going home. One day he knocked on my bedroom door and asked to come in. He sat on the bed and said, "Mommy, two weeks hadn't come yet, but I've already made my mind up. I want to go home."

When we first got back it was like being on a holiday. But, as time passed, I began to realize that I wasn't going back to Canada. And then I worried if I'd done the right thing, leaving my work and all up there. Sometimes I still wonder—maybe I should have

told Siebert to go home by himself and see if he really wanted to
be there.

When I came back home people weren't what they used to be.
Even your own family. When you were in Canada they would write
to you and send you cards, and you would send them money or
gifts. But when you are in Barbados you don't have money to do
that. It makes you wonder if people really care about you, or if they
just want the things that you can give them.

When you have traveled people think you're rich, and they try
to see how much they can get out of you. They don't know how
hard you worked for your money. They think money is picked
from trees. We were only able to achieve this, the house and the
cars, because we worked very hard and saved. Even when we were
making good money in Canada I still sewed all the family's clothes,
except for their winter coats.

When we came back here there was gossip and rumor that we
had won the money and that we were keeping it quiet because our
church is against gambling. They just don't know how hard we
worked. We invested all we had in fixing up this house and in a
shop [general store] in the village. The shop didn't work out. It
took all our time, and then we couldn't compete with the supermarkets. The fellows who import food to Barbados have their own
supermarkets, and they put their price under what you can buy it
for wholesale. Take corned beef. I pay $2.00 a tin wholesale, and,
with the freight or my gas and time to go pick it up, I am paying
something more than that. In the supermarket you can buy the
same tin for $1.79, so who is going to buy from me?

But some people wouldn't buy in our shop because they
thought we were already too rich, because we had a big house and
two cars. They didn't want to know that we have a mortgage and
that one of the cars was the girls'. I heard people say, "I go to the
mini-mart—the Allmans are rich already."

And then we had two break-ins, and we lost $900 in stock. The
insurance didn't cover theft; it didn't even cover the window they
broke to get in. It was in the fine print in the policy that they
wouldn't pay. Now where were we going to make up that $900?

When we first came home my husband said that he'd never go
back to Canada. But when the shop didn't work out he started
thinking about it, and he got a Canadian passport as soon as we

became Canadian citizens. But now that he has a good job he never talks about leaving.

Siebert Allman

I don't think much of the fellow that doesn't want to come back to his own country. Every country has its problems. In Barbados, if you discipline yourself, you can make it; that's what I always tell my kids.

Chapter 12

Richard Goddard

Richard Goddard is white. On the coffee table next to the chair where he sat during our interviews were the books he had been reading: Voyage of Discovery, Decorated Men, Spycatcher, Spyplane, Great Battlefields of the World, *and* North American Indians, *and a copy of* Gourmet *magazine. To me they said reams about his experiences after leaving Barbados at age seventeen to go to Canada, hoping to find work in the oil fields. Richard remained abroad for eight years, working as a hotel cook, a laborer on a road gang in the Canadian Rockies, and finally as a policeman in the Royal Canadian Mounted Police (RCMP) in the bush of northern British Columbia and later in Vancouver. Like Errol Innis (chap. 13), he lived in Calgary for two years, although, being white, neither his skin color nor his Barbadian nationality figured much in his adjustment there.*

The Goddards' family history is part of modern Barbadian folklore. A West Indian rags to riches tale, the Goddards two generations ago were poor whites, descendants of servants, fishers, and field laborers, derisively known as "Redlegs." Richard's grandfather left the isolation and poverty of the Redleg communities in the parish of St. John on the island's east coast. He moved to Bridgetown, where he became a shopkeeper, the beginning of what has become one of the island's largest businesses, involving manufacturing, catering services, and supermarkets.

The following narrative is taken from three interviews done in 1988 at Richard's plantation home, named "Bleak House" after Charles Dickens's novel. Like John Wickham, Richard often pondered my questions before beginning to answer, and, like Roy Campbell, he was greatly concerned with accuracy, wanting to make certain that all his recollections were right. When some detail escaped him, such as the name of the Indians in British

Richard Goddard and one of his pigs, 1990.

Columbia whom he dealt with as a Mountie, he would mull it over after I left and report it to me at the next interview.

Today, fifty-five-year-old Richard manages one of the family's businesses, while operating a former sugar estate of his own. At six each morning, before dressing for work and commuting fifteen miles to Bridgetown, he works side by side with his field hands, slopping sixty pigs and checking several thousand broiler chickens and a few head of sheep on 166 acres of land that straddles a scenic ridge in the northern parish of St. Andrew. Richard is well known in Barbados for his outspoken views on the decline of agricultural land and as the founder of the Barbados National Trust's weekly hikes, which were inspired by his experiences in the Canadian North.

To understand my family you have to go back to about 1620 in England, when there were serious quarrels between Oliver Cromwell and the king. Many British were looking for places overseas to get away from the strife; some went to St. Kitts and later, beginning around 1626, to Barbados. There were prominent families who got big tracts of land. And they brought out indentured servants, who had to serve so many years before they would be given their freedom and land to work themselves. I believe my ancestors were servants and fishermen on a large estate owned by the Haynes in the parish of St. John, but much of our early history has been lost due to all the church records being destroyed by fire and hurricanes.[1]

I know my grandfather, Joseph Nathaniel Goddard, was born in 1874. He was the one who moved the family into town [Bridgetown] and into prominence. But he grew up in Clifton Hall Woods, a very poor area. The acre of land his parents rented was so rocky and unproductive that they paid the landowner just four dollars a year. Most other acre parcels rented for twice that.

My great grandparents had a small wooden chattel house and some goats and what were then referred to as "feathered animals"—ducks and chickens. My great grandfather, Joseph Josiah Goddard, was a rum blender on the Haynes estate—every estate had its own rum still—and he was also an animal speculator. Animals in those days, the 1920s, were brought to Barbados from Venezuela. The ship would anchor off the reef, and the animals, mostly steers, would be thrown overboard to swim ashore. My grandfather would stand on the beach and estimate the weight of each animal as it came running up onto the beach.

My grandfather started work as a yard boy on Union Estate in St. George. But he soon decided he wanted something better than working in the fields all his life. And not wanting to become a fisherman, which is what most of his uncles did, he decided to go to Bridgetown to look for work. He walked the fifteen miles to town carrying his belongings in a bag—no underwear, just a sec-

---

1. In a letter to me in September 1988 Richard Goddard included some additional information on his family background, information that he had just received from a researcher in England. "All the Goddards in Barbados," wrote Richard, "descend from Nicholas Goddard, a mariner and bondsman, from Staples Fitzpaines, near Taunton, Somerset, UK. He and his three brothers, who came out [to Barbados] in the 1640s were small planters. About 1700 they fell on hard times and lost their property and became servants, field labourers, fishermen, and shoe-makers."

ond shirt, trousers, and a pair of hand-me-down shoes. This would have been about 1890, when he was sixteen years of age. There was a train to Bridgetown, but he couldn't afford the six cents fare; in those days an agricultural laborer only made ten cents a day.

In Bridgetown, after much looking, he finally got a job as a shop attendant in a small store in Hope Alley. The place was in a shantytown known as the "Ruins," because it had burned in a major fire in 1845 and had never been rebuilt. Like most of the other 850 shops of its kind in Bridgetown, this shop sold the basics—rice, sugar, biscuits, butter, salt fish, and rum. Selling rum is where most shops made money.

After eight years there my grandfather opened a shop of his own: the John Bull Bar on Tudor Street. He got a good start from a friend who ran a stevedoring gang. This friend paid his men every Saturday night in my grandfather's shop. That gave my grand-father customers, since the men would stay to buy drink. In those days there were lots of stevedores in Bridgetown because there was no deep-water harbor, and all the cargo had to be transferred from ships to lighters and then rowed ashore by six to eight men and unloaded again. The shop prospered, and my grandfather opened a meat stall. From his father he had learned to assess the value of an animal. It was said that, after twenty animals had run past him, he could give the total weight of the meat to within a hundred pounds. He earned a reputation for being the most accurate speculator in Bridgetown. He was a scrupulously fair man, and that, I think, brought people to his business. He always used to say, "The man who raised it is entitled to something, and the man who sells it is entitled to something too."

In 1900 he joined with Norman Roach and Company, to operate an icehouse on Broad Street.[2] In those days block ice was cut from rivers in North America and brought to Barbados by ship. Only the upper class could afford it, as ice then cost twelve cents a pound. Most Barbadians hadn't ever seen ice and couldn't even imagine how water could turn into a solid. When the icehouse was built folks traveled in to Bridgetown from all over just to see it. The icehouse made a profit, but it was the rum shop and store that was the start of what is today Goddard Enterprises.

---

2. It was first opened in 1850 by D. P. Cotton.

I grew up in the country, in Graeme Hall Terrace, Christ Church, about four miles out of Bridgetown. There weren't any other children my age out there, so for a number of years I didn't have anybody to play with. I was always big for my age. When I was thirteen I was 5'9" and weighed 175 pounds, head and shoulders above everyone else. I did very well athletically and won everything in my class, but it wasn't because of skill. I was just bigger than the other boys. As I got older, they caught up to me, but by then I had become very health conscious and spent a lot of time training, trying to keep myself fit. I've never lost that habit.

I always liked being outside. In school I always sat by the window or door so I could look out, and I'd make sure there was a bright fellow sitting next to me who could help me. I spent more time looking outside than inside; I really had no interest in the classroom. As early as fourteen or fifteen, I began thinking about going abroad to Canada. Barbados seemed small and lacking in opportunity to me. And, besides, everybody in my family was always telling me what to do. I just wanted to get away and be on my own. I planned to go to the oil fields; in those days boys my age were making a lot of money as drillers in Canada. Once I made a lot of money, I planned to travel and see some of the world.

I chose Canada because I had relatives there. I wasn't so adventurous as to go off to Australia or some country where I didn't have family. My mother had a brother in Calgary, and she arranged for me to stay with him. And so I left Barbados in September of 1953. I was seventeen years old and just out of school. I remember getting pretty frightened when the engines revved up. We were still on the runway when all my great ideas started to disappear. I thought, What the hell am I doing? I am leaving my family, leaving the house where I sleep, leaving the places where I'm given my meals.

But the next day I arrived safely in Toronto, and my uncle, Carl Hassell, met me and took me to his home. For the next two weeks I stayed with different relatives. Then I went off to Calgary to stay with another uncle, Alfred Hassell, and to look for a job in the oil fields. As it turned out, there weren't any jobs. It was the wrong time of year; winter was coming, and they were laying off men. I had to do something. I didn't want to depend upon my uncle. My family owned hotels in Barbados, so I thought I'd try to work in that field. My uncle's father-in-law, Mr. Donaldson, had worked at the Palliser Hotel in Calgary as a house detective, so he took me down there and introduced me. They signed me on as an apprentice cook; that was November third, 1953. Here I was going to be a cook, and I had never in my life so much as boiled water before. At home we'd always had domestic help.

I worked the split shift from eight in the morning to one in the afternoon and then again from five to eight in the evening. Between shifts I went to the YMCA to exercise and swim. I was a bit fanatical about my health and keeping in shape. Except for a few fellows I knew at the YMCA and at the hotel, I didn't have many friends, and I didn't go out much. It was usually late by the time I got home, as I didn't get off work until eight o'clock, and then I walked the three and a half miles home. And, since I had to get up early to start work the next day, I didn't have time to go out. On weekends I wrote letters home and read, and if I went anywhere at all it was for a long walk, usually by myself.

For two years I worked the winter months in the Palliser Hotel, and during the summer I worked in resort hotels in the Rockies—the Banff Springs Hotel in 1954 and Chateau Lake Louise in 1955. The people I worked with in the kitchen at the Palliser Hotel were mostly "DPs"—displaced persons from World War II. Most were from Central Europe and had been in German POW camps.[3] Some were Germans who had been in Allied POW camps. I became friendly with a butcher named Rudy, an Austrian who'd been a machine gunner in the German army. He'd been in a foxhole when a Russian tank came at him. The tank drove right over him, trying to crush him, like you'd squash a cockroach under your shoe. He survived but was captured by the Russians, and they didn't release him from a prison camp until 1953. Then, like me, he came to Canada.

Rudy and some of the others made a real impression on me; memories of them still come back to me. I listened to all their stories about the war and how they'd lost their families. It was very

3. Displaced persons also included deserters, wanderers, East Europeans fleeing the Russians, forced and voluntary laborers, concentration camp victims, Spanish Republicans driven out of Spain when Franco came to power in 1939, and an assortment of other people (C. Holmes, *John Bull's Island: Immigration and British Society, 1871–1971*, 213).

Kitchen staff at the Banff Springs Hotel. On the reverse side of the photograph Richard had written: "The Kitchen Staff, 1954. This picture was taken on the terrace above the swimming pool, with the Bow Valley, with the golf course, and the Fairbone mountain range in the background. The gentleman in the suit is the manager and the one to his right is the chef."

tragic. Having been brought up during the war, I had come to believe that every German, every Italian, every Japanese, and so on was a bad person. But, after I got to know people like Rudy individually, I realized how much I'd been manipulated by politicians and propaganda.

At the Banff Springs Hotel I worked the breakfast shift with another cook. We prepared breakfast for anywhere from 700 to 1,600 guests. Every day we'd cook 150 dozen eggs—half would go into omelettes, and half were fried. I was fascinated by the quantity of food we could prepare. In Barbados, if 2 people have to prepare meals for 15, they think they are overworked. In Canada 2 of us made breakfast for 700 and more. After awhile, though, I got tired of kitchen work. I also began to realize that I wasn't suited to the hotel business. Hotel business is like show business in that you have to drink with the guests and be sociable. I didn't drink, I didn't like mixing with lots of people, and I liked to go to bed early.

I was thinking of looking for other work when I met a Barbadian guy, Barry Peters, who was in the Calgary police force. His job sounded really interesting, and, after thinking about it, I applied. But I was turned down because I wasn't twenty-one. Then I saw a poster saying that the Royal Canadian Mounted Police were taking troops between eighteen and thirty years of age. I applied, and, while waiting to hear from them, I took a job with a work gang building the Trans-Canada Highway near Lake Louise. Most of the men in the gang were older than me; many were over fifty. Most of them were the dregs of society, and many were on the run from the police. Whenever a police car drove into the camp the fellows would melt away into the bush. One of the things I remember best is the quantity of food we ate. In the morning we'd get out of our bunks and line up for the mess hall. There was no talking; we just sat down at long tables and ate and ate and ate. Cereal, pancakes, eggs, bacon, and sausage. If you wanted something, you didn't say, "Please pass the bread." No. You nudged the fellow next to you and pointed at it. Some fellows put away ten eggs, a pound of bacon, and a half-loaf of bread. We ate four times what a person would normally eat, but because of our work we didn't put on weight.

After breakfast we'd be loaded into a pickup truck and our Indian chief, a kind of straw boss, would drive us to the work site. I had an axe and was paired up with another fellow about sixty, who also had an axe. We chopped down trees on the hillsides that were too steep for tractors to get to. There was real skill to cutting down a tree without wearing yourself out. This old man showed me how to drop a tree at any angle. He could take any point on a compass, regardless of the slope and direction of the wind, and make a mark on the ground and then drop the tree right on it. That was real skill.

At night I listened to the men in the bunkhouse. One old fellow talked constantly about having sex with Eskimo women and how they didn't like doing it in a warm room, that they wanted the window open, even when it was freezing. They talked a lot about the crime they'd been involved in. But getting drunk was what they wanted to do most. They'd go into the beer parlors in Lake Louise and come back totally drunk. The older men couldn't hold their urine and would wet the bed and vomit all over the bunkhouse. It really sickened me, but it opened my eyes to a different strata of people, and that was a strata I'd never known in Barbados.

I was still waiting to hear from the RCMP when I left the work gang to drive around the States with some people I'd known at the hotel. There were six of us, three guys and three girls. We drove down the West Coast, across Death Valley to Laredo on the Mexican border and up the East Coast to New York. About 6,500 miles in fifteen days. A fellow who had been a boy pilot in the Luftwaffe drove the whole way. Each night we'd get a motel room for two, and all of us would pile in. As we approached New York, I heard on the radio that Hurricane Janet had struck Barbados. I had a cousin in New York who was training to be a nurse; she had been on the phone to Barbados and told me that everyone in the family was alright. But I decided to make a trip home anyway. I arrived a week after the hurricane. That was September 1955.

Barbados looked as if it had been beaten down with a broom. Tree limbs were broken everywhere, and many trees had been stripped bare. The sea was still very rough, kind of boiling, and most of the island's fishing boats had been sunk or damaged beyond repair. The beaches were strewn with bits and pieces of fishing boats and schooners. Nine thousand houses had been damaged or destroyed, and twenty-two people had been killed, nine of them in a collapsed church. And then there was the added problem of people in positions of authority running off with the storm rations or turning them to their own private use. I think you had to be older and to own your own house to appreciate what the destruction meant to people. At my age all I saw was the damage.

I stayed in Barbados for several months and worked in the family supermarket until I heard that I had been accepted into the RCMP. I joined the RCMP in Ottawa on the twentieth of January, 1956. They immediately sent me to Regina, Saskatchewan, for training.

I arrived there in January, and for the first thirty days it never got warmer than thirty degrees below zero, and once it got down to fifty-five below. One of my first duties was to dig the grave for an officer who had died while out on patrol. The ground was so frozen that we had to burn tires and wood on it for three days before we could shovel it. Not long after that I was given the task of shoveling snow off the path that led to a creek where the officers lived. The day I started there was a blizzard. The temperature must have been thirty below with forty-mile-per-hour winds. I started at eight in the morning, and by noon I hadn't gotten more than twelve feet. Almost as fast as I shoveled, the wind blew the snow back in. The sergeant came along and asked me how I was getting on. "Sergeant," I said, "this is an impossible task." I remember his response well. "If it's possible, it will be done. And if it's impossible, it will still be done." I thought to myself, This man is a real idiot. Only later did I realize that this was part of our training. They were trying to make us decide that, although something might appear impossible, nothing really was and that you must always do your utmost.

Four years later I was stationed in North Vancouver and was out on patrol with a fellow named Dave Harvey. We got a call that a child was drowning in the Copillano River. We rushed down there, and we were met by a young woman with a lot of ten- to twelve-year-old kids. It was the first day of summer camp, and the boys had gone down to the river edge where one of them had slipped and fallen in and been carried downstream. The water was swift and very cold; there was still some ice on the edges. The child had been gone at least fifteen minutes, and no one had heard him cry out, so I knew that he must have drowned. Nevertheless, my partner, Dave Harvey, who was from a farm in Saskatchewan and had never swam before joining the RCMP, stripped down to his underwear and jumped in. He didn't stop to think that the boy had obviously drowned by now or that he should let me, a strong swimmer, go instead. He could have easily lost his own life for nothing. I realized that this was what police training did to you; it programmed you.

There were thirty-two fellows in our training squad—'B' Troop—in Regina; about half were city boys and half farm boys. What really surprised me was that they didn't seem very close to their families. I come from a very tightly knit family, and I took it for granted that all families were that way. But in my squad only

Richard Goddard in the Royal Canadian Mounted
Police, Regina, Saskatchewan, 1956.

two of us out of thirty-two wrote weekly to our families. The rest
only received two or three letters from their parents during the
entire nine months we were in training. I was brought up to
believe that you wrote regularly to your parents and they replied
back just as often. My mother's letters were very newsy, and they
kept me abreast of what was happening in Barbados.

Being the only West Indian and the only colonial in the squad,
I was often the odd man out. During the Suez crisis, which my
squad discussed in a course on foreign affairs, I was the only one to
support Britain's intervention. I was from Barbados, which was still
under British rule; all the other guys were Canadians, and they felt
that it was an imperialistic act.

Being a teetotaler and into fitness, the instructors were often
tough on me, pushing me to see how much I could take. I'll give
you an example. Once I was given the job of grooming a difficult
stallion named Faux Pas. All the other horses had ropes on them,
but Faux Pas was kept in a loose stall, where he was free to rush at
you, bite and kick you. It could take fifteen minutes just to get a

rope on him. Instead of rotating, each man taking a turn grooming him, they kept me on him for months, just waiting for me to be
kicked or bitten.

Another time the instructors tried to embarrass me at the
pool. We are being taught lifesaving, and I am sent to rescue
Instructor Forbes, who is pretending to be drowning. From the
poolside I extend the bamboo pole to him, but he yanks it back,
pulling me into the water, then he descends on me like a hurricane dragging me to the bottom. Fortunately, I am a strong
swimmer and don't lose my calm. I get a big breath as I hit the
water, and I grab Forbes and take him to the bottom of the pool. I
squeeze him and begin to hurt him. He gives me the signal—a
slap—that is used when you have had enough. But I don't let go
and nearly drown him. Everyone cheered when it was over. Forbes
was sort of a bully; he wanted to humiliate me.

When my training was over in October 1956 I was assigned to
E Division in British Columbia. Since I liked the North I applied
for British Columbia, and they sent me to Fort St. James, which was
only a two-man detachment in winter and a three-man in summer.
I was in real wilderness—fifty-six thousand square miles of land
and a population of less than five thousand. Some of the folks
were homesteaders whose parents had come with the gold rush in
1890. There were only three settlements: Fort St. James, Germanson Landing, and Manson Creek. And there was the Takla Indian
reservation. Germanson Landing and Manson Creek had been
gold mining towns around the turn of the century but were now
down to a half-dozen people. Coming from a small island like
Barbados, I found the vastness of the place overwhelming. Even
when I was living in Calgary the distances between things frightened me, and I often didn't go places for fear of getting lost. But
Calgary was nothing compared to the North. The first time I drove
the police van from Fort St. James to Prince George I was terrified:
it was such a long way, about a hundred miles, and there were so
many ways you could go wrong and nobody around to direct you
back on the right road if you did get lost.

I remember well the first person I had to arrest. He was a half-
breed named Phillip Felix. He was drunk and creating a distur-
bance at Camp 24, a half-breed camp in Fort St. James. As I
approached him in the camp, I was preparing myself for a strug-

gle, thinking of what hold I would use on him, how I would subdue him. In my head I was going over my training. But then when he saw me, instead of putting up a struggle, he begged for a chance and meekly followed me off to be locked up for the night.

On the street in Fort St. James there was a single red light on a post that was used to alert us that there was a call at the police station. On New Year's Eve, 1956, not long after I had arrived in town, I was at the dance in the town hall when someone came up to me and said, "Cop, your light is on. The butcher has gone mad." I walked across the road to the butcher's place, and, as I moved through the crowd, I could see him through the window. He was a big man, nearly six feet and over two hundred pounds, with a meat cleaver in his hand, hacking at everything in sight—meat, food bins, countertops. He was making a right mess of the place. As I mounted the front steps, the crowd watched to see what I would do. I couldn't very well run away and say I'd never gotten the call because everyone was there watching, and in front of the crowd was Phillip Felix saying, "C'mon cop, he's yours, what are you going to do with him?"

So, I knock on the butcher's door, and he comes to it with the cleaver still in hand. I say, "Man, it's nearly midnight, and I've come to wish you a Happy New Year. I hope all goes well for you in 1957." He mumbles a threatening reply, which I pretend not to hear, and look in through the doorway. I say, "Man, it's a mess in there. It'd be bad luck to let the new year catch you in this condition." Then I move in the door past him, keeping a careful eye on the cleaver, and I begin to straighten things up. I was really frightened; my whole life began to pass before me. But I managed to say, "I'm cold and thirsty—do you think I could make me some coffee?" He does, and we both sit down and drink coffee. His wife comes out—she is pregnant and crying and mumbling that they have lots of debts and now everything is destroyed and they'll be worse off than ever before.

Most of the people I had to arrest were drunk Indians who were fighting. In very cold weather you weren't allowed to put handcuffs on people, so you had to wrestle them back to the station or to the police van yourself, up and down the snowbanks. They'd be struggling to break away, and you'd be trying to hang onto them without getting too rough. It was like that all winter long. The Indians had an obsession with drink. In the early days trappers and explorers had given them drink in order to get their pelts, and most Indians had never gotten off it. Some say it's a genetic weakness. Once you'd get to know the Indians you realized what tremendous harm it was causing them. We would monitor the stores to see who was buying yeast, sugar, and raisins, to make home brew. We weren't against Indians; we were just trying to protect them from themselves. Their drinking often meant that they neglected their children. They really loved their children, and when they were sober they would spoil them, but because they were drunk so much of the time the children were often left alone, and there would be fights and serious accidents, especially motor vehicle accidents. Some kids died. Money that was needed to feed and clothe them often got spent on alcohol. But when they were sober they loved their children just like Barbadians do.

I had a good relationship with the Indians. They called me Gordi-Gordi, and they often asked where I came from. I would try to explain that I came from an island in the Caribbean sea, off the coast of Venezuela. But they didn't have a clue where any of that was. South America and the Caribbean didn't mean anything to them. Fort St. James was their world.

I would say, "It's a long way off, very far to the south where there is no winter." And they'd say, "You tell us, Gordi-Gordi, that we are drunk and stupid, but you are more stupid to leave a place that is always summer to come up here."

They mimicked my Bajan accent, and they wondered if other people from where I came from spoke like I did. Because of my accent, which made my voice stand out on the police radio, everybody in the region knew me, or at least they knew the voice.

My first sudden death was Bobby Wells. I think what you remember best is the first of each new experience—first arrest, first death, and so on. The Wells family was from Nova Scotia. During the depression they had driven west, as far as the road would take them, and that was Fort St. James. The Wellses' son, Bobby, and his friend had been out on Stuart Lake stealing boom chains—the chains that are used to tie logs together to form a log boom. Their boat became overloaded with chains and was swamped by a wave during a storm, and the men were thrown into the water and drowned. It was October 1956. We got a note from an Indian who had found their boat, and we went out in the police boat to search for them, but a storm came up and forced us to go ashore for the night. We didn't have the right clothing and no food other than a Hershey chocolate bar. All night we sat around a big driftwood fire. We were hungry and cold. And that taught me a lesson: from then on I always carried emergency food; I always prepared for the worst. Little mistakes that don't mean much at other latitudes can be fatal in the North. That's why people leave caches of food and fuel around the place so that, if you're traveling and run out of food, you will have some. You take just enough to get you to the next point, and you leave a note; then as soon as possible, you return what you have taken, plus some extra. It's an unwritten law of the North that you share with others who were in need. Anyway, we didn't find the men's bodies until six months later, after the ice had gone out.

In November 1957 I was transferred to Vancouver and in June the following year, to North Vancouver, to a thirty-man detachment. It was completely different from Fort St. James—we worked regular shifts six days a week, and we were divided into a traffic branch, a criminal investigation branch, and a court prosecutor's office. I had more time off than in Fort St. James, but I still visited the office on my days off to type up my reports or to help a friend. I worked about forty-eight to sixty hours a week, but that was less than in Fort St. James, where, depending on what was happening, I might be on duty seventy-two to eighty hours in a single week. Up there you not only investigated complaints, made arrests, and charged suspects; you also acted as their guard while they were in the cell, cooked and fed them, and then drove them to Prince George, a hundred miles away, or else you flew with them to Vancouver for prosecution. If it was a juvenile, you'd have to take him on the ferry to Nanimo to deliver him to the Bremman Lake Juvenile Center. Then I'd have to hurry back, because my partner was alone and might need my help. Once I didn't wear civilian clothes for three months. I was paid just $2,800 per year, plus uniforms. But I loved it.

I had one experience in Vancouver that drilled into me the importance of family. One Sunday afternoon in 1960 I got a call to go to the North Vancouver General Hospital, where a woman was reported to be interfering with a patient. The matron took me to the ward where this woman, who was about sixty and appeared to be a bit mental, was trying to remove a patient from the hospital. She was claiming that the man in the bed was her son and that she had come to take him home. But the man had never seen the woman before. He was screaming for us to get the woman out of his room. The woman said to me, "A mother always knows her son, doesn't she?"

I said, "I would expect so, but tell me how you know this man is your son." She told me that, as a young boy, her son had been burned and had a large scald mark on his chest. So, I turned to the patient and said, "Would you take off your top and show this woman that you don't have a burn mark? Maybe she will accept that and leave." He did it, and there was no scar. But the woman was undaunted. "Yes, yes, that's my son," she said. "A mother always knows her son."

I had to take her to the Essondale Mental Hospital, where they committed her. Later I learned that she and her husband and their three sons had been in a German prison camp during the war and that her husband and one son had died there. After the war she and her two remaining sons, who were then quite young, had come to Canada. She worked as a char woman, cleaning toilets and washrooms to support them. Her kids were her whole life. But when they grew up they both went off. One joined the Canadian navy, and the other just disappeared. They apparently had never written to their mother, and she had gone mental over the loss. On the weekend I saw her she had heard on the radio that a John Balowski had been admitted to the hospital following an accident. Her son's name was John Palowski, close enough to snap her mind and convince her that her son was this man in the hospital bed. I will never forget that woman. I'm involved with several youth groups in Barbados today, and I always, in variety of ways, tell them to never forget their parents, to write home often.

In the spring of 1957 five RCMPs were drowned in a boating accident in Lake Simco, Ontario. One man was from Vancouver, and I was on duty when the telex came in to advise the next of kin, his parents. I went to their house in uniform and knocked on their door. His mother opened the door and asked me to come in.

Before I could say anything she took me into the living room and pointed to a photograph of a young man in uniform on the mantelpiece and said, "See, we have a son who is a Mountie too." Then I had to give her the bad news, that her son had drowned. Fortunately, her husband was present, and they took it quite well, considering. But notifying the next of kin of a death was the most unpleasant thing I had to do, although you'd be surprised at how much people's reactions vary. I saw everything from people flying into hysteria and violent sobbing to people saying, "He's been trouble to me all his life. It's the best news I have had for a long time."

One thing that surprised me in the RCMP was discovering that there wasn't anybody who didn't have friends or schoolmates who hadn't served time for criminal acts. In Barbados I had never known anyone who had been to court, much less been to jail. On a small island, where everyone knows everyone else, you can't get away with the things you can in a big place like Canada. In my youth Barbados was a strict place. If you committed a crime, you were shunned, treated as an outcast, not allowed to go to school, not even allowed into a public dance. If you were caught smoking in school, you'd be expelled. Canada wasn't like that, and now Barbados is becoming much the same.

In 1959 I married Ignacita Margaret Auxiladora Delgado van den Branden. She was from Venezuela but living in Barbados when I had met her during my visit home after the hurricane in 1956. We had written letters regularly while I was away. In 1959 she came to Vancouver, and we got married, but she didn't stay very long, as she suffers from rheumatoid arthritis and was advised by doctors in Vancouver to return to Barbados or Venezuela. Also, the life of a policeman's wife, moving around and my being away long hours, wasn't good for her, so she returned to Barbados in 1960. I went home on a leave but then returned to Canada to finish my five years of service in the RCMP. In 1961 I returned home for good, to be with her and our new son, Rene Bruce.

We moved into my parents house in St. Philip, and, although I very much enjoyed being with my parents, I really wanted a place of my own. So, after six months we moved into a flat. I started work with a cousin, David Patterson, at Harrisons [department store]. I was in commissions, representing an overseas manufacturer and going into shops and stores to take orders for merchandise. I worked for a commission of about 5 percent. The money was alright, but the job was dull, especially after the excitement and physical contact of police work, so after a week I moved over to the family supermarket—Goddard's Food Fair—in Kensington. It had opened a year earlier and was only the second supermarket in Barbados. Barbados was quite advanced in those days; in fact, Barbados got its first supermarket in 1950, before England had one.

Working in the family business, I was okay financially, but I still really missed being a policeman. For a long time the RCMP had been my whole life, and, although I was back in Barbados, at heart I was still a policeman from the bush. Police work was so ingrained in me that, rather than concentrating on making sales in the supermarket, I was looking for people doing wrong, looking for theft. Most customers and staff say that I still stand out as a policeman. I have a reputation with the criminal population of Barbados as being a man that will prosecute [shoplifters]. There's a rumor around that, if you steal from my store, I'll beat you up. It's not true, but it's good preventive publicity.

Today my energies are spent more on the preventive side, especially working with young people. For about a decade now I've been involved in the Duke of Edinburgh Awards Scheme, taking young people out hiking around Barbados and on expeditions to other islands.

It took me fifteen years to really adjust, to really feel content being home in Barbados. I don't think I was really content until 1976, when I went back to Canada for my troop's reunion. There I met a close friend of mine from the RCMP whose house I had lived in. Another friend told me about his two sons and how they had gone bad, committing thefts and so forth. The father had found out, and he had to arrest them and put them in jail. That was a real shock to me; I had known how close he was to his children. They were the apples of his eye. More than anything, that story made me realize how much better off I was in Barbados. Had I remained in Canada, I wouldn't have had the same control over my own son that I did here. In Barbados, if my son ever did anything wrong, somebody would have noticed it very quick and taken me aside and said, "Richard, your son is in bad company." Barbados is a much better setting to bring up a child: the island is small, and there are lots of family members around to love and care for kids. Also, the weather allows kids to be outside much of the time, and that's good for them.

But Barbados is not all rosy. I've found it hard to accept the corruption and political favoritism that has become common here since independence in 1966. People turn a blind eye to the wrong-doings of their family and friends; if you have connections with people in power, you can break the law and get away with it. There has been a lot of corruption in land deals. Large landowners and speculators have gotten around the laws designed to preserve agricultural land and have sold it off for development, at huge profits to themselves. Often lawyers are involved in these deals, many of whom are the biggest criminals.

I have a very strong sense of what is right and what is wrong. I have difficulty understanding how people can tolerate obvious wrongdoing. The way people in the government handled the sudden death of the prime minister in office was shocking.[4] When he died there was strong suspicion that it was from a drug overdose. Yet there was no autopsy, no attempt to find out the real cause of his death. None. Instead they all closed ranks and gave him a great funeral. What kind of message does that send to the young people of this island? You will never see me make a donation to a political party in Barbados, no way.

Even our history is being distorted by people in government who know better. I'll give you an example. In 1816 there was a slave revolt in Barbados in which cane fields were set on fire, and one-fifth of the island's sugar crop was ruined. Thirty rebels were killed, and about three hundred people were later executed after the trial. The revolt was organized and led by free coloreds, but credit is now given to an African slave named Bussa. It's now called "Bussa's Rebellion," and a statue of Bussa has been erected, and a street is named Bussa Road. Yet, Bussa was only a minor leader on the plantation where the revolt started. He isn't mentioned as being an organizer of the revolt in any of the accounts written at

---

4. Prime Minister Tom Adams died suddenly on 11 March 1985.

the time. You see, the black politicians and political activists in Barbados wanted a black African hero, like Cuffy in Guyana.

Today we have weak and corrupt politicians who give public contracts on racial grounds. I know of contracts that have been awarded to people who had bid 20 percent above their competitors. Then the politicians turn around and go to developed countries to beg for aid money to run this small country.

Although I work in commerce, running a supermarket, it's not my first love. My main interest is in agriculture, which has been the backbone of this island's existence for the past 350 years. For a long time I have been saying that we must keep our land in production and that we must grow as much of our own food as possible and not be so dependent on the outside for basic necessities. Over twenty-five thousand acres of arable land have been taken out of production since 1963, of which ten thousand were used for housing. That's one-third of Barbados' total arable land. Two to three more acres are now being taken out of production every day. If that rate continues, there will be no arable land left in Barbados by the year 2010, and the island will look like some North American city. That would be a disaster. It's essential that Barbados not let this happen, but a lot of wealthy, powerful landowners, who publicly express great concern over the land situation and the decline of the sugar industry, really don't care. They don't want to preserve agriculture when they can make fortunes by letting their land be developed. People don't like what I say about corruption here; even newspapermen who have interviewed me usually don't print what I say—it's not what their readers want to hear.

Today I'm finally able to practice a bit of what I've been preaching. In 1979 my wife and I separated, and I began to look for a new place to live, a place with land that I could work. I'd done a lot of hiking on this island, and I knew about this place.[5] So, when the house and land [166 acres] was put up for sale I bought it. I won't grow sugarcane here because the land is slipping, and sugar prices are too low. Instead, I'm putting in

5. Known as Bleak House after Charles Dickens's novel, the house was a burnt shell when Richard bought it. It had been the big house to a small sugar estate, named Burnt House Plantation. It is located high on a ridge, with a commanding view of the Scotland district and the island's east coast.

coconuts and bananas, and when the coconuts grow tall I'll run beef cattle under the trees. I am now producing 400 pigs and nearly 125,000 broiler chickens per year to ensure the cash flow I need to make improvements. This place gives me the chance to prove that what I preach, that keeping land in production and finding alternatives to sugar, is practical in Barbados. Although I am still subsidizing this place out of my income from the store, in three years I should be able to live off the land and continue with my plans for crop diversification and make this agricultural land profitable.

Chapter 13
Errol Inniss

Errol Inniss was a student migrant. He received a scholarship to study in Canada and was sent to a technical college in Calgary, a western city with very few blacks. The social environment of Calgary was nearly the opposite of the one Errol came from. "The Barbados I was raised in," said Errol, "was a colonial environment where 95 percent of the people were black, but the whites ran everything. As children, we got the impression that whites were superior people. But in Calgary just about everyone was white, and at that time some folks thought that we blacks were superior."

Errol adjusted easily to student life at the Southern Alberta Institute of Technology in Calgary, which in part was due to his outgoing, at times flamboyant, personality. One of his close friends describes him as a "lover of life, a guy who likes fun and a party, who loves to holler and laugh."

Errol's return home was more difficult. Ignored by the government agency that had promised him a job after graduation, he drove a taxi and "hustled" white female tourists. At first he was unable, or perhaps unwilling, to integrate back into Barbadian society; he clung to his Canadian identity. He wore cowboy boots, plaid shirts, and a leather jacket, ate steak and french fries, and spent his time at the tourist hotels with North Americans. But in time he obtained a white-collar job, and he went back to the university. It was not until he shed his Canadian ways, leaving the tourist nightclub scene and giving up white girls for a steady Barbadian girlfriend, that he was, in his words, "accepted again as a reasonable human being." Although Errol was only away from Barbados for two years, his experiences in Canada had a profound effect on him. He is an example of how even short stays overseas may produce significant changes in an individual's life.

243

Errol Inniss at work, 1984.

I arrived in Calgary in October of 1972, a couple of days before the school term started. I checked into a motel, but the next day I got a place to live in student housing on campus. And the next day it snowed, and all I had was summer clothes. Okay, it's your first time off the island, and here you are in Calgary, a city with 300,000 people, more people than all of Barbados, and they are all white, and it's snowing. All those white people looked the same to you—you didn't even know if you is seeing the same person twice. I was three days in the city before I saw the first black person. He was a Trinidad guy, who turned out to be a pimp. I made friends with him. But before I go on I need to tell you why I was in Calgary.

When I was twenty-two I was working here in Barbados for a telecommunications company. It seemed to me that, as I looked around that company, there were a lot of middle-aged people who were unhappy with their work. You'd hear them complaining that they were at the top of the pay scale and that they'd have to wait four years for the union to renegotiate the contract before they could get another increase. The job was just a paycheck to them. I said to myself, This is not what I want to be doing in ten years. So, I started to look around for other things to do, and I started to think about continuing my education. One of the things that caught my eye was a small ad, in the classified section of the newspaper, in which the Canadian government was offering scholarships to people in developing nations. The ad said you could pick up an application form at the Ministry of Education. So, I went in and took the exam and applied for it.

Well, a month later the Canadian National Development Agency offered me a two-year scholarship. They chose the subject that I was to study and the college. They wanted me to learn a field that was lacking in Barbados, and they decided that technical studies in television would be the best, and they decided that I would go to the Southern Alberta Institute of Technology.

When I received the letter telling me that I would be in Calgary, Alberta, I had to get out my dad's big atlas to find it. It was really far away. I didn't know anything about the place, and here it was the first time I was going to leave the island.

The arrangement was that I would be there for two years, after which I would return and work for the government of Barbados. I had to sign a bond stating that I would return here, and to get out of the bond I would have to repay x amount of dollars per year, since the scholarship was worth about six thousand Canadian dollars. It was to cover all my costs, like tuition, housing, travel, and even clothing.

There was about two thousand students, but only a half-dozen were blacks. One was a St. Lucia guy, who got a scholarship just like mine. And there were a couple of guys from Guyana and Trinidad, who had first emigrated to eastern Canada but didn't like it there; being more adventuresome than most, they had moved out west to try to make their fortune. They were older students and were working at jobs like driving a cab while they went to college.

It was through these guys that I got to meet a few more blacks. But they mainly lived in Edmonton, which was 180 miles north of where I lived. As a student, I couldn't go to Edmonton every weekend, so the guys up there became acquaintances more than friends. They were mostly Jamaicans. They were living in Edmonton but working as welders much further north in Fort MacMurray. They would work three straight months and then have three months off.

After a while most of my friends were white, and even my best

friend was white. We met in class. The first day of class we are
assigned seats in alphabetical order, and the guy sitting on my left
is Wesley Hannemayer. He is an *H,* and I am an *I.* We meet, and we
chat, and he is an extremely nice guy. Two months later, in
December, it's winter vacation, and everybody in the residence hall
is going home. The other guys can travel home because they are
from Saskatchewan, Alberta, and BC [British Columbia], but,
poor me, I am from Barbados, which is nine hours flying and costs
a bundle. I can't go home for the winter break, so Wesley takes me
home with him. I meet his family, and they introduce me to skiing.
They provide me with a ski outfit and all the ski gear and teach me
how to ski.

Wesley and I became great friends. Even to this day he still
comes down to Barbados every year to visit me. I spent last
Christmas with him in Atlanta, where he now lives. Him being
seated next to me in that class made a big change on my life, and it
had a change on his life too. He got to know my background and
my culture, and after he got out of college he joined the Canadian
University Services Overseas and spent two years in Africa teaching
and doing volunteer work. Now he can eat more pepper than I
can.

When it came to meeting women I was in Calgary at a very
fortunate time, for me as a black West Indian. Western Canadians
didn't seem to like black Americans, and they were unsure about
Jamaicans. But if you were from somewhere else in the Caribbean,
they would go absolutely out of their way to make you comfortable.
I met an awful lot of women on campus. And I got involved with
some of them.

It seemed that the myth of the black man being superior in
bed was at its height then. There were an overwhelming number of
women who tried to get you in bed. To give you an example: there
was one time when I was at a hotel bar in Calgary. This girl comes
over and starts chatting to you; within seconds another girl comes
over and starts chatting. By the end of the night the two of them
are squabbling over who is going to be first in bed with you. Now,
that took a little getting used to—not that you minded.

After my first winter, when I learned how to ski, I could go out
onto the highway with my skis and hitchhike to Banff [National
Park], no trouble at all. And it would almost always be a woman

that would stop and pick you up. They would say that they'd never seen a black man ski and they just had to give you a lift to see if you was for real. Then, sometimes, after they found out that this black guy could really ski, they wanted to find out what this black guy could do in bed. I had no problems in that way. It was the right time of my life for that—I was in my early twenties and out of the teenybopper stage and looking for fun.

I was friendly with this one girl on campus, and she invited me to her home for dinner. But she didn't tell her mother that I was black. When I arrived it was like *Guess Who's Coming to Dinner.*[1] The old lady absolutely freaked right out. She was speechless. But after the initial shock wore off she was very nice, and we later became friends.

I never really experienced any open color prejudice in Calgary. There was always prejudice there, but it was mostly toward the Indians, which I couldn't understand because the Indians were there first. The Canadians have them all living on reservations, where they have a real hard life. A lot of the Indians leave the reservation and come into town to drink, and then they get rolled by prostitutes. It's very sad the way they are treated.

Generally speaking, people went out of their way to prove to me that they were not prejudiced against blacks. I must admit that sometimes I took advantage of that. I'd say to myself, Okay, if you want to prove to me that you are not prejudiced, then go right ahead, prove it, I don't care. People would be exceptionally nice, and I'd never say no. I'll give you an example. The first time my buddy Wesley took me home to his parents' place his father had just bought a new '74 T-Bird. The father wouldn't let Wesley drive it, but he offered me the keys on account of my being older. He said that I could drive Wesley around in it. Here you are—you don't know the city at all while Wesley has lived there all his life, and the father lets you have the keys. What do you do? It was dumb, but I didn't say no. I honestly think that the father was trying to prove to me that he wasn't prejudiced. But he was being too nice.

I found that I never had a problem getting anywhere. If really

---

1. The title of a 1967 film in which a young woman (Katharine Houghton) brings her fiancé, a black man (Sidney Poitier), home to her unsuspecting parents.

pushed, I'd stick my thumb out, and some chick would usually give me a ride. And one night it wasn't even a chick. I am walking home, it's around midnight, and I'm the only person on the street. A cop stops and asks me who I am and what I am doing. I tell him I am a student living in the res [residence halls] and that I'm walking home from my girlfriend's place. I show him my student ID, since I'd been warned that in Calgary you always have to have your ID on you, not like in Barbados. Then the cop asks me if I'm Jamaican. I get the strong impression he doesn't like Jamaicans too much. I tell him that I'm from Barbados, and after that he is real nice, and he puts me in his car, and he drives me home.

Going to Canada was a physical shock for me. It was the first time that I had experienced temperatures below about 70 degrees, or maybe on a rare occasion I'd seen it get down to 65 here. Anyway, I went straight from balmy Barbados into 30- and 40-degree temperatures, and since I arrived in October each week would get colder and colder, until in winter the thermometer sometimes would get down to 40 below. My friends always think you are overdressed, but you are really just trying to get warm.

Most of the people I met didn't know where Barbados was. Many assumed it was part of Jamaica. But that began to change when the weather report on the radio started giving the temperature in Barbados. I think it was the Barbados tourist board that got the radio station to do that, and it worked well. When people didn't know where Barbados was I'd show them my passport, which I always had with me. On my passport cover was a map of the West Indian islands, starting with the tip of Florida and coming right down the chain to Trinidad and Tobago. So, I could say, "Okay, here is Florida, here is Jamaica, and there is Barbados." They would always say, "Oh, it's really far south."

I remember how different the scale of things was compared to Barbados. When I moved into the residence hall I was on the ninth floor. At that time the highest building in Barbados was three floors, and I could walk to the top before the elevator would get there. In Calgary the elevator would take right off with you, shoot you right up, leaving your tummy down below.

And all the roads were different. You go to cross the street in

Barbados, and in three steps you are across. You try doing that in Calgary, and you are in trouble. You had to be prepared to cross two roads at the same time. You had to stop when you were halfway across and look again before you could finish crossing. That took getting used to.

Then, in terms of speaking, it took you at least two months before anybody could fully understand what you were saying, in spite of the fact that we were all speaking English. The Canadians were always saying, "Pardon me," and I was forever repeating myself. I got tired of doing that, and I found it was easier to change my speech. It took me about two months to slow down my speech and to learn not to clip off the beginning and ending of words. You had to make sure that you pronounced each word fully. I didn't try to mimic the Canadians but to develop my Bajan speech in a way that Canadians could understand.

Then, too, a lot of the words they used didn't make sense to me, and a lot of words I'd use didn't make sense to them. For example, they would say, "Where is your can?" I'd say, "What do you want a can for? I got a can of juice, and I got a can of beans— what kind of can do you want?" And they would all laugh. You see, in Canada they call the toilet a can. They meant the bathroom. And there were a lot of other words that I didn't know too. One was *dink*. They kept calling certain people dinks. You'd think to yourself, What is a dink? It sounds like *sink*. But why would they call somebody a sink? Then you'd finally discover that a *dink* is a penis, and they are calling these people pricks. That was 1972, so they are probably calling people something else today.

Even their eating habits were different from mine. The food was awful; it had no taste. I wondered if they knew about seasoning. They always cooked their rice plain; they never seasoned it or mixed in peas. And when they cooked rice they'd cook the minute stuff—that's the minute rice you buy at the supermarket, the stuff you just drop in hot water, and it swells up. To me that's not rice.

But after a while I discovered that there were other types of food besides Canadian, and some of it was really good. In Calgary you could have virtually any type of food that you wanted. I couldn't believe that some places would even bring the food to you. Say you wanted Chinese tonight, you could take up the phone and dial a Chinese food place, and they would send it over in a car. In Barbados, if you want to eat Chinese, you have to get in your own car and drive over there.

But when it came to liquor you could only buy that in a special store run by the government. There was a joke on me about this. I was with some of the guys—it was in winter of my first year—and I had brought up a gallon of Mount Gay rum from Barbados. We were sitting around drinking, and we didn't have any pop, or, as we called it, any chasers, so we drove to a corner store to buy some pop. The other guys went inside while I stayed in the car. Then, I thought to myself that I'd better go in and buy some more rum, so I go in and ask the man for a bottle of rum. Well, they all laughed at me, and I couldn't figure out why they were laughing. Only then did I learn that you can't buy liquor at a corner store. In Barbados the corner store will sell you whatever you want, and you don't have to be a certain age. If you want, you can send an eight-year-old kid to the shop to buy you another round.

Another thing that freaked me out was that on Friday evenings everybody would leave class and go line up to get in a bar. It's below freezing, and there in the street is a line waiting to get into a bar, waiting to sit down and drink beer. I could not believe it. You had to stand in line if there wasn't any seating inside the bar, because the bars weren't permitted to let you drink standing up. And there was a rule that, if you wanted to move from one table to another, you couldn't take your drink with you; the waiter has to come and move the drink. Well, there was no way that I was going to stand outside in subzero weather.

After the first year in Canada I realized how much I'd changed by living there—and that I was continuing to change. Sometimes I'd sit down on a quiet night and would think about what I'd be doing if I was back home, compared to what I was doing in Calgary. It was so different. I'd say, Hey, my life's taken a totally different road. And, hey, you know something, this ain't bad. I'm enjoying it. I'm not missing what's happening back home. Only in the quiet moments would I even remember home.

I always felt that I was accepted and that I always had something to do, whether it was going to somebody's home for dinner or out for a drink with a group. I didn't just hang out with one group. I had several different groups of friends who did different things. I had the bad group from town—the pimps and prostitutes—and the goodie group from campus.

Now, not every Barbadian who goes away will go through what I did. Because I was an outgoing person, I got out, and I became part of the Canadian scene. And I tried to learn as much about Canada, about its history and its politics, as I could. And I traveled around during the vacations. I met West Indians who didn't get out, who moped and groaned about the cold and spent all winter in the house.

I came back home to Barbados in the fall of 1974, when I finished my education, just as the scholarship required me to. I'd like to sue the Barbados government. When I came back I reported to the Ministry of Education, the people that granted the scholarship. They said they'd never heard of me. They said they didn't know anything about my being away, that they had no job for me, and that they were very sorry. I said, "Well, if you don't know who I am, then release me from my bond"—the bond that guaranteed that I would return to Barbados at the end of my studies—"so that I can go back to Canada." They didn't like that idea. They then wrote and told me that they had suddenly found my papers, but they still had no job for me. You see, the people in the ministry weren't interested in helping me; they were just a bunch of diehards who had been working there for years and years, thinking only of their own security, thinking they owned the place. They weren't concerned with anybody else. I tried to sue them, but I didn't get anywhere, and it was costing me a lot of money that I didn't have.

I spent until March of the next year literally looking for a job. This was right in the middle of the energy crisis, and there were no jobs. In Calgary I didn't even know there was an energy crisis. It wasn't until I came here and saw everybody lining up to get petrol that I realized how bad it was. People were leaving their cars in line overnight at the gas station so that the next morning they could get the few gallons you were allowed.

I tried to get back to Canada, but you needed a job to get back, and I didn't have one. I thought about going back to get married to a girlfriend I had in Calgary, but I really didn't want to do that. So, with no job, I started partying like I'd done before. By then the tourist industry was well on its way here, so I would go to the hotels at night and look for Canadians. You see, when I came back here I was all western Canadian. I came dressed in a Stetson; I wore plaids and cowboy boots, a leather shoulder bag, and a leather jacket. And I ate Canadian food—steak, fries, salad, and garlic bread. I hardly ate fish anymore. I was all Canadian.

At first I wasn't too worried about not having a job right away, since I had saved some of my scholarship money to live on. But, with renting an apartment, the money started running low, so I had to start driving a taxi. My old man wasn't too happy with that. He had figured the family had gotten above that kind of work. But, as far as I was concerned, I was gainfully employed.

The money wasn't very good. I drove someone else's taxi, and he got 75 percent of the take. If I made twenty-five dollars a week, I was doing well. It didn't pay, but I was young then, and I wasn't so real with money. Besides, there was a little extra benefit. I used to work out of the Paradise Beach Hotel. At first I worked the days, but then I reached the stage where I didn't have to start driving until five o'clock in the evening. I liked to get dinner trips. If I was lucky, I would be giving a ride to a couple of girls to dinner. On the way in the taxi I would usually make a pass at them, and by the end of the night I'd have dinner on their head [expense]. Then I might see them for the next two weeks, and that's how I got money. I got quite good at it—at being a gigolo. And I kept the taxi, too, so that I didn't have to worry about having my own car. I still did some driving in order to make the taxi owner some money. In the morning I'd be in my taxi gear, and in the night I'd be properly dressed in my Canadian clothes. And I ate very well because I used to eat out, and at the best restaurants.

In those days we weren't beach bums like the guys who hustle white tourists on the beaches today. Today you got guys pushing dope, pushing coral [jewelry], and hassling fifteen-year-olds. I am proud to say that in my time we were very professional. It was a different scene back then. Some of the guys who were gigolos on the club scene back then are today executives like me. You had some pretty sophisticated guys then.

In the meantime, I kept pressing the government for a job. Finally, they offered me a part-time, six-month job with the CBC [Caribbean Broadcasting Company]. I went to work every day, and, as I got to know the staff in the department where I worked, I discovered there were a half-dozen people who rarely showed up for work. And two fellows would usually come in drunk and then spend the rest of the day drinking at the shop. Hardly anybody did any work. The place was a wreck. After awhile I begged for a job with another telecommunications company, and they hired me.

By now I've been home for a couple of years, and I am starting to get back into Barbadian society. I am spending less time on the nightclub scene. But by then I have a reputation that I don't like black people, because I was only seen at night and always at a hotel with some white chick.

At the new job I was starting to use some of the things I had learned in Canada. I was being helpful, and I thought I was doing good work. Then I find out that my colleagues are getting hostile towards me because I am working too quickly, and maybe because I know more than they do. When something went down [wrong] I would fix it. And when everything was working okay I would look for things to do. I'll give you an example of the problem I had.

Here I am at this radio and television station, and they don't even have a television in the lobby. I mean, they don't have a house system so that you can hear what is on the air. Unless you are actually in the studio, you wouldn't know what was on the air. So, when somebody calls in to the station to ask a question about what was just on the operator can't even answer the question because she doesn't know. Of all the stations that I visited in Canada, even the little ones, every one had a television in the lobby. So, I decided that I would wire the station for a house system. I went to the chief engineer with my idea. "Yes," he says, "that would be a good idea." So, I get the cabinet wood for the speakers, and I start running the wires all through the place. Then, suddenly, the word comes down that the project must stop. I don't know why; I can only conclude that somebody thought I was a little too pushy. You see the place was staffed with people who left school [who didn't go to college]. They went to work for the radio station when it started. They learned radio by working at radio, and they had no external training. A lot of things that are considered normal in radio and television today, things that I learned as a student, they had not been exposed to. So, here I am, a junior, not a senior, but a junior—a just hired technician off the street. But I have training, and nobody else in there has training, even the chief engineer doesn't have training; the announcers don't have training; the general manager is trained but not in radio and television. So, here I am, this new guy, suggesting that they make some changes. They didn't like suggestions coming from the bottom, and after about six months they fired me out through the window.

Okay, so now I need another job. I go from radio and television, where I have training, to an assembly line, assembling semiconductors for a new firm that had just come to Barbados. But it's all individual people interacting with machines. There is little human interaction. You don't meet anybody new. At eight o'clock in the morning the doors open, and all the workers herd in, put on their starlight gear, and sit in front of the bonders or whatever machine you are working at. When you look up to breathe you see the supervisor looking down at you saying get back on the job. Everything is meeting deadlines—so many units to be finished at a certain quality level by a certain time. Deadlines, deadlines, deadlines.

But now I am really getting back into society. I'm going steady with a Barbadian girl, and I'm off the nightclub scene.[2] I'm starting to be accepted again as a reasonable human being. People finally figured out that I actually liked black people, that I wasn't just interested in whites.

But I'd ask myself, Why am I working in an environment where I must live under the bell? The bell rings for work, the bell rings for break, the bell rings for lunch, and the bell rings at 4:30 to go home. I'd say to myself, I didn't study in Canada to work like this. So, I decided to go back to university. That was 1977. I applied and got into Cave Hill [the University of the West Indies campus in Barbados]. About the same time there is a job advertised for a computer programmer with National Cash Register, a company which is just getting into computers. I don't know anything about computer programming, but, just like with the scholarship to Canada, I apply for the job. The company gives me a bunch of tests, and I come out extremely well. Since the company wants somebody to be trained in computers, I get the job.

---

2. In July 1980 Errol married his girlfriend, Lila. She had also lived overseas, having worked as a nurse in London for five years. Today she is a travel agent in Bridgetown.

So, at the same time I'm able to both get a job and go back to university and do computing courses for a degree. Later the company changed hands and has since become a full computer company. I've been able to grow with the company, from a programmer to an analyst and then into software support and now into computer services. I'm now responsible for all software services within the English-speaking Caribbean.

But I worked damn hard to get where I am. I learned by taking down the manuals and sitting down long hours in front of the computer. People can tell you that anytime they passed the office, whether it be Sunday, Monday, a bank holiday, day or night, my car was always there. I was on the computer learning it. And when I went as far as I could on my own, when I started reading things I couldn't understand without more background, then I went back to the university and took a few more courses. It's because I became knowledgeable about the product, showed interest, and acquired the basic foundations that I'm where I am. Today I have people working for me, and one of them used to be my boss.

But it's also clear to me that none of this would have happened if I'd not gone to Calgary. It changed me. I returned to Barbados a totally different individual. As I said before, I was all Canadian, and I was more broad-minded. Today I know a lot of things that people here just aren't aware of. And I am not talking about business. I'm talking about the basic behavior of people. And taking a course in human relations is not going to teach you that. Having somebody stand up there in a class lecturing to you about behavior is not the same thing as living it. When you do a course you are still in your own environment, in your own society. But when you are placed in a different society you are forced into new situations, real living situations which you must cope with. You are shocked. It's not like the classroom; it's life, and you had better be able to deal with it.

In business I find that a lot of Barbadian businessmen who have never been off the island are narrow-minded. They have a high resistance to change. Very, very high. Unfortunately, it's too late for most of them. They are too trapped in their careers to go live in another environment, to experience another society now. Besides, you have to do it when you are younger, before you get too set in your ways. I would like to see every Barbadian spend a few years away, and I don't mean going to Brooklyn or Toronto, because in going to Brooklyn or Toronto you are not really leaving Barbados. Sure, the climate changes, and the buildings are different, but the social environment—if you're hanging out with other West Indians—doesn't. You see too many Bajans there. I am talking about going somewhere in the middle of Europe, Africa, western Canada, or the western United States, where you can't hang out with other West Indians because there aren't any there. I'm talking about going to a place where you must make it on your own. When you are put in a different environment you discover: Hey, you know what? I can't change all these people—I gotta change. You gotta change yourself if you're going to get along. And your whole scope, your whole thinking, does change. You appreciate people more for what they are; you become more broad-minded, and you learn to listen better. You learn that there are other, better ways of doing things.

As a result of living in Calgary, I've been able to take my licks here, especially during the period of time that I couldn't find any work. The average Barbadian guy in my position, not being able to find work, would have given up his own place and moved back home, gone back to his parents and his brothers and sisters. I didn't. In true North American style I took my licks, and I continued to live on my own and to pay my rent. I continued to manage my own affairs.

If I hadn't been exposed to new things like I was in Canada, I would have never gone into computers. And I probably would have never found the work that I really enjoy doing. So, I'll always be indebted to the Canadian government for placing that little ad in the newspaper. It has had a fantastic effect on my life.

Errol Inniss was the first person I interviewed for this book in 1985. A year later, on my next trip to Barbados, I phoned Errol to ask what he had thought of the draft of his narrative that I had mailed but had never gotten a reply. His secretary said that he had died of prostate cancer five months before. He was thirty-eight years old. He had been seriously ill when I had interviewed him but had never mentioned it. His doctor had lost an early set of X rays and then misdiagnosed his illness. A year passed before Errol learned the real cause of illness, when Wesley Hannemayer, his college friend, asked him to come to Atlanta for a second medical opinion. The time lost in getting the right treatment may have made the difference between life and death. Nevertheless, Errol refused to let his wife sue for malpractice. In planning his own funeral, he asked people to give money to the Barbados Cancer Society rather than buy flowers. On the first anniversary of his death the cancer society sponsored a ten-kilometer race with the slogan "Run for Errol."

Part 4
Interpretations

Chapter 14

Immigrants in the Metropole

In the previous ten chapters thirteen Barbadians talked about their lives as migrants in England and North America then as returnees in Barbados. In reading their stories we have gotten to know them as individuals, and in the process we have seen the great diversity in their experiences and adjustments. While there is no typical Barbadian migrant story, threads do run through their accounts that we can pull together. My aim in the next two chapters is to look for patterns in their experiences. The task now is to use the narratives—these insiders' views of emigration—as data to build some generalizations. I am mindful, however, that the small size of our sample, just thirteen individuals, limits how much we can say.

All of the migrants in *Double Passage* left Barbados with the expectation that they would find better opportunities for themselves abroad. Seven persons (Siebert and Aileen Allman, Cleve Thornhill, Roy Campbell, Gabby, Richard Goddard, and John Wickham) emigrated primarily to find work; four (Errol Inniss, Valenza Griffith, Rose Thornhill, and Janice Whittle) went to further their education or learn a profession; and one (Ann Bovell) went primarily to join her husband. But we also heard many of them talk about their desire to see a "bit of the world," what the "mother country" was really like, and "how the other half lives." Roy Campbell, Norman Bovell, and Valenza Griffith were also influenced by the fact that many other Barbadians were emigrating and that it was the "thing to do."

In short, there were often several considerations in their decisions to emigrate, and economic motives were not always foremost. As Ceri Peach has argued (see chap. 3), poverty or hardship in

261

Barbados was seldom the main factor. In fact, most of the migrants in this book were gainfully employed in Barbados before their emigration. From the narratives we sense that the decisions to emigrate are more complex than what the economic theories of migration suggest—namely, that migration is a response to spatial unevenness in labor markets, with the primary cause of migration being differentials in income and employment opportunities between two or more regions or societies.[1] Moreover, some labor economists, say A. Portes and R. Rumbaut, write about migration as if immigrants "have perfect information about labor market conditions in the receiving country and adjust their locational decisions accordingly."[2] While most of our migrants thought they could earn and save more money in the United Kingdom or North America, we see little evidence of their having had a clear idea of what employment opportunities and wages were open to them. In fact, their information was often inaccurate or overly optimistic, which resulted in some migrants, like Roy Campbell and Cleve Thornhill, being disappointed with the small wages.

For most the journey overseas was a momentous occasion and the beginning of a new life. None of these migrants had traveled abroad before, nor had they been on a ship or airplane. Perhaps one indication of the journey's significance is that many migrants remember the day of the week they left home and the day they arrived abroad. (I wondered if there were any events in my own life for which I knew the day of the week and concluded that there aren't any, except for the faint recollection that John F. Kennedy was assassinated on a Friday.)

For the early migrants who went by sea, the ten- to fourteen-day voyage gave them time to reflect on where they were going, what they hoped to achieve, what their new lives might be like, and so on. On board they met and talked to expatriates and nationals who knew the host country. In Roy Campbell's account we sense that the trip and what he observed in the ports along the way (Tenerife, Barcelona, etc.) helped to prepare him for his arrival in England. Not surprisingly, the trip by airplane didn't offer the same benefit.

The migrants were "sojourners" rather than "settlers" in that they all saw their stays overseas as being temporary. Most of them, both workers and students, expected to be home within 5 years.

Nearly all, however, stayed much longer. The only exceptions were Errol Inniss, who returned on schedule—being on a student visa, he had no choice—and the Allmans, who when leaving for Montreal felt they might be away for 20 years but returned after only 10. The others stayed three and four times longer than they had originally intended. The average length of time abroad was 14 years. In this regard these migrants are similar to the larger sample ($n = 135$) of returnees whom I interviewed in 1982–83, in which three out of every five respondents thought at the time of their emigration that they would be home within 5 years. In that study those who emigrated to work were away an average of 15.3 years, while those who emigrated to study (many of them also worked after their schooling was completed) were gone for 9.7 years.

Settling in the Metropole

The places these migrants went to and the neighborhoods they settled in are typical of the destinations and residences of other West Indians in both Britain and North America.[3] Most traveled to cities and neighborhoods where they had relatives or friends. Roy Campbell went to his sister's flat in London, Gabby to his in-laws' in Brooklyn, Richard Goddard to his uncle's in Calgary, the Allmans to friends' in Montreal, and so on. The exceptions were the students and those who went on labor contracts (Valenza Griffith and Rose Thornhill): their destinations and accommodations were determined in advance, either by the university or an employer.

The migrants in this book settled mainly in large cities (see chap. 3). Nine of the thirteen settled in either London, New York, or Montreal.[4] Their choice of large cities is characteristic of most twentieth-century immigration, not just in the United Kingdom and North America but universally, since these are the places where work is most available. Regardless of their qualifications and experience, most newcomers enter at the bottom of their respective occupational ladders, and low-paying, arduous entry-level jobs are usually most available in large urban areas.[5] Once a few immigrants locate job opportunities there the process becomes self-perpetuating, their having paved the way for relatives and friends back home.

These migrants are also like most immigrants to Britain and North America in that they did not wander far from the city in which they initially settled.[6] Only Richard Goddard and Valenza Griffith moved to new regions. As Portes and Rumbaut explain in their overview of immigrants in America, "By moving away from places where their group is numerically strong, individuals risk losing a range of social and moral resources that make for psychological well-being."[7] Staying in or near areas that have a concentration of West Indians makes it easier for the migrants to maintain relationships with people who share their interests and values and for their children to grow up with other West Indian children. Other West Indians can provide moral support as well as information about jobs and economic opportunities. And even small groups of immigrants can have some economic and political weight if they are spatially concentrated.

Many of the migrants were surprised at what they found upon arriving in the host country. Growing up in Barbados, they had listened to the villagers who had traveled abroad talk about life in Britain and North America, but their anecdotes were not adequate preparation. Gabby was shocked at the rundown condition of the neighborhoods he saw from the car window on the trip to Brooklyn from the airport. In Montreal Aileen Allman found people unfriendly and discovered that Canadians do not greet strangers. Even England did not look or feel like the mother country that these Barbadians had learned about in their school days from English textbooks. Some found the towns gray and grim. Roy Campbell felt that the people were distant and their houses depressingly similar. He immediately made plans to return to Barbados as soon as he could save enough money for the passage. Several complained about the penetrating cold and the burden of wearing so much clothing. Ann Bovell marveled at all the chimneys she saw and the fact that people actually built fires inside their homes. Valenza Griffith, who had never seen attached housing, wondered if the terrace, which stretched from one end of her street to the other, wasn't all one long house. Only John Wickham was really prepared. Having read English novels all his life, only he of the thirteen had a clear idea of what England would be like. The people and scenes he saw on his train trip to Birmingham were right out of the pages of D. H. Lawrence.

A West Indian man and English schoolboys on the streets of Birmingham, England. (Photo courtesy of The Hulton Picture Library.)

While there were many disappointments, the migrants' narratives show them adjusting reasonably well. There is nothing to suggest that any of them experienced prolonged psychological distress. Even the migrants—the Bovells, the Thornhills, and Roy Campbell—who moved directly from rural villages in Barbados to London, a city with a population more than thirty times that of Barbados, coped reasonably well. If their adjustments seem too trouble free, it may be because many of our ideas about the hardships of immigration have come from the experiences of turn-of-the-century immigrants.[8] The lives of these immigrants were often harsh, and most of the sociological studies about them have emphasized their alienation, maladjustment, and anomie.[9]

Most of the migrants in this book stayed with relatives for several weeks until they learned their way around and rented a place to live. Kin and friends were often instrumental in helping the new arrival find accommodations and a job as well as in showing them where to shop and how to ride the bus. Although only a few of them mention it specifically in the narratives, most settled in the same neighborhood as their relatives. The cumulative effect of West Indians, like any group of immigrants, settling in places where they already have friends or relatives—a phenomenon commonly referred to as *chain migration*—is the formation in the host society of little colonies of migrants transplanted from the same villages and districts of their native country or region. Anthropologist Douglas Midgett, for example, who went to England to track down migrants from a village he had studied on the island of St. Lucia, found that half of the 290 migrant households lived in the same London borough of Paddington.[10]

Except for the two students, Inniss and Whittle, the migrants' first accommodations of their own consisted of a room in a boarding house or a small flat. About half of them remained in private rental accommodations, mostly flats, during their entire stay. In both England and North America few West Indians were allocated public housing. In the English Midlands city of Birmingham, for example, immigrants accounted for 10 percent of the population of the city in 1970 but only 3 percent of the people renting council housing. The main barrier to being allotted public housing in England was an eligibility requirement that the immigrants be residents for five years. But even for those who did qualify there were other hurdles to overcome, including the prejudices of officials who assigned houses.[11] Despite this, among the narrators, Roy Campbell and Valenza Griffith did live in council houses for a time before eventually buying homes of their own. Of the seven couples in this book four eventually purchased their own modest single-family dwellings, after having rented for a number of years.

Work

Almost immediately upon arriving in England the migrants began searching for work. Norman Bovell, for example, arrived in London on a Tuesday, found a job on Wednesday, and began work on Thursday. Rose Thornhill arrived at the mental hospital in York at 4:30 A.M. and was told to report to her nursing station for the 7 A.M. shift. The speed at which the migrants were employed indicates the high demand for laborers in England during much of the 1950s and early 1960s. The same urgency to hire migrants did not exist among the migrants to North America. Those who, like Cleve Thornhill and Norman Bovell, went on contracts to do agricultural work were undoubtedly put to work soon after arriving. The others, such as Gabby and Richard Goddard, visited relatives for several weeks before looking for employment. That the migrants lost no time in finding work should not be surprising given that a primary motivation for going abroad was the desire to make money. I found it interesting that most of the migrants, the blue-collar workers particularly, could recall their wages down to the last shilling for each job they held. It was almost as if the wages they earned were a measure of how well they were faring as immigrants.

The work the migrants found, and that which had been arranged for them in advance, was predominantly manual labor. They became van drivers, bus conductors, mail carriers, painters, seamstresses, nurses' aides, and factory operatives—common occupations among colored immigrants generally in Britain and North America. Typically, the jobs available to them were the dirtiest, most boring, and worst paying. Most were jobs that white workers did not want.

For some West Indians these jobs were of lower status than the positions they had left at home in the Caribbean, though the wages were generally higher. Siebert Allman, a self-employed joiner (cabinetmaker) in Barbados, became a bus conductor in London and a factory worker in Montreal; Roy Campbell, a mechanic in Barbados, drove a delivery van and worked in a bakery in London. In a study of Jamaican immigrants in London Nancy Foner found that very few had actually improved their occupation-

Immigrant and English workers during a tea break at the Ford body shop at Dagenham, England. (Photo courtesy of The Hulton Picture Library.)

al status.[12] Several other studies have reported that a sizable percentage of West Indian migrants actually experienced downward mobility while in England.[13] This was most often the case among West Indians who had been white-collar workers at home and were forced to take manual jobs overseas. It should be no surprise that migrants who were forced to take lesser jobs in England, who moved down the occupational ladder a few notches, were bitterly disappointed.[14] None of the migrants in *Double Passage* falls into this category. In fact, the only one who held a white-collar job prior to emigrating was John Wickham.

Despite only being able to find low-status, manual work, most of the migrants were gratified that their wages were considerably higher than what they had been earning in Barbados. Only Roy Campbell was dissatisfied with his weekly salary of £8 10*s*. as a helper in a bakery. Not having enough money for the return fare home, he had no choice but to stay and continue working. From their weekly pay packets nearly all the migrants were able to take care of their room and board and have enough left over both to send money home and to save for a house.

If there is a dominant theme in the narratives, it is work. It is difficult to overstate how hard these individuals worked. Five of the migrants, at various times, held two jobs simultaneously. It seems that each one volunteered for any overtime that was available. As Siebert Allman said:

> I did all the overtime I could get, as my purpose in going to England was to improve my family's standard of living. I was always happy for the extra work.

In a study of immigrants in the English Midlands city of Birmingham, Rex and Tomlinson found in the mid-1970s that twice as many West Indians and three times as many Asian immigrants worked more than forty-eight hours a week than did white British workers. Despite the West Indians' and Asians' longer work hours, their wages were not any greater than white British workers. Rather, the immigrants had to do shift work and overtime to bring their wages up to the level of their British counterparts.[15] Roy Bryce-Laporte describes West Indian immigrants in the United States as fierce believers in and practitioners of the Protestant ethic.[16]

Despite their toil, only John Wickham received a job promotion. Even after as much as two decades of work experience, no other migrant was promoted or markedly improved his or her occupational status. In a similar way John Rex and Sally Tomlinson found in Birmingham that twice as many whites as immigrants had been offered promotion. About one-third of the immigrants they surveyed believed they had not been offered promotion because of racial discrimination. Yet, despite the low wages, menial work, and the unlikelihood of being promoted, most of the migrants in this book remained at the same jobs for long periods of time. Only Norman Bovell and Aileen Allman had more than three jobs during their years abroad, and even they eventually settled with one employer, whom they worked with for a long uninterrupted period until their return to Barbados. Similarly, 68 percent of the West Indians in Rex and Tomlinson's Birmingham sample had been at the same jobs for more than five years.[17]

Given their unskilled work, meager wages, and not being promoted, we might ask why more of the migrants weren't self-employed. Only Cleve Thornhill had his own business (repairing cars), and that was secondary to working for the post office. It is a common sociological observation that immigrants who own their own businesses usually earn more money than those working for wages.[18] It is true that, because prosperous immigrants are less likely to return home—the economic sacrifice being too great—self-employed migrants were less likely to have been selected for my research. But, nonetheless, other sources confirm that West Indians tend not to become entrepreneurs. Frank Fratoe and Ronald Meeks, for example, in a study of self-employment among the fifty largest ancestry groups in the United States, report that for Jamaicans (Barbadians were not listed) only twenty-one in every thousand are self-employed.[19] In contrast, for those of Lebanese, Greek, and Russian origin the rate of self-employment is at least five times greater.[20]

One reason for the low rate of entrepreneurship among Jamaicans and other Caribbean peoples is that most of them view their stay in the host country as only temporary: they plan to return home. According to M. Piore, temporary migrants or sojourners are more willing to accept and tolerate low wages and arduous work conditions than migrants who cannot return home and who plan to remain permanently in the host country.[21]

Children

As a husband and a father, I was struck at how long these married migrants were separated from their spouses and children. None of the three couples (Allmans, Griffiths, and Thornhills) who were married at the time they left Barbados emigrated together. In each case the husband went first, and the couple was apart from two years (Thornhills and Allmans) to five years (Bovells) without seeing one another. I remember wondering during my interviews how well the marriages of my middle-class American friends would have endured under such circumstances. But Valenza Griffith spoke for most of the Barbadian women whose husbands had gone abroad when she explained that, as long as one's husband

At home in Mile and a Quarter, St. Peter. (Photo by Ellen Frankenstein.)

was emigrating to better the family's position, you couldn't cry or complain. Rather, you passed the time until they came back or you could join them by "keeping busy."

Separations between the migrant couple and their children were also common. Six of the nine couples who had children were apart from them for at least one year during their stay abroad. Although the Allmans and Bovells, for example, left their children behind in Barbados when they emigrated, both couples later sent for them, but neither family could afford to bring all their children overseas at once. The Allmans brought their first children over after two years in Montreal, and the Bovells after five years in London. The Campbells and Griffiths were separated from their children when they sent them home in advance of their return. It should also be noted that some of the grown children of the Bovells, Thornhills, and Allmans remained abroad (and still live there) when their parents resettled in Barbados.

Like other West Indian immigrants, most of the children of these migrants were left in the care of grandparents or other relatives. Most migrants believed that their children would be better off in the Caribbean, because the village was a safer and healthier environment than the streets of Brooklyn or London and also because more relatives would be there to look after their welfare. In the metropole, with both parents working, the children would of necessity be left with a child minder. Good child care was difficult to find, and many immigrants had heard stories about children left with babysitters being neglected or abused.

It was not uncommon for immigrant parents to send their children home in response to a family crisis, as a disciplinary measure, or because of divorce, although there are no instances of this in these oral histories. In one Barbadian village in which I did fieldwork, I got to know a teenage boy from New York whose parents had sent him back to Barbados to live with his aunt after he had joined a street gang and, in an unrelated incident, was shot at in the tenement where they lived. Children are also left behind or sent home for their education. Many Barbadian returnees that I have interviewed believe that the schools in Barbados are superior to English or American schools—their assessment that the host society offers an inferior education is not confined to the poor inner-city schools that they knew best. While the immigrants' children were generally left in good hands in Barbados, the separation was difficult on the parents. We heard the Bovells and All-mans talk about their unhappiness and worry; similar sentiments were expressed by Roy Campbell.

On some islands, but not Barbados, the idea of leaving children in the care of others for an extended period of time to enable both parents to work was an accepted practice. In Jamaica, for example, many mothers left their children with their own mothers in the rural areas while taking a job in the city of Kingston.[22] This was different from overseas migration, however, in that it was easy for parents to regularly return to their village to visit their children; for emigrants to Britain the long and costly passage to the West Indies made return visits very infrequent. In some cases the migrants' stays overseas stretched into more years than they had originally planned, and their children grew up during their absence. It was ten years before Norman Bovell saw his eldest child, and then she wasn't sure that he was her "daddy." Another elderly man whom I interviewed in Barbados painfully recalled his homecoming after more than twenty years abroad. His two sons, who were infants when he left Barbados, were in their twenties when they came to the airport to meet him. He had a photograph of them but was unable to recognize them in the crowd. When they finally did locate one another his sons were unconvinced that he was their father.

"Broadening Horizons"

Another prominent aspect of the migrants' experience was becoming acquainted with people of other nationalities. The Allmans lived between Greek and Armenian families and had close French Canadian friends; the Thornhills, Griffiths, and Wickhams made friends with their English neighbors; Richard Goddard, as a Mountie, got to know native Americans as well as Canadians; Gabby explored and tried to learn about the different ethnic groups that he encountered in New York; and so on. All of the migrants became aware of differences in the customs and traditions of people from different cultures. I recall Norman Bovell, the least educated of the migrants in this book, recounting differences in the diet and habits of Indians and Pakistanis.

But it was the West Indians from other islands whom they got to know best. Jamaicans, Trinidadians, Montserratians, Grenadians, and Vincentians, among others, held the same kinds of jobs, lived in the same neighborhoods, shopped in the same stores, and sent their children to the same schools as Barbadians.[23] West Indians from different islands celebrated pan–West Indian cultural activities such as the West Indian Carnival in Brooklyn and its counterpart in Notting Hill, London. Writing about West Indians in New York City, Linda Basch notes that these events nurtured a "developing West Indian consciousness."[24] Many of these migrants acquired a new awareness of the similarities between Barbadians and the people of the other islands of the Caribbean. They also discovered that, although they recognized clear differences between West Indians from different islands, they were all regarded as the same, all lumped together as "black people" or as "Jamaicans," by the host white society.

Racial Discrimination

In all but two of the narratives incidents of racial discrimination are recounted. We learned about it most often in the context of the migrants' searches for employment and housing, such as when they encountered the signs in windows and doors of flats telling blacks they need not apply or when the Allmans were turned away from an apartment just shortly after being told by phone that it was available. But discrimination was also expressed in countless other ways, such as the white woman bus passenger putting her bus fare on the seat next to her to avoid having to touch the black hand of conductor Siebert Allman. There were also a number of incidents in which, though there was no intent to discriminate, in subtle, perhaps unconscious ways whites revealed their biases about black people to the migrants. The receptionist at the store, for example, who didn't ask Roy Campbell to sign for the heaters he had come to pick up did so because she assumed he couldn't write. And the captain of the cricket team at the college in Birmingham that John Wickham attended automatically assumed that John would be a good bowler because he was tall and black.

But against the vast literature on racism and race relations in Britain and North America these migrants mention fewer incidents of color prejudice and less overt discrimination than one might expect. In a study of Jamaicans in London, for example, Foner concludes that an immigrant's skin color is a crucial element in his or her daily life.[25] John Lambert, in a study of police-immigrant relations, argues that black people are subjected to discrimination of such "unrelenting tenacity that it is justified to describe English society as supporting a system of institutionalized racism."[26] And about West Indians in North America many observers have concluded that skin color overwhelms all other criteria in determining a migrant's position in the host society.[27]

In light of these findings should we not have heard more from our migrants about racism? Some might argue that my being white inhibited the Barbadians I interviewed from talking about race. For most of the narrators I don't believe this had much, if any, influence. The better educated migrants, such as John Wickham and Janice Whittle, and the irreverent and often provocative Gabby all spoke freely as did, I believe, the individuals whom I knew particularly well, such as the Allmans. On the other hand, I suspect that the Thornhills, Bovells, and Valenza Griffith may have downplayed their encounters with racism, perhaps in deference to my being white. Among older country people in Barbados there is still a certain reverence for whites, a lingering vestige of English colonialism, which causes people to be cautious when talking about race in the presence of a white man.

But I also think that we don't hear more about racism in these narratives because most of these migrants did not let the racist attitudes of the host society unduly intrude upon their everyday lives, at least not very often. About racism Aileen Allman once said to me, "There are good and bad people in every country. The best thing is to forget about the bad ones and get on with your work." And after a lifetime of having repressed these injustices, the average working-class Barbadian migrant, explained a former Barbadian government minister who is a returnee himself, "can't simply pull these hurts out from under the bed where they have been hiding all these years, and, even if they could, they wouldn't want to for a nice, well meaning, and affable white man." Certainly, every day of their lives overseas the migrants paid a price for being black in terms of being excluded from the best housing and having to work long hours at menial, low-status jobs, earning less than whites who had no more skill or education.

But such disadvantage is not part of most migrants' everyday consciousness. Also, racial prejudice is often very subtle and is manifested, like it is for minorities generally, in the migrants simply being ignored—whites not greeting them, avoiding eye contact, and generally behaving as if blacks are invisible. And when they did encounter racism, such as the derogatory remarks overheard on the bus or in the workplace, they took no notice. The migrants understood that fighting back was futile, that it was more sensible to turn a deaf ear to the remarks, just as when bus conductor Siebert Allman decided that trying to collect bus fares from a rowdy group of Teddy Boys simply wasn't worth the risk of a confrontation.

Finally, it can't be ruled out that time (most of the migrants

had been home in Barbados for several years or more) and distance may have diminished their bitterness and made them appear more tolerant of racism than they had been when they
encountered it. Or even that the unpleasantness of the experience
has led to unconscious repression of the memory. Whatever the
case, racial prejudice in the host society did discourage most
migrants from identifying with mainstream white American or
British society.

Assimilation

Even after living many years abroad and successfully adjusting to
English or North American society the orientation of the migrants
was always toward the Caribbean. The narratives reveal evidence of
this in a variety of ways. Most of their friendships were with other
islanders (the students, Inniss and Whittle, are exceptions, as
there were few West Indians in the places they studied). Nearly all
of the migrants made return visits to Barbados, despite costly
airfares that cut into their hard-won savings. Most regularly sent
remittances home to help support parents and other relatives.
Some sent their children as well or left them behind from the
beginning. In either case, having the children grow up in the
Caribbean ensured that they would learn Barbadian values and
customs rather than those of the English, Americans, or Canadians. Leaving one's children at home undoubtedly also strength-
ened the ties between the parents overseas and the relatives at
home who looked after them. Perhaps it is only logical that these
migrants—migrants who eventually returned home—should have
maintained strong ties with their homeland. But, based both on
the conversations I have had with West Indians in England and on
what other researchers have reported, I don't believe the migrants
of *Double Passage* differ very much from other migrants in the
strength of their orientation toward the Caribbean. In fact, most
West Indians, even after decades abroad, still identify strongly with
their homelands, and many retain what observers call an "ideology
of return."[28]

Part of the explanation for this may be that most West Indians
see their time abroad as temporary; they never intended to leave
the Caribbean for good. But, equally significant, the white host

societies, particularly those of England and the United States, by keeping the colored immigrants at arm's length, did not encourage them to assimilate. In England the migrants were reminded in countless ways that, while the country welcomed their labor, at least as long as there were plenty of jobs to go around, it was not willing to extend to them the privileges of full citizenship. This was a disappointment, a shock for some, like John Wickham and Siebert Allman, who in emigrating to England had believed that they were going to the "mother country," to a society they assumed would treat them as equals, on the "basis of merit rather than on the basis of their color."[29] Encounters with racism also diminished the migrants' respect for whites.

In the Caribbean the only foreign-born whites they knew were in high positions and were generally well educated. Abroad they saw whites doing menial work. They discovered that many whites were not particularly well educated; many did not even know where Barbados was or that it had until recently been a British colony and was now independent. Hearing people ask, "What part of Jamaica is Barbados?" or "What part of Africa is Barbados?" made Valenza Griffith laugh at first, but then she wondered how the English could be so "stupid." "It gave me second thoughts about England," she said. "With all the tales we'd heard about England we thought everybody would be brilliant." The mystique of whiteness, notes Nancy Foner, was eroded when the immigrants discovered that "whiteness no longer correlated with other attributes of respectability and authority." And when whites are no longer seen as special, she argues further, immigrants begin to question the legitimacy of racial prejudice and white notions about the inferiority of blackness.[30] It follows that, in such a social context, black immigrants are unlikely to try to identify strongly with the larger society.

The situation was somewhat different for Barbadians and other West Indians in North America. In the United States there was already a large American black population when the West Indians arrived, and the new immigrants settled in neighborhoods that were predominantly black. White Americans, knowing perhaps even less about the Caribbean origins of the migrants than was the case in Britain, merely lumped them in with American blacks. Their status as immigrants was "invisible." By being treated as black Americans, argues Connie Sutton, the West Indians have been discouraged from assimilating: the immigrants see that the group they are being identified with "possess[es] the lowest incomes and the highest school dropout and unemployment rates." There are few incentives to become Americanized when it means that your identity will be with a low-status group. In their pursuit of higher socioeconomic status in North America West Indian immigrants know they are better off retaining their Caribbean-based identity and cultural heritage.[31]

What experiences or aspects of life are missing from the narratives? Noting what the migrants fail to talk about may be revealing. There is, for example, no mention of politics or political activity, not even of them having had an interest in British, American, or Canadian elections. The political concerns that are expressed invariably deal with Barbados, usually in the context of trips home or after the return to Barbados. But their disinterest in the domestic politics of a host country is no different from that of most immigrants, regardless of national origin. Oriented to their homeland and without intending to settle permanently in the host country, there is little reason, other than curiosity, to take much interest. Moreover, the migrants' lives overseas were already fully occupied with work—with doing any available overtime and maintaining multiple jobs, all the while raising a family.

Except for Ann Bovell, the migrants also scarcely mention religion, whether it be attending Sunday services, participating in church activities, or just having joined a congregation. I do not know to what degree their failure to talk about religion accurately reflects its unimportance in their lives abroad. As I mention in chapter 15, one of the changes that local Barbadians notice about migrants when they return home is that they are less religious than when they left. The scarcity of references to religion may also be due to my own influence—my not showing an ample interest in it or not asking the right questions about religion.

Finally, while many migrants, in talking about their reasons for emigrating, mentioned wanting to see the mother country and "a bit of the world," few of them ever talked about actually having traveled in the host country. They don't seem to have seen much of Britain, Canada, or the United States, outside of the cities they lived in. The notable exceptions are the students, who traveled widely (Errol Inniss across Canada, Janice Whittle to London and Paris, and John Wickham to Holland and the Continent).

Can We Compare?

Before we turn to the migrants' repatriation to the Caribbean in the next chapter, one interesting question remains: Have differences within the host societies themselves—those of England, the United States, and Canada—differentially shaped the migrants' experiences? We get a few clues from the narratives. Recall, for instance, the different reactions of Gabby and Ann Bovell upon arriving in their new environments, Brooklyn and London, respectively. Finding three locks on the inside door of the house in which he was staying, Gabby wondered if it was safe to go outside. He decided it was not and stayed indoors for nearly a week before getting up the courage to explore his environs. In contrast, Ann Bovell, a small woman from a rural background, arrived in her London home and shortly after wandered off by herself to explore the neighborhood. While there may be several explanations for their different behavior, it is quite likely that New York, with its more frequent crime, reputation for violence, and considerably larger buildings, may have been a more intimidating environment for new immigrants than was London. But, of course, it would be foolhardy to generalize from these two incidents. Any comparison between the two or three host societies we might wish to make from the oral histories means having to subdivide our already small sample into even smaller and thus insignificant units.

Rather than ignore such an interesting question altogether, let us turn to Nancy Foner's excellent "comparative analysis" of West Indians in New York and London. Her study focused on the occupational attainment of all West Indians, second-generation as well as new immigrants. In brief, she found that, occupationally, West Indians in the United States have been far more successful than West Indians in Britain. In the United States in 1970, for example, about 45 percent of the West Indians in the labor force held nonmanual jobs compared with only 25 percent of West Indians in Britain.[32] The same pattern of "success" holds true for business, with a far higher percentage of West Indians in the

United States being self-employed than those in Britain.[33] Foner offers several explanations for the difference, beginning with the fact that a higher percentage of West Indians have lived in the United States for a longer period of time than is the case in Britain. West Indians arrived en masse in Britain only after 1951, while a substantial number of West Indians had come to American shores in the early part of the twentieth century. By 1920, for example, one-fourth of the black population of Harlem was West Indian. The result is that more of the West Indian population in the United States are second-generation than is the case in Britain, and second-generation West Indians in both countries are more likely to achieve white-collar positions.[34]

Differences in the social contexts in which West Indians live and in the character of race relations in the two countries also play a role, according to Foner. In the United States, as noted earlier, most West Indians have settled in cities with many American blacks. In Britain West Indians moved into a rather homogenous, largely white society.[35] For West Indians in the United States, living in areas of mainly black residence means a much larger market or clientele for local businesses. In British cities there are proportionately fewer potential black customers; also West Indians fear that English whites will not patronize their businesses. It is also true that, in the United States, West Indians often are competing with American blacks for good jobs. With schooling and university degrees more prized among West Indians than among American blacks the West Indians are often at a competitive advantage in the job market within the black community in America.

What the migrants have learned and experienced overseas is not only important to their adjustment to life in the host societies, but it also influences their readjustment in Barbados, as the next chapter will demonstrate. Let us now turn to what it means to go home, what local Barbadians think of the returnees, and what the social and economic impacts of return migration are.

NOTES

1. See M. Piore, *Birds of Passage: Migrant Labor and Industrial Societies.*
2. Ibid., 28.

3. N. Foner, *Jamaica Farewell: Jamaican Migrants in London;* and R. B. Davison, *Black British: Immigrants to England.*

4. Although the specific location of their new residence is not always stated in the oral histories, most in fact were in inner city areas. West Indians in both Britain and the United States tend to be clustered in the inner city. The reason for this, as Ceri Peach notes of British cities, is that the older, more dilapidated, and therefore less costly housing is found near the center (*West Indian Migration to Britain: A Social Geography,* 85). Not surprisingly, as British towns evolve the newer and more desirable housing is built further from the center.

5. A. Portes and R. Rumbaut, *Immigrant America: A Portrait,* 45.

6. Ibid., 53; see also C. Holmes, *John Bull's Island: Immigration and British Society, 1871–1971.*

7. Portes and Rumbaut, *Immigrant America,* 53.

8. Ibid., 146.

9. See, for example, L. Wirth, "Urbanism as a Way of Life"; and Portes and Rumbaut, *Immigrant America.*

10. D. K. Midgett, "West Indian Migration and Adaptation in St. Lucia and London," 173.

11. J. Rex and S. Tomlinson, *Colonial Immigrants in a British City,* 143, 141.

12. Foner, *Jamaica Farewell,* 108–9.

13. R. Glass, *Newcomers: The West Indians in London,* 70–72; and P. Wright, *The Coloured Workers in British Industry,* 83.

14. Foner, *Jamaica Farewell,* 108–9.

15. Rex and Tomlinson, *Colonial Immigrants in a British City,* 113–15.

16. Cited in P. Marshall, "Black Immigrant Women," 89.

17. Rex and Tomlinson, *Colonial Immigrants in a British City,* 114, 118, 115–16.

18. Portes and Rumbaut, *Immigrant America,* 73.

19. See, for example, F. Fratoe and R. Meeks, "Business Participation Rates and Self-Employed Incomes: Analysis of the Fifty Largest U.S. Ancestry Groups."

20. Discussed in Portes and Rumbaut, *Immigrant America,* 75.

21. Piore, *Birds of Passage.*

22. R. B. Davison, *Black British: Immigrants to England,* 7.

23. L. Basch, "The Politics of Caribbeanization: Vincentians and Grenadians in New York," 167.

24. Ibid., 167.

25. Foner, *Jamaica Farewell,* 53.

26. Quoted in ibid., 43.

27. See, for example, the essays by E. Chaney, P. Marshall, and L. Basch in C. Sutton and E. Chaney, *Caribbean Life in New York City.*

28. See H. Rubenstein, "Remittances and Rural Underdevelopment in the English-speaking Caribbean"; and Foner, *Jamaica Farewell.*

29. Foner, *Jamaica Farewell,* 41.

30. Ibid., 51.

31. C. Sutton, "The Caribbeanization of New York City and the Emergence of a Transnational Socio-Cultural System," 21.
32. Foner, "West Indians in New York City and London: A Comparative Analysis," 120.
33. In Britain, where only 3 percent of West Indians work for themselves, the *West Indian Digest* noted that West Indians are "reluctant to go into business, small or large" (ibid., 120).
34. Ibid., 122, 123; see also V. Dominguez, *From Neighbor to Stranger: The Dilemma of Caribbean Peoples in the United States*, 61.
35. Foner, "West Indians in New York City and London," 124.

Chapter 15
The Meaning of Return Migration

While the migrants' narratives paint a vivid picture of their experiences in Britain and North America, they reveal less about what it means to come home. The time abroad is a completed life event, and through reflection and the telling and retelling of their experiences this period in their lives has crystallized into a set of memories. In contrast, the return migrants are still in the process of living their return, and in most cases they are too close to the experience to see it as clearly. It is also perhaps less interesting to them, since Barbados is the society in which they grew up; compared to their lives overseas, there are fewer opportunities for adventure and self-discovery at home. I believe it is for these reasons that they speak less, or more tentatively, about the return to Barbados. The following discussion, although based on the migrants' narratives, is also informed by other field research, including roughly a year, divided between several stays, of ethnographic fieldwork and my earlier (1982–83) survey of 135 Barbadian returnees.[1]

The return migration of our narrators, like that of most West Indians, involves a movement from a highly developed and usually urban area to a less developed region. While this is the most common pattern of return migration worldwide, we should note two other types: (1) the movement of people between countries with roughly equal standards of living and levels of economic development (e.g., Americans migrating to and from Canada, Europe, and Japan); and (2) the movement of "developed" migrants back from undeveloped, typically colonial or ex-colonial

West Indian immigrants leaving Britain to return home, 1961. (Photo courtesy of The Hulton Picture Library.)

countries (e.g., French from Algeria, British from Kenya, Dutch from Indonesia).[2] The movement from the United Kingdom, United States, or Canada back to Barbados is similar to that of Mediterranean migrants returning home from northern Europe or Puerto Ricans and Mexicans returning to their countries, and therefore there are many parallels between the experiences of these narrators and migrants in other cultures. Nevertheless, in this chapter my primary aim is to make sense of the Barbadian experience and to focus on the patterns in the narratives.[3]

Why They Return

For most returnees, certainly for all the people in this study, return migration is best understood as the natural completion of the

Home—the beach and Caribbean Sea at Speightstown. (Photo by Bill Case.)

migration cycle. At the time they left Barbados most migrants only planned to stay long enough to save enough money to buy a house and perhaps a car and to see something of the world. Roy Campbell was typical of many:

> On the way over to England my thinking was that I'd be away no more than five years. I had a goal of saving a certain amount of money and then coming back to Barbados and getting a little house.

Only 9 percent of the returnees interviewed in the survey believed they were leaving Barbados for good at the time of their emigration.[4] Nevertheless, most overseas Barbadians never manage to return home, at least not to stay. Some simply cannot afford the passage or plane ticket back. More often, those who have not bettered themselves economically while overseas are disinclined to return because they think they will lose face.[5] Student emigrants are expected by Barbadians to come home with a diploma, while working emigrants are expected to have at least enough money to buy a home of their own. Furthermore, unless they will be receiving a pension, most migrants will not return home without good prospects of a job.[6] Without a guaranteed job they are better off staying abroad, since Barbados has few benefits for the unemployed. Returning home can also mean costly obligations to share their wealth with less well-off family members. Ann Bovell, Valenza Griffith, and Aileen Allman found that even neighbors who were unrelated to them expected them to spread their wealth around, such as in buying them presents.

Conversely, the very successful also seldom return home because to do so would mean giving up well-salaried positions and a standard of living that cannot easily be equaled in Barbados. Among our migrants only John Wickham gave up a high-paying job to come home. When migrants make the decision to return, especially those who are comfortably settled abroad, they must believe they can attain a comfortable standard of living in Barbados. For most this means being able to start a business or to find a job somewhat comparable to what they had abroad. For returnees of retirement age or those who are otherwise living on fixed incomes it means that housing and the cost of living in Barbados must be affordable. The state of the Barbadian economy, employment opportunities both at home and in the host society, and exchange rates all significantly influence the flow of return migrants.[7] Although there is little reliable data on the return migration to the islands of the eastern Caribbean,[8] no one who knows the region disputes the fact that, since the late 1960s, Barbados has seen a higher rate of return migration than any of its neighboring islands. This has been due primarily to a growing economy, high per capita income, and the increasing availability of modern amenities, which have greatly narrowed the gap in living standards between Barbados and the host societies of the migrants.

The realization that it was possible to have all the material comforts they have become accustomed to abroad, and that life in other ways may be even more fulfilling at home, often came for these migrants during a holiday visit.[9] It was then that over half of them saw how much Barbados had prospered during their absence and, significantly, that black Barbadians, and not just the white elite, had benefited from the new prosperity. They could not help but notice the increasing number of high-quality wall houses; islandwide electrification; the extension of piped water, which has allowed indoor plumbing in most homes; new roads; new restaurants; and recreational facilities—much of the improvements associated with the increasing number of tourists who visit the island. Some who had left Barbados during the 1950s and 1960s saw that during their absence the country had truly become independent—that the people now running the island were black and large numbers of blacks had entered the middle class. They saw that all Barbadian children, no longer just those of the wealthy, were guaranteed an education through secondary school. They were impressed and proud of the great strides that Barbados had made while they had been away. Then, exalted by sunny blue skies, warm air, the inviting sea, an easygoing pace of life, and the friendliness of their village neighbors, migrants often began seriously to consider a new life at home. Since it was usually Christmas or summer holidays when they made their visits, the atmosphere was especially festive, and their relatives were in good cheer; they were eager to please, willing to drive the migrants here and there to see sights and old friends.

It is not surprising that it was either during such a visit or immediately upon their return to Britain or North America, while memories were still fresh, that migrants often reached a final decision and made concrete plans to return home—setting a date, buying a house site, and opening a Barbadian bank account. Rose Thornhill, who wanted the family to stay in England, recalled how her husband brushed aside her reservations and instead only talked about "how beautiful Barbados was," that the country was "doing much better, that there were better homes, and that now they had a deep-water harbor, which could bring more commerce." Many migrants later discovered, however, that perceptions of home acquired during these short holiday visits could be deceptive.

While migrants are drawn home primarily by what life in Barbados promises, there must also be some discontent with their lives abroad, even if it is only the vague feeling that something is missing. People who are entirely satisfied with their lives rarely uproot themselves. John Wickham, for example, despite having a secure, well-paying job that he enjoyed, made the decision to come home suddenly one day while looking out his apartment window in Switzerland onto the park where his children were playing and realizing that they would always be outsiders in Switzerland. Unemployment, racial tension, and personal problems also push people home. The British economy has been slow to recover from the 1979–82 recession, and what gains have been made have done little for West Indians, whose unemployment rate is nearly triple that of white Britons. Recently, four nonwhite members of parliament noted, "The economy doesn't need their labor, and in some ways the society has junked them like so much garbage."[10] Jobs for young West Indians are so scarce that, in an ironic reversal of their own parents' emigration, some who were born and raised in England are now leaving to seek their fortunes in the Caribbean.

Migrants have been disturbed by new signs of racism in Britain, including the rising popularity of extreme right-wing groups like the National Front. The rhetoric and policies of Margaret Thatcher's conservative administration also contributed to the West Indians' growing uneasiness. Several right-wing members of parliament proposed that the government offer cash incentives to West Indians to encourage them to go home. One forty-year-old returnee I interviewed said that the final straw for him was the British Nationality Act of 1981, which decreed that children born in Britain of West Indian parents would no longer qualify for British citizenship. "The notion that my children," he said, "would not be citizens of the country that I had given the best years of my life to was a slap in the face."

Some return migration is precipitated by personal crisis: the breakup of a marriage, the death of a spouse, trouble with children, or ill health. A hotel maid in an English resort town, who returned after being divorced, said, "After my husband left it was just me and kids in the house, and that's not good for anybody. I was lonely and bored. We needed more relatives around." An engineer in the London Post Office returned when his wife developed severe allergies; a construction worker in Toronto came home after suffering a stroke; and a mechanic in Brooklyn brought his family back when his mother, at home in Barbados, was diagnosed as having cancer. Ann Bovell came back when her father sent word that he was seriously ill and needed her help, and Roy Campbell, though planning to return for nearly a decade, finally moved when he injured his back at his post office job and could no longer work. In Britain doctors often advise West Indians with serious health problems, especially mental disorders, to re-emigrate. The change of scene and climate may be good for the patient, but it also helps to reduce the burden on the National Health Service.

Migrant parents have also been disappointed in the education their children have received abroad, especially in inner-city schools. In Britain many West Indian children drop out of school, and a disproportionate number of those who remain in school perform at or near the bottom of every category of academic skill. Many Barbadian parents, who value education and will proudly tell you that Barbados has one of the world's highest literacy rates, believe that their children will do better in Barbadian schools.

Despite such complaints, most migrants who return home go primarily because of their attachment to the land of their birth.[11] As one elderly man, who chewed a stick of sugarcane as he spoke, said, "The money [in Canada] was good, and the people treated me with fairness, but in the end I wanted to be home with my own people, in my own land." A woman who had graduated from Colgate University and worked as a housing research analyst in Washington, D.C., returned to Barbados to teach high school because, she said, "Barbados is still a developing country, and I felt that any contribution that I make in my lifetime I want to make here."

Adjusting to Home

Most of the migrants in this book succeeded at finding good jobs. Some are employed by someone else: John Wickham, journalist and senator; Janice Whittle, schoolteacher; Valenza Griffith, nurse; Siebert Allman, construction supervisor; and Roy Campbell, bus inspector. Others are self-employed: Gabby, calypso performer; Richard Goddard, estate owner and businessman; Cleve and Rose Thornhill, bus owners; and Aileen Allman, seamstress.

A similar pattern of success can be seen among the returnees I surveyed. When the occupations of the surveyed returnees are compared with those of the total Barbadian people in the 1980 census we find that the returnees are disproportionately represented in high-status occupations. Forty-three percent of returnees, for example, are in the professional/technical category compared to just 9 percent of the general population, and 22 percent are in administrative/managerial jobs compared to only 2 percent of all Barbadians. Only 3 percent of returnees work in production, while 31 percent of the total labor force works at these jobs.

The oral histories show a picture of returnees who have complaints about Barbados and who have experienced some difficulty readjusting but who are generally satisfied to be home. Only Ann Bovell and Aileen Allman have serious regrets. The survey (1982–83) compared the returnees' levels of satisfaction after their first year at home and then again after three years at home. It found that over half (53 percent) the respondents were dissatisfied during their first year back in Barbados; they believed that they would have been more satisfied had they remained abroad. Over time, however, most of them adjusted. By the third year at home only 17 percent of all the returnees surveyed were still dissatisfied.

What problems do migrants encounter in their readjustment? A serious disappointment for some migrants is their inability to develop satisfying social relationships. Friendships do not materialize as expected. Relatives and friends from their youth, known for years only at a distance, often proved, at closer quarters, narrow and greedy. Neighbors who had appeared affable or chummy during return holiday visits when presents were distributed became distant or disinterested once the migrants returned for good. In the words of Ann Bovell:

> The people [villagers] say that I don't want friends. They say I don't want to share. Them that do the talking [gossiping] are the same ones that I brought goods for. I give them rice, I give them coffee, I give them dinner plates. I give all around, and I

try to keep friendship with them. They took my things, but then they cut me up.

About her situation Aileen Allman said, "It makes you wonder if people really care about you, or if they just want the things that you can give them."

Sometimes the old friends that the migrants had looked forward to seeing—those with whom they might recapture some lost memories of their youth—are no longer there, having themselves left the area. One man was disappointed to find upon his return home that all his former friends were gone, having emigrated or moved to Bridgetown. He did not know the younger crowd of men at the rum shop or any of the children. A stranger in his own village, he wondered if he had made the right decision in returning to Barbados after more than twenty years away.

In their interactions with villagers and workmates returnees often conclude that Barbadians who have never lived abroad are provincial and narrow-minded, which only makes it more difficult to establish friendships. One woman said to me, whispering as though she were afraid of being overheard:

> I have no good friends who have never been away. There are very few here I would want to call friends. . . . Their outlook on life is so small, so tiny, it's like they have blinkers on, like they're always going down a one-way street.

A man who had spent twenty-three years in England complained that the Barbadian women he met were boring, that he could not make conversation with them: "They sit there like great lumps of pudding with nothing at all to say." A woman in a remote village in St. Lucy, who had returned from New York, said:

> People here don't know what is going on in the outside world. People have walked on the moon; it be twenty years ago they were on the moon, and some [people] here is still saying it isn't so.

Some returnees feel they no longer share the same interests as their neighbors; their own interests, they feel, are more cosmopolitan and transcend the local community and the island. Aileen Allman, Ann Bovell, and Rose Thornhill, who all live in villages, complain that their neighbors are gossipy and preoccupied with the affairs of others in the village. Having grown accustomed to the anonymity of life in the metropole, they, like many other returnees, especially those who return to live in villages, feel a loss of privacy as their every action and even their new possessions come under public scrutiny. In the words of one woman, "People go out of their way to make gossip. You can't lead your own life here. It's so small, and everybody knows everybody. It's terrible." This same woman confided to me that she and her husband had made a mistake resettling in the village. "Maybe it wouldn't be so bad," she said, "if we had moved to Bridgetown."

Moreover, many sense, often accurately, that the villagers who stayed behind are jealous of their prosperity—of their large houses and new cars and their children's higher education. Resentment may be behind the frequent attempts by villagers to diminish the migrants' accomplishments and high status: money is said to be easy to earn abroad, and anyone who goes away, it is said, can come back rich. In the village of Sutherland the Allmans, rather than being credited with having worked hard, were rumored to have received a "blessing" or to have won a lottery. Villagers rarely came to their shop, lest they add to the family's wealth. Siebert Allman complained:

> Even the people from our church don't shop here. They don't want us to have their business, except for an occasional small thing when they run out and don't want to go into town. You can't win. If you come back with money, they are jealous. If you come back with nothing, they ridicule you. . . . When I was a poor shopkeeper, before I first left Barbados, we had more friends than we have today. Then we were all at the same level.[12]

On the other hand, it is also true that returnees are sometimes insensitive. They can strain relationships with friends and neighbors by their frequent comparisons of Barbados to the society from which they have returned. Some talk too much perhaps about the metropolitan society they have just left and their experiences abroad when they should be trying to find common ground with people at home.

An irritation, commonplace among migrants everywhere who return home to a developing society from the metropoles of the industrial world, is the slow pace of life and the difficulty of getting things done.[13] The migrants whose accounts are given here have been frustrated at the delays in getting service workers to make repairs, in getting a telephone installed, in clearing an overseas parcel at the local post office, and in having to wait in line while salesclerks chat with other customers. Having grown accustomed to the punctuality of Britons or North Americans, they are often impatient and frustrated by its absence at home. "If people agree to meet you at eight o'clock," said Roy Campbell, "they don't turn up until eight-thirty or maybe even nine o'clock, and they don't say they are sorry for being late." Valenza Griffith felt there were only two speeds in Barbados: "slow and dead stop."

Some migrants even describe their adjustment as a process of slowing down to the Barbadian pace of life. Some claim this takes a year or more. Ironically, the slowness of life at home, which annoys the recently returned migrant, often later becomes valued. Similarly, returnees who initially find the tropical heat hard to take, once acclimatized, regard the climate as one of their homeland's merits.

Returnees who are retired and living on pensions or otherwise fixed incomes often find the cost of living at home higher than they had anticipated. Those whose savings are being eroded by the high cost of goods and energy often speak of little else: canned fruit is four times what they paid abroad, milk and eggs twice, water and electric three times, and so forth. For them the cost of living becomes an obsession. A sixty-six-year-old retired welder said:

During my last five years in England I set aside money for my passage home. I did that and saved $3600 which I brought with me, thinking it was a fortune. But when I got here I found the cost of things like lumber and masonry for my house so high that my money disappeared fast. I could not even hold onto my passage money to England in case I ever wanted to go back.

Many returnees, however, reduce their household expenses by producing some of their own food—having kitchen gardens, fruit trees, and a few animals. One man, who earns half as much in Barbados working as a waiter as he did at the same job in Toronto, motioned to his backyard:

> In Toronto I lived ten floors up in an apartment. Here I can grow my own food. I can go out in the yard and pick a coconut, a lime, or a banana, and I raise my own animals. In Canada I had to buy all that stuff.

For women returning home can present special problems. Almost universally they held wage-paying jobs while abroad, yet they have more difficulty than their husbands finding work at home, particularly jobs with decent wages. Faced with accepting low wages or early retirement, some become self-employed. Aileen Allman sews uniforms for hotel staff, Ann Bovell sells soft drinks from her house, and Rose Thornhill keeps the books for the family bus operation. Their wage work overseas helped women gain a measure of independence and autonomy they had not enjoyed before. Their greater access to economic resources, if not outright control of their paychecks, enhanced their status and their claims for power and respect in relations with their husbands.[14] Listening to Aileen Allman or Ann Bovell describe the mind-numbing tasks and daylong repetition of the work they did in the sweatshops of Montreal and London makes it easy to underestimate the importance of work to these women. It is easy for the middle-class observer to see many of these jobs—as domestics, sewing machine operators, nurses' aides—as menial, low-paying, and demeaning. And from this perspective the work associated with being a homemaker in Barbados and perhaps tending a vegetable garden and a few animals—having land, fresh air, and open spaces—appears to be an attractive alternative. But this perception is not often shared by women who, prior to their emigration, had never earned a weekly paycheck nor enjoyed the autonomy, stimulation, and status that go with having a full-time job. For them wage work, menial or not, is an improvement over not working at all.

In village Barbados some returnee women find there are not enough things to do; some especially miss shopping. While living abroad, they had come to enjoy browsing and looking for bargains in the large, urban department stores, and they liked the wide range of foodstuffs available in the large supermarkets. In Barbados, especially outside Bridgetown's Broad Street, most retail stores are small, the range of goods limited, and the prices higher than overseas. Many women have lost a favorite pastime.

For women who have returned to Barbados without their grown children the most serious source of unhappiness is often the separation. Fathers, of course, also miss their children, but the sense of loss is greater for women. Ann Bovell spoke for many women when she confided at the end of one interview, "To tell the truth, I feel real bad the children being over there [England] and me being here." Aileen Allman's response to being cut off from her children has been to work even harder, often rising before dawn, in order to earn enough money to travel overseas each year to visit them in Canada, England, and Belgium. Rose Thornhill hopes that her children, whom she raised in London, will someday move to Barbados, but she is not optimistic.

Listening to the woes of returnees begs the question: why do so many migrants who are familiar with Barbados and who have usually visited the island several times before their actual return home have difficulty readjusting? As one local who had never been away said, "You'd think they'd know what they do be getting into." I believe the problem is best explained in terms of the changes that have occurred in the migrants themselves during their time abroad and, to a lesser degree, the changes that have taken place in the homeland during their absence. Migrants often do not realize how much their attitudes have been altered by their experiences in a metropolitan society until they come home. While abroad, they only see themselves in opposition to mainstream English or North Americans, and they tend to think of themselves, and the other Barbadian emigrants they live among, as being no different from people back home. It is when they return to Barbados and try to resume relationships with old friends and relatives that they first see the differences. To the returnees the changes are largely in their becoming what they see as more "broad-minded." In anthropological parlance the migrants have become less ethnocentric: they are no longer convinced that the Barbadian or West Indian way of life is necessarily the only right way. And they are less inclined to do something simply because of tradition. They have seen alternative ways of doing things, and, in some areas, these ways are better than those used at home. Hence, when they know a better method they sometimes become impatient with the time-honored Barbadian way.

Many come back with a changed attitude toward work. Most of them say they learned the value of hard work or how to work more efficiently. An architect who returned from Toronto, for example, said, "I now recognize that it takes work to be successful. I didn't really understand that before." And a female office worker, who had lived in Brooklyn for thirty-seven years, said:

> I learned that money doesn't grow on trees, that even in America you have to work hard to make money. Everyone should go away and see for themselves—it would be good for Barbados.

Many come back with a clearer idea of what they want in life. As one middle-aged man explained the change he saw in himself:

> I'm not interested in hanging around the way I did before I left. I want to go forward, to make something of myself. A lot of people here [a village in St. Andrew] don't want a lot. As long as they have a roof over their head, own their own home, they're happy.

Meanwhile, Barbados is not the same place the migrants left a decade or two before. Although most welcome the new prosperity, the doubling of the number of cars since 1970 has snarled traffic in Bridgetown, crime and drug use have increased, the development of hotels for tourists has driven up land prices on the coast so that there is no opportunity of buying a house near the sea, and young Barbadians are less courteous than they were a generation ago. These changes do not fit the image of Barbados that many migrants have retained from their youth, images that brief vacations at home had not entirely been able to correct or update. In short, the cause of dissatisfaction among many migrants is the lack of fit between what they expected to find at home and the reality. The most disgruntled are those who were most unrealistic about what Barbados could provide them. Their discontent is caused less by the actual social, economic, and environmental conditions at home than by their expectations.

With the passage of time, however, most returnees' dreams and fantasies fade, and they learn to cope with the inefficiency and petty annoyances of life at home. Gradually, expectations about what can be accomplished in a day's work are lowered, and the slow pace of Barbadian life is no longer an irritant. The better-off also cope by occasionally getting off the island, whether on business, to visit relatives, or just for a holiday. Even the less well-off may manage an occasional trip, usually a cheap charter package to Miami. In either case, a trip to a North American or British city can satisfy their appetites for the things they miss in Barbados, whether it be good movies, particular foods or cuisines, or discount merchandise. But being abroad also serves to remind them of the drawbacks of life in the metropolitan society—the impersonality, not feeling safe on the streets at night, racial prejudice, and the "rat race"—and that makes them appreciate Barbados and enables them to accept island life more easily.

Local Perceptions of Returnees

What do Barbadians who have never lived abroad think of returnees? Do they look up to them? Do they see them as role models? From the beginning of my research I informally asked Barbadians their opinions about return migrants. In speaking about neighbors and coworkers who have lived abroad, most Barbadians readily agree that returnees have been changed by their overseas experiences. There is a consensus that returnees are more broad-minded than Barbadians who have never left the island. The term *broad-minded* is such a typical response that it seems almost a cliché. When pressed to explain exactly what they mean by it people usually say something about the returnees having had more "experience" or having a greater knowledge of people and of the world. Recall the considerable contact the migrants in this book had with people from other cultures, and especially with other West Indians. Writing about immigrants, in general, Robert Park in 1928 noted how they had been changed by their experiences: "Energies that were formerly controlled by custom are released. . . . [Immigrants] become in the process not merely emancipated but enlightened." He goes on to say that the immigrant, in being freed from the constraints of tradition, becomes in certain respects cosmopolitan, and relations that were formerly "sacred" become secularized.[15]

Another widespread perception among Barbadians is that returnees are harder working and more goal oriented. One man remarked:

> When they come back here they know what they want from life, and they go forward. In that score you have to give them full credit, because they apply themselves diligently.

If asked directly, most Barbadians will also concede that returnees are less tolerant of racism and sexism and are more willing to support unpopular causes, such as putting protection of the environment before business interests.

But Barbadians are also critical of returnees, particularly of those who do not make enough effort to meld back into society or who think they are superior to their nonmigrant compatriots simply because they have lived abroad. One of my neighbors in the village of Free Hill said, "They feel that because they've been overseas in a big country and you ain't been nowhere that they are better than you." Another man said:

> They think because you were here in Barbados all the time that you didn't learn anything, while they being abroad learned all about life. Some of them, because they've been in a big country, come back down here to this small country, and they think they is the world.

Several villagers related incidents to me in which a returnee tried to appear worldly by pretending to have forgotten or never to have known some local custom:

> Sometimes they try to play the stranger. Like if you have a breadfruit in your hand, they might ask you, "Is that a breadfruit?" Now, you know they haven't forgotten what a breadfruit is.

Speech and dress are often mentioned as ways in which returnees stand out. Many have an English or North American accent when they return. And, as one villager explained, "They try to put their words in the proper places; they try to raise their language up." If the returnee's accent is pronounced, locals may suspect it is intentionally put on: "You find that lots of them pick up a foreign accent whether it's genuine or not. It's something they put on to let you know that they've been somewhere." It is said that migrants who have been away for a short period, say three or four years, often have stronger accents than those who have been away much longer.

One explanation given for this is that local people are more likely to forget that a person who had been away for only a short period had in fact lived abroad, whereas no one forgets the experience of the man or woman who had been away many years. About the latter one woman said, "They don't need to remind people by talking like they've just left England. You know they have been away." The speech of most returnees changes back to the Bajan dialect fairly quickly, but some traces of their foreign accent always remain. From speech alone, many Barbadians say they can tell whether or not a person has lived abroad even after they have been home for a decade or more.

Returnees are also said to stand out because of their clothes:

You can tell them by the way they dress. They wear stockings and sweaters and clothes like they were still living in a cold country. I always wonder how they manage underneath all them clothes—it must be so hot.

Most local Barbadians that I questioned believed that returnees were less conservative in their dress:

When they come back here they have a different manner of dressing. We Bajans feel that unless a man is in a tie and a waist coat and a woman is in a hat and long sleeves, they is not properly dressed for church. But these people who have traveled [lived abroad], well, you see the women in church bareheaded and in armhole dresses and some of the men with no tie. Now, we Bajans feel that is a sin.

Older Barbadians recall that in the past the attire of returnees stood out even more than it does today. When Barbados was poorer and the island had less contact with the outside world those migrants who came home were often a spectacle and the object of much attention. Speaking of the 1950s, one man recalled:

> Them back from England would wear these three-piece suits and stockings, and they'd all come back with a watch. Even if it was a really cheap watch, they'd want you to see it. If you hadn't noticed it, they'd pick up their wrist and look at the watch and say, "Gee, it's already two-thirty!" That was just to draw your attention to it, because having that watch was a great achievement.

Today most Barbadians deny being impressed by the speech or dress of returnees, although their wall houses and cars are a different matter.

Many locals are also of the opinion that Barbadians who have "traveled" are less religious when they come back. They are also said to be less strict with their children. "They no longer flogs their children to put them right," said one man. "They think that talking to the child, more than whipping it, is the better way. But I don't see their kids turning out any the better."

Nothing annoys Barbadians as much as hearing returnees complain about their country. This is often done in the context of comparing Barbados with the country from which the migrant has returned. Barbados invariably comes out on the short end of most comparisons. Locals say they do not want to hear how expensive the vegetables are in Barbados or that the cashiers are slow and discourteous or that medical service is not what it is in Britain or Canada. They have heard it all before and do not want to hear it again. One woman told me about two migrants back from England whom she overheard on the local bus:

> They were laughing at our buses, making fun of our buses— about how much better the buses were in England and that the roads there don't have no holes in it. It's not fair to stack up Barbados against a big country like England.

Return Migrants as Agents of Culture Change

Because most migrants move from areas of underdevelopment to areas of greater economic development, migration has become inextricably associated with issues of national development.[16] One question governments and anthropologists alike have begun to ask about return migration is whether returnees have any developmental impact when they return home. Do they bring back new ideas and attitudes that might rub off on local people? Do they bring back work skills or invest their overseas savings in ways that contribute to their society's development? Or are they a conservative force, not really adding anything new to society, who, in returning home, merely add to the island's overcrowding and the pressure on its scarce resources?

Most social scientists who have studied the impact of return migration have taken the latter view, that returnees play a minimal role, at best, in introducing modern ideas.[17] They also find that returnees rarely invest their repatriated earnings in new enterprises that create jobs or benefit the region. Russell King, writing about the Mediterranean, concludes: "The notion that returnees help in the development of their home country is falsely utopian."[18] For the English-speaking Caribbean Hymie Rubenstein suggests that return migration and remittances may actually add to the "deterioration of already trouble-ridden economies."[19] And in a review of the literature Michael Kearney concludes that "few migrants learn any new skills, or, if they do, rarely are they able to put them to use in the home community."[20] But these conclusions have largely been drawn from research conducted among peasant or worker migrants who have returned to rural areas, where undifferentiated agrarian economies provide little opportunity for them to make use of the new skills and training they acquired in urban-industrial settings abroad.[21]

The return experience described in the oral histories paints a different picture. Gabby, for example, introduced the North American "block party" to his own neighborhood, and it is now being repeated in other Barbadian communities to bring people together. And Richard Goddard organized and leads wilderness hikes to different parts of the island, patterned after what he saw in Canada; he now draws several hundred Barbadians every Sunday.

The survey offers even more evidence of Barbadian returnees being innovative influences for social change.

About half of the surveyed migrants who held jobs believed they had initiated at least one constructive change in their work-places based on knowledge they had acquired overseas. Those who were college educated or who had received technical training abroad, such as Valenza Griffith, John Wickham, and Janice Whittle, were twice as likely as the nontrained workers to believe they had been innovators. Some examples of innovations, cited by both the returnees as well as their employers, were the following: an American-trained certified public accountant, who became the head of the accounting department for a Bridgetown firm, implemented the electronic processing of financial accounts; an obstetrician, trained in Montreal, introduced new techniques for monitoring babies before birth; and a rector instituted policies he had learned in England that expanded the participation of his parishioners in church services.

In some fields major new innovations were attributed to the influence of return migrants. A movement to deinstitutionalize child care in Barbados came from returnees in the Ministry of Social Service who had become familiar with the new approach while working in Canada. Similar examples were given in computers, medicine, and engineering, all areas in which there is no graduate training offered in Barbados, and thus a large number of the practitioners are returnees.

Opportunities for migrants to apply their foreign experience appears to be greater in private sector jobs than in the public sector. Foreign work experience, in fact, is considered important by many in the Bridgetown business community. An owner of a retail sales firm said he preferred to hire returnees because of their wider experience. Perhaps with some exaggeration, Errol Inniss claimed, "There is nobody in business in Barbados who is moving up who has not been away. Any progressive young businessman would have left the country for awhile."

There is less room for innovation in government. Barbados' civil service, established by the British and modeled after their own system, is hierarchical and rigid. Its bureaucrats are said to be primarily interested in defending their own positions. Unlike the business community, where the pressure of competition forces people to be at least minimally open to new ideas, there is really no incentive for change in the civil service. One civil servant who had returned from England talked about his superiors, who had not been away:

> Because you've been away and maybe know more about something, they feel threatened. They don't want to admit that maybe you have the answer, especially when you've only been on the job half as long.

Recall the resistance Errol Inniss encountered from management in his efforts to install a television in the lobby of the Caribbean Broadcasting Service so that the telephone receptionist could respond to callers' queries and complaints about programs on the air.

But resistance to the foreign ideas of returnees is by no means restricted to government bureaucrats. Barbados is a conservative society in which people are slow to accept change, especially foreign ideas brought back by other Barbadian citizens. "When proposing some change to my parishioners," said an Anglican rector, "I have to be very careful not to let them think I learned it in England." Another man said of returnees:

> They have the same ideas as North Americans who live here. The difference is that people will listen to what the foreigner has to say but not to their own kind. They'll say, "Who the hell is he to tell us what to do? He's only a Barbadian like us."

As a rule, it is the returnees in professional or managerial positions who are most likely to introduce change. Whether managing a supermarket or teaching at the university, they have the authority and the freedom to put into practice the ideas and techniques they have learned abroad. Returnees who are on the shop floor rather than in the front office make it abundantly clear that, as "workers" rather than "bosses," they lack the opportunity to change things along the lines they learned while abroad. A diesel mechanic, trained in England and now employed in one of Barbados' six sugar factories, found that he knew much more about his job than his nonmigrant counterparts, but he had little effect:

They're [the other workers] not interested. If you tell them something new, they think you're trying to fool them. The guys here don't wear protective clothing when they're welding, and the factory won't make them until there is a serious accident. I've tried to show some of them that they should do it the right way, to look after themselves or they'll get injured. Some listen, but most don't.

In occupations where there are many return migrants, however, they may have an impact collectively. This was the case with nurses at one hospital, who, by strength of numbers, modernized some procedures and upgraded their positions. In the words of one:

If you try to change things, there is opposition. But there are certain standards in the hospital, and one is that they have meetings, and nurses are allowed to give their opinions. Since a lot of us have worked or were trained overseas, some things we say are heard.

Outside the workplace, however, the influence of migrants as purveyors of new ideas is much more difficult to measure. Certainly, we can find a few concrete examples in the narratives, such as Gabby's instrumental role in reviving the popularity of calypso, but most influences are difficult to pin down. There is no evidence, for example, of returnees having influenced the attitudes of local residents toward racism. Yet I am certain that it occurs. While some migrants may not say much about their encounters with racism overseas, others freely recount their experiences to neighbors and friends. The Allmans have told friends about being turned away at the door of an apartment after the landlord only a half-hour earlier had told them by telephone that an apartment was vacant. Similarly, Roy Campbell has told others of being denied a bus driver's job while all the white applicants got through. And many other returnees relate the stereotyped remarks they have overheard white Britons and Americans make about black people as being dirty, ignorant, loud, lazy, living off the backs of taxpayers, and eating smelly food.

Anthropologists Constance Sutton and Susan Makiesky found that, in the two Barbadian villages they studied, return migrants had a significant influence in awakening the racial and political consciousness of villagers who had not been away.[22] It was largely from migrants that villagers learned how black people were regarded in predominantly white Britain and North America. It is not that Barbadians had never known racism, for there is ample white bias in Barbados; rather, they had long assumed that the prejudice of their own whites was a perversion of the "true" metropolitan culture, that whites in England or North America somehow were different. By living abroad, the migrants had learned a different reality, which they communicate in various ways to Barbadians at home.[23] Sutton and Makiesky considered the returnees' influence in raising racial consciousness to be greater than that of either the Barbadian middle class or student radicals.[24] They also noted that, while the media keep Barbadians abreast of happenings in the outside world, it is often the returnee who interprets the news from overseas for the villager and, in the course of doing so, shapes public opinion.

We might look to technology for further evidence of the influence of returnees, as items of material culture are typically more easily transferred than ideas from one culture to another. In an earlier period Barbadians returning from work on the Panama Canal, with what local Barbadians referred to as "Panama money," introduced better household sanitation and window screens.[25] But today's returnees seem to be introducing little in the way of material culture other than their curious use in a tropical climate of wallpaper, wall-to-wall carpeting, and drapes, none of which has yet been imitated by other Barbadians. As a group, however, the returnees who have become accustomed to new technology abroad are likely themselves to be quicker to adopt new ideas and goods when they appear in Barbados.

One problem with assessing the influence of returnees in the larger community is trying to disentangle their role as agents of cultural change from other external influences on Barbadian society. Barbadians today have much contact with the outside world through films, foreign television programming, tourists, and travel. In the realm of material culture there is little that migrants can introduce that locals have not already seen.

But returnees do have a clear impact in another way. After years of hard work most emigrants arrive home with a sizable amount of capital from savings and from the sale of overseas assets, such as a house, a car, and furniture. Most use their savings to purchase housing or to improve the home or property they already own.[26] Returnee housing is almost invariably of high quality; as a rule, migrants buy or build substantial and high-status wall houses, rather than the more common wood houses most of them grew up in. In the villages large, solidly constructed, and brightly painted returnee housing often sets a standard that others aspire to.

Most returnees also buy a car. Successful migrants are expected to buy a car or bring one home when they return. Among our migrants only the Bovells, because they had never learned to drive, and Gabby, for ideological reasons, do not own an automobile. Several of the others own two vehicles. Car ownership is an important status symbol among middle-class Barbadians, who shun public transportation. Buying an automobile, however, provides no benefit to the island's economy, since all are manufactured outside Barbados. The potential balance of payment benefits of the returnees' repatriated earnings is canceled when the money is spent on imported items.[27] Worse yet, car ownership adds to the already severe congestion on Barbados' main roads.

Anthropologists in other settings have argued that it would be far better if return migrants invested their savings in business enterprises that create new jobs and capital rather than on housing and automobiles.[28] And it is largely the returnees failure to do so that has led these scholars to conclude that returnees have little or no impact on their homelands. Only one in seven Barbadian returnees in the survey had invested his or her savings in a business. One forty-five-year-old man, for example, spent the $16,000 he had saved during five years in Montreal on setting up an auto body repair shop. (When I met him in 1983 he was repairing a car in a field while at the same time doing business on a cordless telephone.) The Allmans opened a small general store when they first returned, and another family opened a typewriter repair shop. Still another had a fishing boat built with money the husband had earned over twenty years working on an assembly line in a Liverpool glass factory. Other migrants who brought cars home from abroad set themselves up as taxi drivers. Although these are not new enterprises and they do not employ many people, they do provide needed services and contribute to the smooth running of the economy. The new typewriter repair service, for example, is an enormous improvement over the slow and inefficient repair shops run by nonmigrants.

Moreover, while Barbadian returnees admittedly spend their repatriated savings mostly on consumption—on housing, furnishings for their homes, and automobiles—these investments do raise their living standard and their social status, which in most cases were their reasons for emigrating in the first place. It seems unreasonable to expect them to invest their savings in a business before providing for their own shelter. Often the problem is not the returnees' investment priorities but, rather, simply not having enough capital. Many more returnees would start businesses if they had enough money remaining after taking care of their housing needs. And some returnees, if they are financially successful at home, will later start up businesses of their own. It was nearly twenty years after Richard Goddard returned from Canada that he finally had enough capital to buy a large sugar estate, which he then diversified into different crops and livestock. His estate is a small but important part of the national effort to find alternatives to growing sugar.

In the aggregate Barbados' returnees, who bring back new ideas, work skills, and capital, are an important resource for the nation's development. And by "development" I mean more than simple economic growth; rather, I am referring to a broader concept, one that implies an open-ended type of social change in which there is progress toward the establishment of a self-reliant society.

Since the bulk of postwar English-speaking Caribbean migrants emigrated to North America and Britain, the skills and cultural knowledge they return with are Western ones. Hence, in the Caribbean context *development*, at its roots, means becoming Western. At the national level, progress, or development, becomes a measure of the country's proximity to the institutions and values of British and North American society.[29] The ethnocentrism inherent in this position is unfortunate, but in assessing the impact of migrants returning from Western metropoles it is difficult to avoid. The problem is mitigated, however, by the fact that Barbados is not a traditional non-Western society. It is neither Bali nor Nepal nor Samoa. The aboriginal Arawak and Carib inhabitants of Barbados were gone by the time of British settlement in the 1600s, and from that time until 1966 the island was a colony of Britain.

Furthermore, both black and white Barbadians have always been oriented toward Britain and, more recently, North America and still look to these countries for their social and economic goals. In short, in the minds of most Barbadians the transfer of culture and capital from the metropolitan countries to their island nation represents development. Curiously, from a labor and capital point of view, the return of migrants to their homelands is also beneficial to the host countries. It is in the interests of the United Kingdom, the United States, and other metropolitan countries to have migrant laborers go home as they age and become less productive and as their children begin to take spaces in the schools and universities. When migrants return home Barbados, like other developing countries, bears most of the cost of reproduction, education, and, at the other end of the life cycle, retirement. As Kearney affirms, as capitalist economies mature and their populations grow, circular labor migration becomes preferred over permanent immigration.[30] It is not surprising that most industrial countries in the post–World War II era have preferred "guest" worker programs.

Finally, it is legitimate to ask, though we can never know the answers, what would have happened to Barbados had these migrants, and the many more who permanently remain abroad, not left their island. Young, healthy, and ambitious at the time of their emigration, how would they have changed their society had they stayed behind? And how would Barbados have responded to and been changed by the increased unemployment and pressures on scarce resources that would have inevitably resulted?

NOTES

1. An interview schedule containing 140 items was used to gather data on the circumstances of the interviewees before their emigration from Barbados, the emigration experience (i.e., work, housing, and adjustment), the reasons for returning to Barbados, the post-return adjustment, and

the social and economic impact of the migrants in the workplace and community. The study also involved open-ended interviews concerning the impact of return migrants with officials and executives representing different sectors of Barbadian business, government, and academe.

2. R. L. King, "Return Migration: Review of Some Cases from Southern Europe," 175–76.

3. For comparisons with other cultures, see the literature reviews by Bovenkerk; G. Gmelch, "Return Migration"; and King, "Return Migration."

4. The pattern was similar among the Irish and Newfoundland returnees that I surveyed: in both populations only 22 percent of the return migrants said they had expected to remain away permanently at the time they first left home.

5. I have heard Barbadians tell stories about migrants who came home and discovered that their wives or families had frittered away the remittances they had sent home. These frustrated and unhappy migrants, often with nothing to show for the years of effort and saving, reemigrated.

6. I have also heard of students who went abroad to earn a college degree but dropped out or were dismissed for poor grades and then remained overseas to avoid the shame of returning home a failure.

7. For more detailed discussions of the influence of macroeconomic conditions on return flows in other settings, see J. Hernandez-Alvarez, *Return Migration to Puerto Rico;* S. Paine, *Exporting Workers: The Turkish Case;* R. Rhoades, "Intra-European Return Migration and Rural Development: Lessons from the Spanish Case"; and M. Piore, *Birds of Passage: Migrant Labor and Industrial Societies.*

8. Most governments do not have good measures of return migration because of the difficulty in distinguishing overseas nationals who have only returned home to visit from those who have returned to stay.

9. Similarly, many Irish and Newfoundland returnees said the favorable experiences during a holiday visit home were also the impetus for them to return permanently (Gmelch, "Who Returns and Why," 52).

10. S. Monroe, "Blacks in Britain: Grim Lives, Grimmer Prospects," 32.

11. The desire to return is usually stronger among men than women. In all three of the oral histories where we hear from both husband and wife, for example, the wives—Aileen Allman, Ann Bovell, and Rose Thornhill—initially resisted the decision to come home.

12. This quotation was taken from an interview I did for a video documentary, and therefore the wording is slightly different than the version that appears in the oral history.

13. For examples from other cultures, see Gmelch, "Return Migration," 143–44.

14. Michael Whiteford's observations among Columbian migrant women that migration is a "liberating process which results in a modicum of sexual equality" applies equally well to Barbadian migrant women ("Women, Migration, and Social Change: A Columbian Case").

15. R. Park, "Human Migration and the Marginal Man," 887–88. Also discussed in A. Portes and R. Rumbaut, *Immigrant America: A Portrait,* 146.

16. M. Kearney, "From the Invisible Hand to Visible Feet: Anthropological Studies of Migration and Development," 332.

17. See, for example, B. Dahya, "Pakistanis in Britain: Transients or Settlers?"; Rhoades, "Intra-European Return Migration"; and H. Rubenstein, "Remittances and Rural Underdevelopment in the English-speaking Caribbean."

18. King, "Return Migration," 17.

19. Rubenstein, "Remittances and Rural Underdevelopment," 298.

20. Kearney, "From the Invisible Hand to Visible Feet," 246.

21. Gmelch, "Return Migration," 146–47.

22. C. Sutton and S. Makiesky, "Migration and West Indian Racial and Political Consciousness."

23. Quoted in ibid., 115–16.

24. Ibid., 124–25.

25. B. C. Richardson, *Panama Money in Barbados, 1900–1920.*

26. The preference to use one's savings to buy and improve housing has been widely described among returnees elsewhere. For a detailed example, see Rhoades, "Intra-European Return Migration"; and, for a review of similar cases, see Gmelch, "Return Migration," 148.

27. Rubenstein, "Remittances and Rural Underdevelopment," 298.

28. For good examples of this argument, see Rhoades, "Intra-European Return Migration"; R. E. Wiest, *Rural Community Development in Mexico: The Impact of Mexican Recurrent Migration to the United States;* and King, "Return Migration."

29. E. Thomas-Hope, "Return Migration and Implications for Caribbean Development."

30. Kearney, "From the Invisible Hand to Visible Feet," 344.

Chapter 16

Reflections on Oral History and Migration

At the beginning of this book I stated that I thought the best way to get beneath the abstractions of migration theory in order to understand migration from an insider's perspective is through oral history. In this final chapter I would like to offer some reflections on the uses of oral history in this work and in the study of migration generally. I will also address some questions that early readers of this book have raised, which are not only relevant to *Double Passage* but to all retrospective accounts.

Memory and the Reliability of Personal Narratives

How well do people recall their pasts, and, if they do, can we rely upon them to tell it accurately? The vagaries of memory have been a concern of critics of oral history.[1] In the recounting of most experiences, and especially an entire life, a person is bound to leave out some things. Human memory is never a perfect blueprint of past life events; many details are, with the passage of time, forgotten.[2] A lot more is simply never stored in long-term memory. Social psychologists have found that accurate recall depends on the initial perception of the event, so that people, things, and details that individuals did not notice when the experience occurred are never entered into memory and, therefore, cannot be recalled, no matter how much probing or prompting by a researcher.[3]

To a large degree we remember best those experiences and events that are, or were: (1) important to us (e.g., rites of passage, major achievements); (2) unique or unusual events, rather than commonplace ones; and (3) occasions with a strong emotional content (e.g., birth of a child, death of a parent).[4] All three factors come into play in many aspects of migration. Just consider what migration involves for most Barbadian men and women: the first experience away from home; travel overseas by ship or plane (which most had never experienced before); a new job, usually in a new line of work; new accommodations in an English or American house, whose features are markedly different from Caribbean homes; being a racial minority for the first time; and so on. Many of these feelings and experiences are out of the ordinary, which means they impress themselves indelibly on the mind. All of the migrants I have worked with—Irish, Newfoundlanders, and Barbadians—have particularly strong memories of their migration, and I believe this is so because it was the paramount experience of their lives. In listening to migrants talk I was sometimes reminded of the stories my grandfather told of his life in the U.S. army in France during World War I and those of my father-in-law, as a pilot during World War II. Migration, like war, creates vivid memories, and vivid memories are more likely to be reliable than dim ones.[5]

There are also small ways a researcher can enhance memory. One advantage to doing not one but a series of interviews spaced over time is that memories forgotten at one interview sometimes come back to the subject in the interim and are reported at the next session. Photographs can also help. I asked all the subjects to show me their family photo albums, if they had one. Their looking at the pictures and explaining them to me helped them to remember details they had forgotten or overlooked in the interviews. In recording the life of an Alaskan Eskimo I found by accident that an excellent aid to memory is to take the subject to the setting in which the experiences being described had actually occurred.[6] In this case I had spent several weeks interviewing my Eskimo assistant about traditional land use and subsistence—when, where, and by what method he and his people hunt, fish, and gather a wide range of resources (whales, salmon, caribou, fox, wolf, berries, etc.). The interviews were done in my cabin, and we used maps to plot the locations and seasons of different activities. Then, by chance, we traveled together down the Noatak River in a boat to the Bering Sea, where many of the villagers had summer fishing and whaling camps. On the trip, with my questions still firm in his mind, his memory came alive. With each bend in the river another forgotten place and details of the Eskimos' activities associated with that place, past and present, came to him.

Later I learned that psychologists call this "environmental context-dependent memory,"[7] and it relates to much of our experience being integrated with environmental information. When we move to a new location, such as my Eskimo informant to a village or a migrant's return home from abroad, we become physically separated not only from our former residence but also from the habits, routines, and people associated with that place. Without being in the physical presence of these reminders of our past, memory decays. Simultaneously, the new habits, routines, and friends of our new environment cause the disuse of old memories.[8] Of course, it was not possible to take my Barbadian narrators overseas, back to their neighborhoods and workplaces in London, New York, and so on, but had it been possible, I have no doubt that their stories would have been richer for it. (In the Eskimo case I also found that my actually seeing the places that figured prominently in my assistant's stories greatly increased my own understanding of the Eskimo past, enabling me to ask better questions.)

Also of concern to oral historians and their critics is not just how completely people can recall the past, but whether their recollections are selective.[9] Because oral histories can never be more than portions of lives, they inevitably involve selection.[10] I am sure that the migrants in these narratives sometimes omitted or played down experiences they were not proud of or that might have put them in a negative light. Most people avoid memories that are painful or embarrassing. But it is usually true that people will talk about them when directly asked, at least that has been my experience with the narrators in this book. Roy Campbell, for example, never mentioned his regret over living apart from his children for many years, but when I asked about it he was forthcoming and open.

Likewise, rarely did the migrants recount painful encounters with racism independent of my asking. But, when I asked, usually with a question phrased something like, "Do you recall any incidents in which you were discriminated against?", most spoke without hesitation. Rarely did I have the feeling that a narrator was intentionally distorting or censoring a story or information that he or she was telling me. Most of the migrants, I believe, held the attitude that I put forward in the first interview: that the interviews were a chance to record for all time what it had been like to leave one's home and to be a Barbadian in Britain or North America and that their aim as a narrator was to set down the story in as much detail and as accurately as possible. I am not suggesting that the migrants were never selective in their recollections; certainly, they sometimes were. But I have no reason to believe that this selectivity has created an inaccurate picture or has led to false conclusions about their lives.

Let us take Valenza Griffith's story, one in which I suspect there was some selectivity. In her narrative there is little mention of her husband, Randall, from whom Valenza had recently separated. Because Randall has such a low profile, the reader might easily conclude that it was Valenza who made the decisions and ran the household in England. Actually, given her assertive and outgoing personality, she may well have been the pillar of the household, but that is another matter. For the sake of argument let us assume that she was not. Does the impression of her dominance in the household invalidate the rest of her story? Of course not. Perhaps if this volume were a single life history and Valenza was presented as a typical West Indian woman migrant, the reader might conclude that West Indian women have more authority and power in the household than they actually do. But Valenza is only one of five women in *Double Passage*, and, even with a small sample, we are not likely to generalize from her case alone.[11]

A different kind of selectivity, though not an intentional one, may occur when a change in the attitude of the narrator, subsequent to the event, causes him or her to view the event differently today than at the time it occurred. The past is never simply the past but, rather, a prism through which subjects filter memories according to their worldview and self-interest.[12] It is not that the events themselves are recalled differently but that the subject's feelings about the events may be different today, and that can color or shape the memory. The bitterness, for example, that Roy Campbell expresses today when recalling his being denied a bus driving job in London solely because of his color may be the result of an awareness of racism that he did not have at that time. The specific events he describes are not in question; I would expect that he relates the facts of what took place much the same today as he would have years ago. Rather, what is more susceptible to change are his feelings about it. One might argue that Roy, as a young, recent immigrant to Britain, had not yet experienced any racial prejudice, and, therefore, when he was turned down for the job he was not certain that it was due to prejudice. Then his subsequent experiences in London revealed that racism was the real reason, which, of course, changed his feelings.

To bring this closer to home, how accurately do Americans who were students or adults in the 1960s recall their attitudes toward the Vietnam War (or, say, the civil rights movement) at that time? I imagine that, for many citizens who once supported the war, disclosures about the conduct of the United States government during the Vietnam years and the events that have unfolded in its aftermath have not only changed their opinions but also their memories of the attitudes they once held.

That human memory is fallible and subjective must be taken into consideration in all research that relies upon retrospective accounts. More than oral history, this includes a good deal of ethnography and survey research that routinely calls upon their subjects to remember past behavior and events. And for historians the selective reporting and recording of data in written documents is no less of a problem. As Paul Thompson notes in *Voices of the Past*, many of the social historian's sources—such as census data, registrations of birth and marriage, government commissions, and social surveys—are themselves derived from interviews. And the questions that need to be asked of the documents that historians depend on generally—whether they are forgeries, who the author was, for what purposes they were produced—can more easily be answered for oral testimony than for written documents.[13] This is especially so when the oral testimony comes from the researcher's own fieldwork.

Anthropologists get a sense of the accuracy of their informants' accounts by living with the people and knowing them over a long period of time. In having many conversations with the same individuals there are opportunities to check and recheck the information given. The researcher also compares the information given by one informant with that of another, uncovering inconsistencies and fabrications.[14] When the research concerns behavior that occurred outside the community, however, such as international migration, then these normal checks on the reliability of personal accounts become somewhat problematic. Most of the migrants I interviewed, for example, did not live in the same village as I, and most of the people in my village had never been migrants; therefore, they were not in a position to refute or validate stories told by my narrators. On the other hand, my residence and fieldwork in a Barbadian community allowed me to informally check many of the stories the narrators told me about return migration. And, of course, my observations and conversations with returnee families in my village increased my general understanding of migration, an informal check of sorts.

The Influence of the Researcher

The oral life histories in this volume are not just the creation of the individual narrators. Rather, they are the result of a collaboration between the narrators and a researcher, and hence there are important epistemological considerations. We need to recognize, says John Knudson, that life histories are a "shared composition," in which the relationship between the two parties is inseparable. In a similar vein others have referred to life history as "joint productions" and "collaborative biography." Marjorie Shostak tells us that life histories cannot exist independently of the collaborative process involved in their collection, for an interview is an interaction between two people. James Freeman says life histories do not just happen; they are "staged and directed by the investigator," despite the concerted attempts by most researchers to be as nondirective as possible.[15] Moreover, in anthropology life histories are seldom an integral part of the culture in which they are collected; rather, they happen because a foreign researcher provoked and guided their creation.[16]

These observations are useful reminders both to investigators engaged in collecting oral history and to readers assessing the material. But some critics overstate the influence of the researcher on their subjects' narratives to the point where it is taken as a crippling limitation of the method. Gelya Frank, for example, says that the process blends together the consciousness of the investigator and the subject so much that it's not possible to disentangle them. She even suggests that we consider them as "double autobiographies."[17] I believe such claims are exaggerated. Had the interviews in this book been conducted by someone else, I do not doubt that they would be different in some respects, but I would also expect that their essential characteristics would remain the same. In an apt analogy Freeman compares his influence as the recorder of a life history to that of a portrait photographer who shapes the image by controlling the lighting in his studio and by cropping the composition in the darkroom.[18] Some features of the subject may be emphasized or enhanced by the photographer, but no one would mistake the subject's likeness for someone else.

Today some life and oral historians insist that the readers should not only know what procedures were used in the research, but they should also know something about the researcher's background. It is important, they say, so that the reader can place the work in context and know something about how the researcher might have influenced the work.[19] Accordingly, I reflected on my own background, looking for clues that might explain why I did this research and how I might have left an imprint on it.

Why migrants? My interest in recording the experiences of Barbadian migrants may be due in some measure to my having been a migrant of a sort and in the same countries—Canada and England. After graduate school my wife and I moved to Montreal, where I took up my first teaching position (at McGill University); and in 1980–81 we lived in England while doing research for the English Department of the Environment. Some of the subjects of our research—Gypsies and Travellers—had moved to cities and were neighbors to West Indians.[20]

My interest in migrants may also stem, in part, from the similarity of my own experiences as a young man leaving home to play professional baseball and those of the migrants: both involved relocation and all the attendant logistical problems, adjusting to a new environment and social group, and some acculturation into a new culture for the migrants and a subculture for the ballplayer. Moreover, the study of migrants fits well into a theme that runs through most of my work. That is, an interest in adaptation, in the strategies that people develop to cope with the demands of the physical and social environments in which they live. It first shows up in my dissertation research twenty years ago, in which I examined how Irish Travellers, as migrants from rural Ireland, adapted to cities and how urbanization changed their lives, society, and culture.[21]

The interest in migrants also fits a pattern of studying marginalized groups of people—Irish Travellers, English Gypsies, and Native Americans. All have been disadvantaged in some fashion by racial and ethnic prejudice. Seen against my own upbringing, an interest in such groups may seem curious. I am a white male from a solidly middle-class, West Coast, Protestant family. I grew up in the suburbs and went to a middle-class high school, where my main interest was baseball and my identity was as a "jock," which was what I then wanted to be. Although there were some Asian Americans in school, I do not recall any blacks or Latinos, or, if there were, they were invisible to me. I had no awareness of ethnicity, and I could not have told you which of the kids I knew at school were Protestant, Catholic, or Jewish. I scarcely knew the meaning of racism. This was the early 1960s.

Ironically, my first exposure to racism, and perhaps the beginning of my interest in minorities, occurred in professional sports. I was living in North Carolina, playing first base on a Detroit Tigers farm club. It was our first road trip of the season, and in the middle of the night we stopped at a restaurant to eat. While my sixteen white teammates and manager entered the restaurant through the front door, my black teammates went around to the back. Back on the bus, I learned that they were not allowed to eat with the white folks and, moreover, that in some towns on our road trips they would be staying in hotels separate from the rest of us. Then, returning to Rocky Mount, the town I played for, I discovered there were separate drinking fountains and waiting rooms for blacks. On foot I explored the town's black neighborhoods, much as Gabby had examined his new environs in New York, though without the same concern for my safety. I remember thinking that the black side of town, just a mile from my comfortable neighborhood, looked like a different country.[22]

But a curiosity about other cultures, despite my ignorance of cultural groups within my own society, had occurred for me at a younger age. My father was an executive in the shipping business, which each year took him on a lengthy trip to the "Orient," as we then called it. My mother sometimes went along. At the dinner table in the weeks after they had returned I would hear descriptions of other peoples and their customs. Our house was decorated and furnished with artifacts from the places they had been— cinnabar and cloisonné from China, scrolls and sumie (ink paintings) from Japan, rosewood and carved teak chests from Hong Kong, rattan furniture from the Philippines, and so on. We also adopted a few customs from the Far East, such as not wearing shoes in the house, and my mother learned to cook "Chinese," which, of course, we all ate with chopsticks. There was a considerable gap in time between these experiences and my decision as a disillusioned biology major at Stanford University to switch my major to anthropology, but I would be surprised if they did not contribute to my interest in other cultures.

My mother was (and remains) an avid reader and throughout my upbringing was always attending courses at the community college. She traveled and, being a photographer, took lots of pictures. Her images of the Far East and Mexico hung on our walls. I suspect my own interest in using photographs in research, both as projective techniques (as an aid in getting informants to talk about things) and as illustrations in my writings, has come largely from her. So, asking my Barbadian narrators to show me their pictures then later borrowing them for use in this volume to illustrate their stories came naturally.

Why did I choose to work in Barbados rather than somewhere else? I first went to Barbados not out of any special interest in the Caribbean but because of the frequency of migration there. Prior to this I had completed a comparison of return migration in Ireland and Newfoundland, and I was then interested in comparing the findings from the North Atlantic with another region. Several colleagues suggested the Caribbean. In discussions with Caribbeanists I narrowed down the possible locations to Barbados, Jamaica, and Trinidad and bought a plane ticket that would take me to each. I ruled out Trinidad because its ethnic diversity and much larger size would have complicated the study; Jamaica posed similar problems, and also I was warned that the students that I might ultimately take to the field with me might not be safe there. Barbados felt right and was easily my first choice for both academic and, I must admit, aesthetic reasons.

In chapter 1 I explained that the idea for doing oral histories of migration arose from my dissatisfaction with the survey approach I had used earlier and that I wanted to convey what migration meant to its participants. But I now suspect there were other reasons as well. Having some loss of hearing (due to a high school classmate discharging a rifle near my ear), I am more comfortable talking to people one-on-one, which, of course, is the format of interviewing. In groups I often don't hear the little witticisms, quips, and asides that can be revealing, and for an anthropologist this is extremely frustrating.

Hopefully this biographical information explains why I did this particular research, but I wonder if it says very much about how I, as the researcher and editor, might have biased the material. I suppose one might argue that my interest in the experiences of individuals has caused me to overlook the role of groups, such as voluntary associations, in the migrants' adjustment—but I doubt that. I inquired, and for most of the narrators organized groups do not figure very prominently, if at all. Or perhaps there is a clue here about why, as I mentioned in chapter 14, politics and religion are given little attention in the migrants' stories. If so, I am unaware of what that may be. I am not suggesting that, as the one who asked the questions and who edited the verbal accounts into written ones, I did not have an influence; rather, I am saying that I simply don't know what it is. The problem may be that beneath our life experiences and conscious attitudes and values are a host of unconscious tendencies that do influence the kinds of questions we ask and how we interpret the answers. But without a psychoanalytic search these are things that we have very little knowledge of or easy access to. And, as Freeman notes, self-analysis is often self-delusion.[23]

Margaret Blackman, who has written two life histories of native American women, says that, if it were not for the investigator's questions, which suggest to the subject a structure for his or her stories, a subject might organize the stories in a different way. She gives the example of James Nageak, an Eskimo, who was recording his grandfather's life story. He began by locating his grandfather in a large kinship network and then gave all the geographical places he was connected to. Obviously, this is quite different from how Barbadians begin their own life histories, as their ancestry in

Barbados is rooted in slavery and, with it, landlessness and trun-
cated genealogies. I cannot say how Barbadians might structure
their own life histories, unaided or uninfluenced by the inquiring
anthropologist. My guess is that the stories would not be very
different than those that appear in this volume. Although most
Barbadians are of African heritage, their worldviews and orienta-
tions are today far more Western than African, the result of several
hundred years of living in a small colonial society, the replacement
of their native languages with English, and, in more recent times,
education with a British curriculum and books. So, unlike
Eskimos, or, say, the Moroccan subjects of Vincent Crapanzano
and Kenneth Dwyer's life histories,[24] the chronological organization of my interviews was not alien to the ways in which the
narrators think about their own lives.

The Place of Oral History in Migration Studies

Having considered some limitations of oral history—the fallibility
of human memory, selective reporting of the narrator's past, and
the unknown influences of the investigator in shaping an
account—let us now turn, in conclusion, to some of the strengths
it brings to the study of migration.

Migration, unlike many other cultural phenomena, is not a
readily observable event. There are no artifacts or special material
culture; there are few, if any, rituals and little public behavior
related to migration. If one is investigating the adaptations of
migrants after they have arrived in the host society, then, of course,
a wide range of behavior is observable. But, ordinarily, most of the
stuff of migration involves spontaneous discussions, debates, and
decisions, which usually take place in the privacy of the home. And
in most communities few families are actively planning to migrate
at any one time. There are exceptions: famine, natural disasters,
and war provoke large-scale migration. (But we then call the
subjects "refugees" rather than "migrants.") In the course of an
anthropologist's normal term of fieldwork migration is a rare
event. In fact, during my entire stay only one family emigrated
from the Barbadian village in which I lived. It makes sense, then,
to rely on the migrants' own detailed accounts of their decision
making and behavior, and what better way to do that than in a

series of intensive, open-ended interviews in which migration is explored in the larger context of an individual's life?

Migration invariably involves two or more locations—namely, the communities that migrants leave and the places they move to. Because of this, it is usually not feasible, financially and logistically, for the investigator to do research in both locations. This is particularly so when the migration is international. Traditionally, there has been a division of labor: some anthropologists work in the villages and towns of the sending societies, often examining the reasons for the migrants' departure and the impact of their absence, while others work in the host societies, often studying the migrants' adaptation in the new, usually urban setting.

One consequence of social scientists working at only one end of the migration chain has been a failure to appreciate the systemic nature of migration—that, while migrants may be far from their homelands, they are still embedded in and affected by social networks and dyadic relations that reach back to the village. Robert Rhoades speculates that the kind of fieldwork that anthropologists do—participant observation in a single community for a set period of time (usually one year)—has led to a view of migration as a one-way movement, as a static event.[25] Put differently, the snapshot view of migration produced by this fieldwork often fails to note that many migrants eventually return home, that for every migration flow there is a counterstream. Oral history is not constrained by time and space, so that, in recording the lives of migrants, it reveals migration's cyclical nature.

There is also, I believe, a good fit between oral history, with its focus on documenting individual experience, and migration, which is usually an individual act (although family, kin, and friends both at home and abroad also play a role). In the Caribbean, as in many societies, the majority of migrants are single when they leave home. And even after marriage it is common for family members to go individually (usually men going in advance of their wives and children). As Caroline Brettell put it, "Ultimately it is individuals, or at most families who migrate, not cultures, societies, nor even social groups."[26]

The open-endedness of oral history interviews—the narrators being free to talk about whatever they want—can produce information about behavior that has been overlooked in studies using other approaches. One example that comes readily to mind from the present narratives is the migration journey. In most studies the trip is usually ignored, whether it be from village to city within a single society or across an ocean and national (and cultural) borders. Perhaps this is because few researchers ever have the opportunity to make such a journey with their subjects, as migration is not an everyday occurrence, and there may be considerable expense involved in traveling to another country. In any case, the Barbadians' accounts suggest that the journey is often a significant event. It is usually the individual's first time away from home and first experience on an airplane or ship; there are weeks of anticipation and preparation before embarking and often much anxiety. And for long trips, such as the sea passage to England, the journey itself may help the migrants to mentally prepare for what is to come. In short, oral histories can give us hunches about behavior that we need to investigate in greater depth with other methods.

Finally, in providing an insider's account, oral history reveals the subjective world of attitudes, ideas, and emotions. This is a perspective not often found in studies of migration, which are typically based on etic methods, where the emphasis is on the general rather than the individual. In the migrants' narratives the reader learns the contexts in which decisions, choices, and social acts occur. And these paint a picture of migration that is not only rich in detail and texture but is often more complex and varied than etically based generalizations and models of migration suggest. (See, for example, the discussion of migration motives in chapter 14). In their focus on the community or societal level most migration studies homogenize the individuals. In place of the varied individual experiences we get abstract descriptions or statistical frequencies of behavior, like the following, taken randomly from books on the shelf of my home library:

Social relations among [the migrants] in the capital are based on dyadic contacts in which mutual expectations and obligations exist within a system of reciprocal, multi-purpose ties.

Economic motives were cited by 68.2 percent of the respondents . . .

Nearly 35% of the migrants had visited home at least once every three years.

The migrants mentioned 3.7 factors as having had an influence on their decision to return home.

Of course, these kinds of generalizations and statistical summaries of what is normative are essential to our understanding of migration and to developing theory. Oral history data is quite unsuitable for determining frequencies, averages, and relationships between variables. But from narratives we learn the particular as opposed to the general, and we can understand what the abstract categorizations and generalizations about migration look like on the ground, from the individual's point of view. We get a sense of the degree to which migrants are free actors shaping their own destinies as opposed to pawns merely responding to constraints imposed upon them by their society. In all this I believe oral history offers an invaluable alternative to the increasing tendency in the social sciences to reduce people to categories and abstractions.

NOTES

1. Michael Frisch notes in *A Shared Authority* that memory has always been difficult for historians to confront, "committed as they are to notions of objectivity beyond the definitive subjectivity of individual and collective recall" (21). For other discussions of the concerns over subjectivity of memory, see R. Grele, *Envelopes of Sound: The Art of Oral History;* and P. Thompson, *Voice of the Past: Oral History.*
2. Some research has shown, however, that, after rapid loss, or "degradation," of memory in the months immediately following any experience, memory then stabilizes with very little subsequent loss, even over decades. See Thompson, *Voice of the Past,* 101–3.
3. R. Gant, "Archives and Interviews: A Comment on Oral History and Fieldwork Practise," 28.
4. See articles by Barclay and DeCooke, "Ordinary Everyday Memories"; Barsalou, "The Content and Organization of Autobiographical Memories"; and Brewer, "Memory for Randomly Sampled Autobiographical Events," in *Remembering Reconsidered: Ecological and Traditional Approaches to the Study of Memory,* ed. U. Neisser and E. Winograd. See also S. Larsen and K. Plunkett, "Remembering Experienced and Reported Events."

5. F. Heuer and D. Reisberg, "Vivid Memories of Emotional Events: The Accuracy of Remembered Minutiae," 496–506.

6. The research involved traditional land-use and subsistence patterns among Inupiaq Eskimos in Noatak National Park and Preserve and was conducted for the U.S. National Park Service.

7. A good review of this literature is found in S. M. Smith, "Environmental Context-Dependent Memory."

8. Ibid., 15.

9. I suspect there is often a difference in the candor (i.e., memory selectivity) of preliterate peoples compared to literate ones. All of the Barbadian narrators read newspapers daily; some have read biographies, and John Wickham has written one. Hence, most of them had some sense that what they said in the interviews would eventually appear in print for others to read. I don't believe the Ikung woman, Nisa, or the relatively uneducated Mexican peasant, Pedro Martinez, or the Moroccan lower-caste tile maker, Tuhami, whose life histories have been recorded by anthropologists, had the same awareness. Nor in this volume do I believe that the rural working-class migrants understood, despite my explanations, what would happen to their spoken words in the same way that John Wickham, Gabby, and Janice Whittle did.

10. Grele, *Envelopes of Sound*, 244.

11. Paul Thompson in *Voice of the Past* notes that distortion or suppression in a life story may "provide an important clue to the family's psychology and social attitudes" (110). In short, it need not always be a negative.

12. L. Watson and M. Watson-Franke, *Interpreting Life Histories: An Anthropological Inquiry.*

13. Thompson, *Voice of the Past*, 92. Despite this, Thompson notes, many historians even feel more comfortable citing a published autobiography rather than an interview, "just because it is printed rather than recorded on tape." Yet, bias and subjectivity are potentially much greater in autobiography, where "the author cannot be cross-questioned, or asked to expand on points of special interest. The printed autobiography is a one-way communication, and with its content definitely selected with the taste of the reading public in mind" (94).

14. L. Langness and G. Frank, *Lives: An Anthropological Approach to Biography*, 8.

15. J. Knudson, "Cognitive Models in Life Histories"; M. Shostak, *Nisa: The Life and Words of an !kung Woman;* J. Freeman, *Untouchable: An Indian Life History.* Ron Grele in *Envelopes of Sound* writes about the oral history interview as performance: "Since the interview is not created as a literary product is created, alone and as a reflective action, it cannot be divorced from the circumstances of its creation, which of necessity is one of audience participation and face-to-face confrontation" (136).

16. Grele, *Envelopes of Sound*, 398.

17. G. Frank, "Finding the Common Denominator: A Phenomenological Critique of Life History Method," 85, 12. This is akin to Clifford Geertz's

sweeping claims in *The Interpretation of Culture* that all anthropological data are interpreted, that "what we call our data are really our own constructions of other people; constructions of what they say and what their compatriots are up to" (9).

18. Freeman, *Untouchable*, 392.
19. See, for example, Watson and Watson-Franke, *Interpreting Life Histories;* V. Crapanzano, *Tuhami;* Schneider, *Oral Histories from the Field.*
20. Travellers have an adaptation based on commercial nomadism and a lifestyle similar to European Gypsies. While Gypsies are of Indian ancestry and first arrived in Britain in the 1500s, travellers are indigenous.
21. See, for example, G. Gmelch, *The Irish Tinkers: The Urbanization of an Itinerant People.*
22. The strongest feelings I remember concerning racial discrimination occurred one evening when I chanced upon a youth league baseball game being played on a weed-choked field. All the kids on both teams were black. I asked a man in the stands where the white kids were, and, perhaps detecting a "foreign" accent or my naive sincerity, he patiently explained to me a social system of race relations not unlike apartheid.
23. Freeman, *Untouchable*, 392–93.
24. Crapanzano, *Tuhami;* K. Dwyer, *Moroccan Dialogues.*
25. R. Rhoades, "Toward an Anthropology of Return Migration," 1.
26. C. Brettell, *We Have Already Cried Many Tears: The Stories of Three Portuguese Migrant Women,* 2.

Bibliography

Allen, S. 1971. *New minorities and old conflicts*. New York: Random House.

Barbados Improvements Association. 1913. *The Tourist Guide to Barbados*. Bridgetown.

Barbados Statistical Service. 1985. *Monthly Digest of Statistics*. Bridgetown: Barbados Statistical Service.

Barrow, C. 1977. Migration from a Barbados village: Effects on family life. *New Community* 5 (4): 381–91.

Basch, L. 1987. The politics of Caribbeanization: Vincentians and Grenadians in New York. In *Caribbean life in New York City*, ed. C. Sutton and E. Chaney, 160–81. New York: Center for Migration Studies.

Bertaux, D., ed. 1981. *Biography and society: The life history approach in the social sciences*. London: Sage.

Bohning, W. R. 1972. *The migration of workers in the United Kingdom and the European Community*. London: Oxford University Press.

Bolles, A. L. 1981. "Goin' abroad": Working class Jamaican women and migration. In *Female immigrants to the United States: Caribbean, Latin American and African experiences*, ed. D. Mortimer and R. Bryce-Laporte, 56–85. Research Institute on Immigration and Ethnic Studies, Occasional Papers No. 2. Washington, D.C.: Smithsonian Institution.

Brettell, C. 1982. *We have already cried many tears: The stories of three Portuguese migrant women*. Cambridge, Mass.: Schenkman.

Brooks, D. 1975. *Race and labour in London transport*. London: Oxford University Press.

Brown, C. 1984. *Black and white Britain*. London: Heinemann Educational.

Bryce-Laport, R. S. 1973. Black immigrants. In *Through different eyes: Black and white perspectives on American race relations*, ed. P. I. Rose, S. Rothman, and W. J. Wilson, 44–61. New York: Oxford University Press.

———. 1979. New York City and the new Caribbean immigration: A contextual statement. *International Migration Review* 13 (2): 214–34.

———. 1982. Preface to *Return migration and remittances: Developing a Caribbean perspective*. Research Institute on Immigration and Ethnic Studies, Occasional Papers No. 3. Washington, D.C.: Smithsonian Institution.

Bryce-Laport, R. S., and D. Mortimer, eds. 1976. *Caribbean immigration to the*

United States. Research Institute on Immigration and Ethnic Studies, Occasional Papers No. 1. Washington, D.C.: Smithsonian Institution.

Carnegie, C. 1982. Strategic flexibility in the West Indies: A social psychology of Caribbean migrations. *Caribbean Review* 11 (1): 10–13, 54.

Castles, S., and G. Kosack. 1973. *Immigrant workers and class structure in Western Europe*. London: Oxford University Press.

Chandler, A. A. 1946. The expansion of Barbados. *Journal of the Barbados Museum and Historical Society* 13:106–36.

Chaney, E. 1987. The context of Caribbean migration. In *Caribbean life in New York City*, ed. C. Sutton and E. Chaney, 3–14. New York: Center for Migration Studies.

Clarke, E. T. 1981. *Mental illness among Barbadians in Barbados and England*. Ph.D. diss., University of Surrey.

Conway D., and U. Bigby. 1987. Where Caribbean peoples live in New York City. In *Caribbean life in New York City*, ed. C. Sutton and E. Chaney, 74–84. New York: Center for Migration Studies.

Coombs, O. 1976. Illegal immigrants in New York: The invisible subculture. *New York Magazine* 19 (March 15): 33–41.

Cottle, T. J. 1980. *Black testimony: The voice of Britain's West Indians*. London: Wildwood House.

Crapanzano, V. 1977. The life history in anthropological fieldwork. *Anthropology and Humanism Quarterly* 2 (2–3): 3–7.

———. 1984. "Life-histories" *American Anthropologist* 86: 953–60.

Cross, M. 1979. *Urbanization and Urban Growth in the Caribbean*. Cambridge: Cambridge University Press.

Cumper, G. E. 1957. Working class emigration from Barbados to the United Kingdom, October 1955. *Social and Economic Studies* 6 (1): 76–83.

Dahya, B. 1973. Pakistanis in Britain: Transients or settlers? *Race* 14:241–77.

Daniel, W. W. 1968. *Racial discrimination in England*. London: Penguin.

Dann, G. 1984. *The quality of life in Barbados*. London: Macmillan.

Davison, B. 1968. No place back home: A study of Jamaicans returning to Kingston, Jamaica. *Race* 9:499–509.

Davison, R. B. 1962. *West Indian migrants: Social and economic effects of migration from the West Indies*. London and New York: Oxford University Press.

———. 1966. *Black British: Immigrants to England*. London: Oxford University Press.

Deakin, N. 1970. *Colour, citizenship and British society*. London: Panther Books.

Dominguez, V. 1975. *From neighbor to stranger: The dilemma of Caribbean peoples in the United States*. New Haven, Conn.: Yale University Press.

Dunaway, D., and W. Baum. 1984. *Oral history: An interdisciplinary anthology*. Nashville, Tenn.: American Association for State and Local History.

Dwyer, K. 1982. *Moroccan dialogues*. Baltimore: Johns Hopkins University Press.

Family Welfare Association. 1960. *The West Indian comes to England*. London: Routledge Kegan.

Field, F., and P. Haikin, eds. 1971. *Black Britons*. London: Oxford University Press.

Fitzherbert, K. 1967. *West Indian children in London*. Occasional Papers in Social Administration No. 19. London: Bell.

Foner, N. 1976. Male and female: Jamaican migrants in London. *Anthropological Quarterly* 49 (1): 28–35.

———. 1977. The Jamaicans: Cultural and social change among migrants in Britain. In *Between two cultures: Migrants and minorities in Britain*, ed. J. L. Watson, 120–50. Oxford: Basil Blackwell.

———. 1978. *Jamaica farewell: Jamaican migrants in London*. Berkeley: University of California Press.

———. 1979. West Indians in New York City and London: A comparative analysis. *International Migration Review* 13 (2): 284–97.

———. 1986. Sex roles and sensibilities: Jamaican women in New York and London. In *International migration: The female experience*, ed. R. Simon and C. Brettell, 133–51. Totowa, N.J.: Rowman and Allanheld.

Frank, G. 1979. Finding the common denominator: A phenomenological critique of life history method. *Ethos* 7 (1): 68–94.

Fratoe, F., and R. Meeks. 1988. *Business participation rates and self-employed incomes: Analysis of the fifty largest U.S. ancestry groups*. Los Angeles: Center for Afro-American Studies, UCLA.

Freeman, J. 1979. *Untouchable: An Indian life history*. Stanford, Calif.: Stanford University Press.

Frisch, M. *A shared authority: Essays on the craft and meaning of oral and public history*. Albany: State University of New York Press.

Frucht, R. 1968. Emigration, remittances, and social change: Aspects of the social field in Nevis, West Indies. *Anthropologica* 10:193–208.

Gant, R. 1987. Archives and interviews: A comment on oral history and fieldwork practise. *Geography* 7:27–35.

Geertz, C. 1973. *The interpretation of cultures*. New York: Basic Books.

Glass, R. 1960. *Newcomers: The West Indians in London*. London: Allen and Unwin.

Gmelch, G. 1980. Return Migration. In *Annual review of anthropology*, 135–59. Menlo Park, Calif.: Annual Reviews.

———. 1985. Barbados odyssey: Some migrants fulfill their dreams by returning home. *Natural History* 94 (10): 34–38.

———. 1985. *The Irish Tinkers: The urbanization of an itinerant people*. Prospect Heights, Ill.: Waveland Press.

———. 1987. Work, innovation, and investment: The impact of return migrants in Barbados. *Human Organization* 46 (2): 131–40.

Gonzalez, N. S. 1961. Family organization in five types of migratory wage labor. *American Anthropologist* 63 (6): 1264–80.

———. 1988. *Sojourners of the Caribbean*. Champaign: University of Illinois Press.

Gooding, E. 1974. *The plant communities of Barbados*. Barbados: Ministry of Education.

Greenfield, S. 1966. *English rustics in black skin.* New Haven, Conn.: Yale College and University Press.

Grele, R. 1985. *Envelopes of sound: The art of oral history.* Chicago: Precedent Publishing.

Griffith, D. C. 1983. The promise of a country: The impact of seasonal U.S. migration on the Jamaican peasantry. Ph.D. diss., University of Florida.

Harlow, V. T. 1969. *A history of Barbados, 1625–1685.* New York: Negro Universities Press. (Original edition 1926).

Harper, R. 1965. *Colour in Britain.* London: British Broadcasting Corporation.

Hernandez-Alvarez, J. 1967. *Return migration to Puerto Rico.* Berkeley: California Institute of International Studies.

Hill, C. 1970. *Immigration and integration: A study of the settlement of coloured minorities in Britain.* Oxford: Pergamon Press.

Hill, D. R. 1977. The impact of migration on the metropolitan and folk society of Carriacou, Grenada. Anthropological Papers of the American Museum of Natural History, 54 (2). New York.

Hinds, D. 1966. *Journey to an illusion.* London: Heinemann.

Hiro, D. 1971. *Black British, white British.* London: Eyre and Spotiswood.

Hoefer, H., and R. Wilder, eds. 1986. *Barbados.* Singapore: APA Productions.

Holmes, C. 1988. *John Bull's island: Immigration and British society, 1871–1971.* London: Macmillan.

Hope, K. R. 1982. *Economic development in the Caribbean.* New York: Praeger.

Heer, F., and D. Reisberg. 1990. Vivid memories of emotional events: The accuracy of remembered minutiae. *Memory and Cognition* 18:496–506.

Hutt, M. B. 1981. *Exploring historic Barbados.* Bedford, N.S.: Layne.

Kearney, M. 1986. From the invisible hand to visible feet: Anthropological studies of migration and development. *Annual Review of Anthropology* 13:331–61.

Kenny, M. 1976. Twentieth century Spanish expatriate ties with the homeland: Remigration and its consequences. In *The changing faces of rural Spain,* ed. J. Aceves and W. Douglass, 97–121. New York: Schenkman.

King, R. L. 1978. Return migration: Review of some cases from southern Europe. *Mediterranean Studies* 1 (2): 3–30.

Knudsen, J. 1990. Cognitive models in life histories. *Anthropological Quarterly* 63:122–33.

Langness, L., and G. Frank. 1981. *Lives: An anthropological approach to biography.* Novato, Calif.: Chandler and Sharp.

Larsen, S., and K. Plunkett. 1987. Remembering experienced and reported events. *Applied Cognitive Psychology* 1:15–26.

Lomask, M. 1986. *The biographer's craft.* New York: Harper and Row.

Lowenthal, D. 1972. *West Indian societies.* New York: Oxford University Press.

Lowenthal, D., and L. Comitas. 1973. *Consequences of class and color.* New York: Anchor Press / Doubleday.

Mandelbaum, D. G. 1973. The study of life history: Gandhi. *Current Anthropology* 14:177–96.

Marcus, G., and J. Clifford. 1985. The making of ethnographic texts: A preliminary report. *Current Anthropology* 26 (2): 267–71.

Marcus, G., and M. Fischer. 1986. *Anthropology as cultural critique: An experimental moment in the human sciences.* Chicago: University of Chicago Press.

Marks, A., and H. Wesson, eds. 1983. *White collar migrants in the Americas and the Caribbean.* Leiden, Neth.: Department of Caribbean Studies, Royal Institute of Linguistics and Anthropology.

Marshall, D. 1982a. The history of Caribbean migrations: The case of the West Indies. *Caribbean Review* 11 (1): 6–9, 52.

———. 1982b. Migration as an agent of change in Caribbean island ecosystems. *International Social Science Journal* 34 (3): 451–67.

———. 1983. Toward an understanding of Caribbean migration. In *U.S. immigration and refugee policy,* ed. M. Kritz, 113–31. Lexington, Mass.: Lexington Books.

Marshall, P. 1959. *Brown girls, brownstones.* New York: Random House.

———. 1987. Black immigrant women in *Brown girls, brownstones.* In *Caribbean life in New York City,* ed. C. Sutton and E. Chaney, 87–91. New York: Center for Migration Research.

Massey, D., et al. 1987. *Return to Aztlan: The social process of international migration from western Mexico.* Berkeley: University of California Press.

Midgett, D. K. 1977. West Indian migration and adaptation in St. Lucia and London. Ph.D. diss., University of Illinois at Urbana-Champaign.

———. 1980. West Indian Ethnicity in Great Britain. In *Migration and development,* ed. H. I. Safa and B. DuToit, 57–81. The Hague: Mouton.

Mintz, S. 1984. The anthropological interview. In *Oral History: An Interdisciplinary Anthology,* ed. D. Dunaway and W. Baum. Nashville, Tenn.: American Association for State and Local History.

Mintz, S., and S. Price. 1985. *Caribbean contours.* Baltimore: Johns Hopkins University Press.

Monroe, S. 1988. Blacks in Britain: Grim lives, grimmer prospects. *Newsweek* 111 (4 January): 32–33.

Moxly, J. H. 1886. *An account of a West Indian sanatorium and a guide to Barbados.* London: S. Low, Marston, Searle, and Rivington.

Mullard, C. 1973. *Black British.* London: George Allen and Unwin.

Neisser, U., and E. Winograd. 1988. *Remembering reconsidered: Ecological and traditional approaches to the study of memory.* Cambridge: Cambridge University Press.

Nurse, L. 1983. *Residential subdivision of Barbados: 1965–1977.* Cave Hill, West Indies: Institute of Social and Economic Research, University of the West Indies.

Paine, S. 1974. *Exporting workers: The Turkish case.* London: Cambridge University Press.

Park, R. 1928. Human migration and the marginal man. *American Journal of Sociology* 33:881–93.

Pastor, R. 1985. *Migration and development in the Caribbean*. Boulder: Westview Press.

Patterson, O. 1968. West Indian immigrants returning home. *Race* 10 (1): 69–77.

Patterson, S. 1965. *Dark strangers: A study of West Indians in London*. Harmondsworth: Penguin.

———. 1969. *Immigration and race relations in Britain, 1960–1967*. London: Oxford University Press.

Peach, C. 1968. *West Indian migration to Britain: A social geography*. London: Oxford University Press.

Peterson, W. 1958. A general typology of migration. *American Sociological Review* 23 (3).

Philpott, S. B. 1968. Remittance obligations, social networks and choice among Montserratian migrants in Britain. *Man* 3 (3): 465–76.

———. 1970. The implications of migration for sending societies: Some theoretical considerations. In *Migration and anthropology*, ed. R. F. Spencer, 9–20. Proceedings of the 1970 annual spring meeting.

———. 1973. *West Indian migration: The Montserrat case*. New York: Humanities Press.

Piore, M. 1979. *Birds of passage: Migrant labor and industrial societies*. Cambridge: Cambridge University Press.

Plotnicov, L. 1967. *Strangers to the city: Urban man in Jos, Nigeria*. Pittsburgh: University of Pittsburgh Press.

Plummer, K. 1983. *Documents of life: An introduction to the problems and literature of a humanistic method*. London: George Allen and Unwin.

Portes, A., and R. Rumbaut. 1990. *Immigrant America: A portrait*. Berkeley: University of California Press.

Pryce, K. 1979. *Endless pressure*. London: Penguin.

Rabinow, P. 1977. *Reflections on fieldwork in Morocco*. Berkeley: University of California Press.

Rex, J., and R. Moore. 1967. *Race, community and conflict*. London: Oxford University Press.

Rex, J., and S. Tomlinson. 1979. *Colonial immigrants in a British city*. London: Routledge and Kegan Paul.

Rhoades, R. 1978. Intra-European return migration and rural development: Lessons from the Spanish case. *Human Organization* 37 (2): 136–47.

———. 1979. Toward an anthropology of return migration. *Papers in Anthropology* 20:1–111.

Richardson, B. C. 1983. *Caribbean migrants: Environment and human survival in St. Kitts and Nevis*. Knoxville, Tenn.: University of Tennessee Press.

———. 1985. *Panama money in Barbados, 1900–1920*. Knoxville: University of Tennessee Press.

Roberts, G. W., and D. O. Mills. 1958. A study of external migration affecting Jamaica: 1953–55. *Social and Economic Studies* 7 (2): 119–28.

Rose, A. 1969. *Migrants in Europe*. Minneapolis: University of Minnesota Press.

Rose, E. J., et al. 1969. *Colour and citizenship*. London: Oxford University Press.

Rubenstein, H. 1983. Remittances and rural underdevelopment in the English-speaking Caribbean. *Human Organization* 42 (4): 295–306.

Runnymede Trust. 1980. *Britain's black population.* London: Heinemann Educational Books.

Sheppard, J. 1977. *The redlegs of Barbados.* New York: KTO Press.

Shostak, M. 1981. *Nisa: The life and words of an !kung woman.* Cambridge, Mass.: Harvard University Press.

Smith, D. 1977. *Racial disadvantage in Britain.* London: Penguin.

Smith, M. G. 1965. *The plural society in the British West Indies.* Berkeley: University of California Press.

Smith, S. M. 1988. Environmental context-dependent memory. In *A memory in context,* ed. G. M. Davies and D. M. Thomson. New York: John Wiley and Sons.

Soto, I. M. 1987. West Indian child fostering: Its role in migrant exchanges. In *Caribbean life in New York City,* ed. C. Sutton and E. Chaney, 131–49. New York: Center for Migration Studies.

Sutton, C. 1987. The caribbeanization of New York City and the emergence of a transnational socio-cultural system. In *Caribbean life in New York City,* ed. C. Sutton and E. Chaney. New York: Center for Migration Studies.

Sutton, C., and S. Makiesky. 1975. Migration and West Indian racial and political consciousness. In *Migration and development: Implications for ethnic identity and political conflict,* ed. H. I. Safa and B. DuToit, 113–44. The Hague: Mouton.

Thomas-Hope, E. 1985. Return migration and implications for Caribbean development. In *Migration and development in the Caribbean,* ed. R. A. Pastor, 157–73. Boulder: Westview Press.

———. 1986. Transients and settlers: Varieties of Caribbean migrants and the socioeconomic implications of their return. *International Migration* 24:559–70.

———. 1988. Caribbean skilled international migration and the transnational household. *Geoforum* 19 (4): 423–32.

Thompson, P. 1978. *Voice of the past: Oral history.* New York: Oxford University Press.

United States Emigration and Naturalization Service. 1981. Emigration and naturalization service, 1980 annual report. Washington, D.C.: U.S. Government Printing Office.

Watson, J. L. 1977. *Between two cultures.* Oxford: Basil Blackwell.

Watson, L., and M. Watson-Franke. 1985. *Interpreting life histories: An anthropological inquiry.* New Brunswick, N.J.: Rutgers University Press.

Whiteford, M. 1978. Women, migration, and social change: A Columbian case. *International Migration Review* 12:236–46.

Whitehead, J., and W. Schneider. 1987. The singular event and the everyday routine: The interplay of history and culture in the shaping of memory. *Oral History Review* 15 (Fall): 43–79.

Wickham, J. 1975. The thing about Barbados. *Journal of the Barbados Museum and Historical Society* 35:223–30.

Wiest, R. E. 1975. Wage-labour migration and the household in a Mexican town. *Journal of Anthropological Research* 29:180–209.

——. 1978. *Rural community development in Mexico: The impact of Mexican recurrent migration to the United States.* University of Manitoba Anthropology Papers No. 21.

Wilson, P. 1973. *Crab antics: The social anthropology of English-speaking Negro societies of the Caribbean.* New Haven, Conn.: Yale University Press.

Wirth, L. 1988. Urbanism as a way of life. In *Urban Life,* ed. G. Gmelch and W. Zenner. Prospect Heights, Ill.: Waveland Press.

Wood, C. H., and T. McCoy. 1987. Migration, remittances, and development: A study of Caribbean cane cutters in Florida. *International Migration Review* 19 (2): 251–77.

Worrell, D. 1987. *Small island economies.* New York: Praeger.

Wright, P. 1968. *The coloured workers in British industry.* London: Oxford University Press.

Index